Knowledge Management in Practice

Knowledge Management in Practice

Anthony J. Rhem

CRC Press
Taylor & Francis Group
Boca Raton London New York

CRC Press is an imprint of the
Taylor & Francis Group, an **informa** business
AN AUERBACH BOOK

CRC Press
Taylor & Francis Group
6000 Broken Sound Parkway NW, Suite 300
Boca Raton, FL 33487-2742

First issued in paperback 2022

© 2017 by Taylor & Francis Group, LLC
CRC Press is an imprint of Taylor & Francis Group, an Informa business

No claim to original U.S. Government works

ISBN-13: 978-1-466-56252-3 (hbk)
ISBN-13: 978-1-03-233993-1 (pbk)
DOI: 10.1201/9781315374376

Library of Congress Cataloging-in-Publication Data

Names: Rhem, Anthony J., author.
Title: Knowledge management in practice / Anthony J. Rhem.
Description: Boca Raton, FL : Auerbach Publications, 2016. | Includes bibliographical references and index.
Identifiers: LCCN 2016002475 | ISBN 9781466562523 (alk. paper)
Subjects: LCSH: Knowledge management.
Classification: LCC HD30.2 .R5195 2016 | DDC 658.4/038--dc23
LC record available at http://lccn.loc.gov/2016002475

**Visit the Taylor & Francis Web site at
http://www.taylorandfrancis.com**

**and the CRC Press Web site at
http://www.crcpress.com**

I dedicate this book to my mother, my angel, and to whom I owe all that I am and all that I will ever be; Marine McCloud Rhem is my angel in heaven constantly looking over me.

Also, I dedicate this book to my wife Tanya and to my son Jaren and daughter Jasmine, who remain my inspiration to continuously strive to be the best I can be every single day!

And ... for all of those who have a dream and the will to pursue it!

Contents

Foreword

People and civilizations desire and cherish wisdom—inspired wisdom or the kind from experience that leads to deep expertise. In knowledge professions, the pathway to wisdom is data → information → knowledge. As the penultimate step, knowledge involves notions of the nature of an expert versus a novice, heuristics based on experience, and depth versus narrow intelligence. The pathway starts with the imperative for clean, relevant, error-free data in a form suitable for analytics and scientific analysis. Information should be relevant to the needs of the users, in an appropriate format for interpreting and archiving, and should be presented for convenient visualization.

People in small communities and large organizations collaborate and share their experiences, so capturing and reusing their knowledge are important for increasing group effectiveness and efficiency as well as for fostering innovation. For organizations, a key challenge is to identify needs for collaboration and to share collective knowledge. This means understanding who holds knowledge and what knowledge they have. Tools, techniques, and processes are thus needed to capture, store, and reuse the many types and instances of knowledge in an organization.

KM includes practices and procedures, as well as the people and systems, that support societies' information and knowledge needs. This includes ways to encourage organizations and individuals to add value and share knowledge. Managers and knowledge professionals then implement KM methods and techniques, differentiating them for specific industries and subject areas. In practice, KM must address the varying requirements in specific industries such as healthcare, human resources, military, and finance. The different environments and cultures require consistent procedures that identify and analyze relevant content, organize knowledge, create effective access, and promote a knowledge-sharing culture through education and training.

Organizations need detailed information on applying KM practices to solve real-world problems. They need to establish organizational policies that lead to successful KM adoption and to understand reasons why KM projects fail. Organizations need to apply known lessons and tips to ensure successful implementation of KM practices and to elevate the value of adopting KM policies.

Dr. Anthony Rhem's *Knowledge Management in Practice* is unique in the degree to which his extensive experience informs his insights and writing. At a time of such great attention to Big Data and data analytics, this book reminds us that knowledge is after all the ultimate goal of careful work with data and the creation of accurate information. Identifying, capturing, and managing knowledge as a critically important asset are formidable tasks in our large corporate and governmental organizations. This evidence-based book provides the framework and guidelines that professionals need for working with the contemporary explosion of data that is creating opportunities and challenges to all phases of our society and commerce. To our benefit, this book captures the considerable wisdom Dr. Rhem has acquired over his career as a KM professional.

Larry R. Medsker
Research Professor in Physics and Data Science
The George Washington University
Washington, DC

Preface

Knowledge is recognized as a valuable asset in organizations across many industries. How knowledge is shared, leveraged, obtained, and managed will be the difference in how successful and sustainable an organization will become. This book is a culmination of my years of experience in the knowledge management (KM) discipline. Since 1998, I have been involved in various KM activities such as researching, developing processes for capturing and codifying knowledge, developing KM systems, developing and operationalizing KM strategies across several industries, writing articles and books, developing and teaching KM curriculum, and speaking at numerous KM conferences.

Why I Wrote This Book

The use of KM principles, practices, and procedures has expanded enormously since 2010. This expansion has also brought about the proliferation of KM systems in its many forms such as contact center knowledge repositories, expertise locators, content management, document management, knowledge repositories/libraries, social media applications, and decision support systems. The inclusion of KM from a strategic point of view to streamline revenue, increase revenue, improve performance, attract/ retain customers, and manage human capital has enabled organizations to maintain and/or improve their competitive edge. To compete in a local, national, and/or global market, organizations, including educational, government, and military, are looking for that differentiator, and KM has proved to be just that. I wrote this book to capture and make available my experience in implementing and practicing KM across many organizations to scholars and practitioners of KM. This book is a resource that presents how KM is being implemented along with specific KM methods, tips, techniques, and best practices to get the most out of a KM investment.

What This Book Is About

This book covers how knowledge management is leveraged in several industries. The various uses of KM practices, policies, procedures, and methods, including tips and techniques, to create a competitive advantage are examined. Industries such as first responders, military, healthcare, insurance, financial services, legal, human resources, merger and acquisition (M&A) firms, and research institutions are covered in this book.

Essential KM concepts are also explored not only from a foundational perspective but also from a practical application. These KM concepts include capturing and codifying tacit and explicit knowledge, KM methods, information architecture, search, KM and social media, KM and Big Data, adoption of KM, and why KM initiatives fail.

The following are the subjects that are covered, and what you can expect from the various chapters:

■ Chapter 2: The Case for Implementing Knowledge Management
This chapter details the factors you must consider before implementing KM in your organization and details the various practices and policies of KM. Moreover, the needs for your organization to launch a KM initiative/ project and/or establish a KM program are addressed.

■ Chapter 3: Being Social: Knowledge Management and Social Media
This chapter examines how social media tools and techniques are becoming facilitators of knowledge for the organization. Specific guidance and insights are given to develop your organization's social media strategy and to determine the social media tools, techniques, and platforms that can be used to take advantage of what social media can bring to KM.

■ Chapter 4: Dude, "Where's My Car?": Utilizing Search in Knowledge Management
This chapter details the importance of search in KM, in particular a KM system. Several aspects of implementing search are examined, including the importance of having user-centric information architecture.

■ Chapter 5: The Age of Discovery: Knowledge Management in Research Institutions
Research institutions play a key role in product innovation. KM is a catalyst for stimulating and sustaining a high level of innovation. This chapter examines how KM is used, focusing on various KM methods that can and in some cases are being incorporated at research institutions.

■ Chapter 6: "Where Have All My Experts Gone?": Knowledge Management in Human Resources and Talent Management
When it comes to talent management, KM can play a critical role in ensuring that the knowledge assets are captured and made available to the enterprise. KM in talent management when applied holistically involves capturing and sharing employee knowledge from onboarding to exit interview.

■ Chapter 7: "Sound the Alarm!": Knowledge Management in Emergency and Disaster Preparedness
Emergency and disaster preparedness is enhanced through the incorporation of KM. Putting the right knowledge in the right context at the right time

in the hands of first responders could be the difference in saving lives and preventing casualties. It is important to begin with a comprehensive KM strategy to establishing a plan to deliver the knowledge in a timely manner.

■ Chapter 8: Happily Ever After: Knowledge Management in Mergers and Acquisitions

When organizations merge or are acquired, there is a level of uncertainty both from a macro (organization) level and from a micro (employee) level. Applying KM to M&A will enable the organization to know what knowledge is important to retain, who those knowledge holders are, what are the knowledge gaps, and how to quantify the knowledge of the organization. From an employee standpoint, having the organization share knowledge about the pending transaction as well as incentify employees to share what they know and to assist employees in transitioning (within the new organization or to a new organization) will go a long way to ensure a smooth M&A transaction.

■ Chapter 9: "Is There a Doctor in the House?": Knowledge Management in Healthcare

The healthcare industry has become individual centric. As the healthcare community moves to electronic record keeping and capturing patient information at the point of initial interaction, having accurate knowledge about that patient as well as having the patient knowledgeable about his or her own health is essential to the success of caring for that patient. KM is an essential ingredient for healthcare success, especially in the areas of drug interaction analysis, sharing of patient diagnosis between hospitals and doctors, and furthering the development of healthcare informatics.

■ Chapter 10: "Show Me the Money!": Knowledge Management in Financial Services

KM in the financial services sector centers on being able to attract, serve, and retain customers. Delivering the tools to customers that provide knowledge to make sound financial decisions is at the heart of what KM will provide. To bring innovative financial services and products to the marketplace and to have an understanding of their potential benefits to customers, imparting training to customer service representatives on specific knowledge will also be a critical component of KM.

■ Chapter 11: "Are You in Good Hands?": Knowledge Management in Insurance

In this chapter, you will learn how KM is used in the insurance industry to communicate knowledge to customers, agents, and customer contact centers while providing mechanisms for employees to share, capture, and catalog knowledge. KM in the insurance industry will provide the knowledge to (among other things) complete applications, bind insurance, and service a claim.

- Chapter 12: "Sign Right Here!": Knowledge Management in the Legal Profession

  In this chapter, use of KM to enhance the management of a law firm and to execute client engagements will be presented. KM in law firms is primarily executed through the building and fostering communities of practice around practice specialties. This enables legal representatives to respond to a situation with the right expertise, equipped with the right knowledge to resolve a legal matter.

- Chapter 13: "A Mind Is a Terrible Thing to Waste!": Knowledge Management Education

  This chapter examines the state of KM education. This examination includes KM certification programs, KM curriculum at institutions of higher learning, as well as KM education policies, procedures, and future direction of KM education. In addition, specific criteria to be considered while selecting a KM education option are presented.

- Chapter 14: "Big Knowledge!": Knowledge Management and Big Data

  In this chapter, use of KM to gain knowledge from your Big Data resources will be examined. The use of KM on Big Data to provide a rich structure to enable decisions to be made on a multitude and a variety of data is the essence of this examination. Along with specific analysis of the various types of data and KM methods for examining this data, a detailed understanding of KM's impact on Big Data can be realized.

- Chapter 15: "What Have You Done for the War Fighter Today?": Knowledge Management in the Military

  KM in military has a rich history. Use of KM in the military, with special attention to events such as Base Realignment and Closure (BRAC), will be examined. In addition, a look at the various branches of the military (army, air force, and navy) and their KM strategies, KM systems, and KM methods are presented.

- Chapter 16: Drinking the Knowledge Management Kool-Aid: Knowledge Management Adoption

  Adoption of KM programs, policies, methods, and systems is a challenge for all organizations. This chapter is all about adoption! If your organization does not adopt its KM principles, practices, processes, procedures, or systems, it may be recognized as a failure. Specific guidance on improving KM adoption and positioning your KM initiatives for success is also presented.

- Chapter 17: Failure Is Not an Option: Why Do Knowledge Management Programs and Projects Fail?

  With lofty promises come unrealized results. KM gained widespread popularity in the 1990s; however, many KM initiatives failed and this popularity has tapered quite a bit. Since the mid-2000s, KM started to experience a renaissance; some disparate KM achievements were witnessed (call centers, research, human resources, and military), and KM is now considered as a discipline to gain a competitive advantage over competitors. Although KM is being used with some level of success in this new knowledge economy, many KM initiatives still fail. This chapter details the factors that contribute to the failure of KM initiatives as well as measures to adhere to in order to achieve successful KM.

An in-depth synopsis of each chapter and an overall introduction to the book are included in Chapter 1. The concluding chapter (Chapter 18) provides a summary of the book and an insight into what's next for KM.

Who Should Read This Book

This book will provide KM educators, practitioners, and those who are new to KM an insight into how KM is being implemented by providing tips and techniques that will enable the reader to be more productive in their application of KM and those who are being educated in KM an understanding of how KM is used in a variety of industries to solve pertinent issues. In summary, *Knowledge Management in Practice* will be a definitive KM reference for anyone entering into the field and/or currently practicing KM.

What You Will Learn

This book is intended to provide comprehensive guidance on how KM is implemented in several industries. The following points identify what the reader will learn:

- Key learnings identified based on the specific industry
- Tips and techniques for the KM practitioner and novice to be productive
- Major concepts and solutions to problems addressed by KM
- A KM reference for practitioners to aid in solving actual problems
- Practical approach to presenting KM concepts and their application
- Identifying the benefits of implementing a KM solution
- Specific guidance on delivering and executing KM strategies
- Guidance on selecting the "right" educational option for KM education
- Foundational and practical application of KM methods
- Real-world application of KM

How to Leverage This Book

There are several ways to leverage this book. An immediate way is to read the book cover to cover and understand how KM is being used in several industries, as well as understand the various concepts that are being presented. However, a more pragmatic approach would be to focus on a specific industry presented in the book and refer to the related chapters that delve deep into the KM methods, procedures, and best practices that were indicated in the industry-specific chapter. Either way, you are sure to gain the insights you need to make KM successful and to increase your KM acumen.

Anthony J. Rhem
A.J. Rhem & Associates, Inc.
Chicago, Illinois

Acknowledgments

I thank the many people who have influenced my career in KM, particularly Dr. Larry Medsker and Dr. Jay Liebowitz. I have had the pleasure of knowing both these distinguished men for nearly 20 years. They have been my mentors, friends, colleagues, and advisors.

I also thank the many corporations and brilliant people I have had the pleasure to work with since 1998, implementing KM strategies, programs, projects and systems, and without this valuable experience, this book would not be possible. Special thanks go to Sydney Torain who served as my research assistant throughout the completion of this book.

Author

Dr. Anthony J. Rhem serves as the president and principal consultant of A.J. Rhem & Associates, Inc., a privately held knowledge management (KM) consulting, training, and research firm located in Chicago, Illinois. Dr. Rhem is an information systems professional, with over 30 years of experience, a published author, and an educator. He has presented papers on the application and theory of software engineering methodologies, knowledge management, and artificial intelligence.

As a KM consultant, Dr. Rhem consistently serves as a KM advisor, KM strategist, information architect, and KM governance strategist. He has played an integral role in the successful implementation of KM systems, KM methods, and KM strategies in several industries, including financial services, insurance, retail, telecommunications, and military.

Dr. Rhem has conducted research in the knowledge engineering domain since 2004. His research experience includes conducting webinars through the Principal Investigators Association addressing various research problems and issues; Dr. Rhem received an Small Business Innovation Research (SBIR) phase I grant award for his work on a process to capture and codify tacit knowledge in which he holds a patent. He has also participated in several research projects, playing an integral role in successfully commercializing software methodologies and software products.

In his advisory work, as a member of the Gerson Lehrman Group Technology Council of Advisors, Dr. Rhem consults with venture capitalists and investment firms specifically as they pertain to technology innovations, best practices, and trends. Dr. Rhem's current advisory work also includes Board of Trustees at the Knowledge Systems Institute, Industry Advisory Board—International Conference on Software Engineering and Knowledge Engineering (SEKE), International Bar Association (IBA) Law Firm Management Sub-Committee on Knowledge Management and IT, Advisory Board for American University Professional Science Master's Degree Program, Member of the National Science Foundation Research Review Panel, and Corporate Advisory Board of the ASCII Group Inc.

Chapter 1

Introduction

Have you ever wondered about all the fuss concerning knowledge management (KM)? What is KM anyway? At its core, KM is about sharing and collaborating what you know, capturing what you know, and reusing that knowledge so as to not reinvent the wheel and/or to combine with other ideas to foster innovation. A KM meeting that I attended, conducted by the American Productivity and Quality Center (APQC) (APQC's January 2011 KM Community Call), included representatives from Conoco Phillips, Fluor, IBM, GE, and Schlumberger; I returned from this meeting understanding that it is necessary to have KM part of an organization's culture. I believe that this is important because we do not want KM to be "another task to complete on the checklist," but the way we conduct business. This includes the business between the various individuals and entities within our corporations as well as with our customers. Talking, listening, capturing, and applying what we learn from each other is a constant, never ending, and always evolving process.

Knowledge Management in Practice provides KM professionals and those undergoing training in KM a practical examination on how KM is being applied. Specifically, this book leverages the experience gained while practicing KM to solve some of the more pressing KM problems faced in organizations today. This book addresses challenges such as search engine optimization, content categorization and searching, building taxonomies and ontologies, capturing and managing tacit and explicit knowledge, KM adoption, and failure of KM projects. In addition, this book examines how KM is being applied to specific industries, including insurance, healthcare, legal, human resources and talent management, military, research institutions, and finance.

Overview

This book will provide detailed information on applying KM practices, procedures, and techniques to solve real-world problems. The applications of KM that will be examined include social media; content management; search engine optimization; capturing and codifying tacit and explicit knowledge; KM in disaster preparedness, action, and reaction; KM adoption process in an organization; the reason for failure of KM projects, and specific industry KM applications. This book will contribute to the advancement in application of KM principles, practices, and procedures, as well as the systems that support KM.

Each chapter will include key learnings as well as tips and techniques for those who are currently instituting KM in projects and/or programs. The following sections contain a synopsis of each chapter in this book:

The Case for Implementing Knowledge Management (Chapter 2)

This chapter examines why your organization may need a KM program. What factors determine that it is time to consider implementing policies, procedures, practices, and processes that will not only be the catalyst for specific KM initiatives, but also the development of a KM program, including KM Center of Excellence? This chapter will answer this question as well as examine the need to collaborate and share knowledge; understand who the key knowledge holders are and what knowledge they know; and the need to respond to internal employees and/or customers by identifying, capturing, storing, reusing, and learning from the myriad of explicit knowledge in your organization. All of this and more will be examined, because it contributes to your organization's need for KM.

Implementation of KM must consider the necessary resources to address the problem(s) being identified that call for KM. In our case for KM, we must communicate a payoff (Rhem, 2005). Why should our organization invest in KM without knowing the payoff and when it will occur? Another aspect of our case for KM is actually selling KM as an organizational effort and benefit and not just limited to a department or business unit.

The case for KM represents a well-argued and logically structured document that puts forward the business rationale for investing in a KM initiative. The case for KM as with any business case must clearly establish the following:

- The driving forces for the initiative
- The costs and risks of doing nothing
- A description of the proposed action(s)
- Comparison of the proposed action to other alternatives

- Accommodation of the proposed actions with the current and future goals of the organization
- The cost–benefit, risk, and financial assessments of the proposed action(s)
- A tentative, high-level strategy and a project plan outlining the key initiatives
- A statement on how the proposed action(s), if implemented, would improve the organization

This chapter will include a template for presenting your organization's business case for KM as well as some proven tips and techniques to enable your business to be approved!

Being Social: Knowledge Management and Social Media (Chapter 3)

KM at its core is people centric. Social media is driven by people and the interactions they have with each other. Many employees and customers of organizations are now engaged in social media. It is now engrained in our society, and new generations of current and future workers are shaping the way it is used and the impact it is been having. Through the implementation of KM, organizations are aligning social media principles, practices and tools to among other things expedite the sharing and the dissemination of knowledge and information real time. KM that utilizes social media will facilitate in building an environment that will facilitate how people interact outside the organization to within the organization. However, this must be accomplished by implementing much more stringent policies and guidelines concerning social media and related technologies. In this chapter, a look at constructing a social media strategy will bring to light how these capabilities must be managed by the organization.

Organizations have also committed resources to contribute to the social media voice. By employing social media specialist (among other titles), organizations tweet about their latest company products, news, specials, and so on, while also responding to others in the "twitter space." You will often find organizations with a Facebook presence, knowing that a great percentage of their customers are also on Facebook. Organizations are benefiting from social media, knowing that the virtual world is filled with knowledge, and they monitor that knowledge within the various social channels.

Social tools and mediums such as blogs, wikis, Twitter, Facebook, and LinkedIn represent the mechanisms to enable people to engage and share openly. These social tools put knowledge-sharing power in the hands of the users themselves, and this power has business and government taking notice. In this chapter, social media as it pertains to the key principles of KM will be examined. These key principles include knowledge sharing, knowledge capture, and knowledge reuse. As it pertains to social media, Twitter, Facebook, and LinkedIn will be the mechanisms that are included in this analysis. This chapter will also include input from my own experience, and the experiences that have been documented by others as contributors to the analysis will be conveyed in this chapter. In addition, this chapter will include a template for developing your organization's social media strategy as well as some proven tips and techniques to successfully execute this strategy.

Dude, "Where's My Car?": Utilizing Search in Knowledge Management (Chapter 4)

This chapter is all about search and "findability" of knowledge within the enterprise and/or customer-facing websites. In this chapter, concepts such as search engine optimization, ontology, taxonomy, information architecture, and information modeling are covered. To increase the chances, content and knowledge are properly located within the knowledge repository; having properly categorized content and knowledge is essential. Knowledge base concepts such as "tagging," metadata, keywords, and synonyms will also be covered. When we understand these concepts along with our specific requirements, we will be better equipped to select the right tool to satisfy our searching needs.

When it comes to selecting a software tool to facilitate the management of our knowledge, whether it's replacing a current tool or if it's the first time implementing a KM tool, we must have a plan on how we are going to get the content on to the knowledge repository. Having a clear, concise, and workable plan for content migration is a critical ingredient in our ability to later find all content and especially those "knowledge nuggets" that will help us in performing our tasks. This chapter will cover the steps that should be considered when developing your content migration strategy. These steps and concepts include the following:

- Content identification
- Content analysis
- Stakeholder/management engagement
- Knowledge repository design
- Taxonomy, content types, and metadata mapping
- Training
- Content migration

Finally, to conclude this chapter, a discussion on where search is heading toward and the tools enabling findability of knowledge will be examined. This chapter will include the examination of Web 2.*x* through Web 4.*x* paradigms. Search paradigms such as PIK-Map, Syntactic/Semantic Frames, intelligence/rules-based content retrieval, Natural Language parsers, and Spiders will all be included. A distension between the search needs of the enterprise and the search needs of the customer facing websites will be examined. The discussion on software tools could not be complete without examining some of the most widely used tools and the criteria established to use when selecting an enterprise search solution.

The Age of Discovery: Knowledge Management in Research Institutions (Chapter 5)

Research institutions are critical to innovation and new product creation. The speed to market for new products are essential to stay ahead of your competitors. KM plays a central role in innovation through the use of collaboration and knowledge sharing.

At its core, the nature of research is to nurture open access to extensive amounts of tacit knowledge (knowledge within the minds of people) and explicit knowledge (knowledge that is written down) by applying a model that reflects the natural of flow of knowledge. The model of Connect → Collect → Reuse and Learn depicts a knowledge flow model that supports KM within research institutions and R&D functions within organizations. For KM to work within a research environment (as with other environments) a culture and structure that supports, rewards, and proves the value KM will encourage the continued use and adoption of the KM practice.

In addition, the choice of IT tools (which is of secondary importance) should be brought into the organization to automate the knowledge flow and its associated process. The KM tool(s) must support KM goals/strategies, and provide a means to connect, collect, catalog, access, and reuse tacit and explicit knowledge. In addition, the KM tool(s) must capture new learning to share across the organization and provide search and retrieval mechanisms to bring pertinent knowledge to the user. Research institutions and departments utilizing KM effectively will have an advantage over their competitors who are not utilizing KM by getting better products to market quicker, increasing the level of innovation at their organizations, and establishing an environment of empowerment for research professionals.

This chapter will cover the KM strategy (including a strategy template), techniques, best practices, and application of KM necessary for research institutions to innovate more effectively and shorten the time to bring new products to market. Topics such as knowledge sharing techniques (communities of practice [CoP], collaborative workspaces, and after action reviews); techniques for innovation (knowledge café, root cause analysis, and problem finding); tools to facilitate KM within the research organization; ways to quickly institute the KM procedures, practices, and principles into the organization; and the key benefits of KM will also be covered.

"Where Have All My Experts Gone?": Knowledge Management in Human Resources and Talent Management (Chapter 6)

Talent management is often referred to as human capital management. Many organizations are faced with the problem of retaining talent as well as capturing the knowledge of the talent as it moves in and out of the organization. KM plays an important role in converting individual knowledge into corporate knowledge, thereby making it available to be cataloged and shared throughout the organization.

As part of a comprehensive KM strategy applied to human capital management, it is vital to establish a program that is executed when your staff enters the organization and continues until the time that staff member leaves the organization. How is this accomplished? Initially, through employee orientation; establishing a mentor–protégé relationship; mapping their roles, responsibilities, and their work products to the specific duties that are being performed; and executing a comprehensive exit interview. All these are aspects of a KM strategy aimed at moving your human capital to corporate capital.

This strategy does not begin and end here! As staff members evolve in their roles, the sharing and cataloging of knowledge continues through the use of CoP, the creation of knowledge repositories, capturing lesson learned, and instituting a culture that values lifelong learning and sharing of knowledge. Getting started with a KM strategy entails a collective vision as to how sharing of knowledge can enhance organizational performance, and that the knowledge of the organization is a valuable commodity that must be collected, cataloged and reused.

In this chapter, the following concepts and topics will be examined:

- Human capital management critical success factors
- Human capital challenges facing organizations
- Capturing employee tacit and explicit knowledge
- Knowledge mapping for identifying key knowledge holders and what they know
- High impact talent management framework

"Sound the Alarm!": Knowledge Management in Emergency and Disaster Preparedness (Chapter 7)

First responders (i.e., police, fire, and emergency medical teams) many times are not able to respond quickly and effectively, causing the increase probability of seriously injured people not receiving care in a timely fashion. This has led to loss of life in situations where one's life could have been saved. Nationally (as seen by the response to Hurricanes Katrina and Rita, and 9/11 attacks), there is a problem in effectively and efficiently enabling first responders in their effort to prepare, respond, and provide recovery during an emergency and/or crisis situation.

KM applied to the preparedness, response, and recovery mission of first responders will enable them to arrive at the scene in a timely manner, be equipped with the right knowledge of the situation, and have the right tools and technology to execute their job, resulting in saving lives. In many urban areas of the United States, when a first responder team is dispatched, they often do not arrive in a timely manner, are not fully aware of the situation, and are not fully equipped to handle the situation. Applying KM to disaster preparedness, response, and recovery will save lives not only in the communities' first responder serve but also within the first responder teams themselves, resulting in a safer, fully knowledgeable team responding to a crises event.

This indicates a need to apply a comprehensive KM strategy that will incorporate the necessary KM policies, principles, practices, and technology to enable knowledge sharing, knowledge harvesting, and knowledge delivery, including alerts to the right people, at the right time, in the right manner.

In this chapter, a KM strategy focused on emergency preparedness and response by first responders will be examined as well as aspects of that plan will be presented. A details analysis of a comprehensive emergency alert system will be presented. This chapter will examine the following areas of a comprehensive emergency alert system: emergency alert interaction (two-way interaction), geographical information system-based real-time alert delivery, leveraging a cloud-based architecture, scalability, and interoperability.

Happily Ever After: Knowledge Management in Mergers and Acquisitions (Chapter 8)

Mergers and acquisitions are a way of life in corporate America and around the world. The results in most cases are mixed. The basic premise is that the acquiring company and/or the merging companies are looking for synergies, increase market share, and overall a stronger and a more viable entity.

Synergy allows for enhanced cost efficiencies of the new business entity. When companies decide to go through a merger/acquisition, the organizations involved anticipate benefiting from the following:

- *Staff reductions*: More often than not, it means job losses. Cost savings are realized from reducing the number of staff members from departments across the organization(s).
- *Economies of scale*: As we all know size matters, it is no surprise that a larger company placing the orders can save more on costs. Mergers often translate into improved purchasing power to buy equipment or office supplies. When placing larger orders, larger companies (i.e., Wal-Mart, Microsoft, and Boeing) have a greater ability to negotiate prices with their suppliers.
- *Acquiring new technology*: To stay competitive, companies need to stay on top of technological developments and their business applications. By buying a smaller company with unique technologies, a large company can maintain or develop a competitive edge.

■ *Improved market reach and industry visibility*: Companies buy companies to reach new markets and grow revenues and earnings. A merge may expand two companies' marketing and distribution, giving them new sales opportunities. A merger can also improve a company's standing in the investment community: bigger firms often have an easier time raising capital than smaller ones.

More often than not, understanding the synergies or the lack thereof when it comes to personnel is absent. Understanding the personnel challenges of a merger/acquisition will be the key to the success of the transaction and the ongoing operation of the new entity.

This understanding will be enhanced by applying the KM principles leveraged within human capital management (see Chapter 6). In this chapter, the specifics of mergers and acquisitions and the application of KM (more precisely human capital management) to improve the process and outcomes as it pertains to retaining staff, conducting staff reductions, identifying key knowledge holders, and understanding knowledge gaps are examined.

"Is There a Doctor in the House?": Knowledge Management in Healthcare (Chapter 9)

With the advent of healthcare reform and the move to digitize health records, streamline medical costs, and to enable better medical decisions, many organizations in the healthcare industry are turning to KM. A prime method in utilizing KM in healthcare is through healthcare informatics. Healthcare informatics incorporates information technology and healthcare to support clinical workflow, collect, organize, and secure health related data, information, and knowledge. It also supports the growing knowledge base of physicians in order for them to make better decisions, reduce the costs of treatments, eliminate (severely cut) mistakes, and improve overall patient care.

Healthcare informatics combines the fields of information technology and health to develop the systems required to administer the expansion of information, advance clinical work flow, and improve the security of the healthcare system. It involves the integration of information science, computer technology, and medicines to collect, organize, and secure information systems and health-related data. As a result, the extraordinary explosion of medical knowledge, technologies, and ground-breaking drugs may vastly improve healthcare delivery to consumers, and keeping the information and knowledge related to these advancements organized and accessible is the key.

Some of the keys to patient care are the ability to evaluate large amounts of data and information, which includes the use of medical informatics. These are the keys to deliver medical knowledge to the right people, at the right time, in the right context. Electronic health records, data warehouses, laptops, and other mobile devices now provide access to information at the point of care. This access facilitates a continuous learning environment in which lessons learned can provide updates to clinical, administrative, and financial processes. Given these advancements, it is imperative that data, information, and knowledge are managed for effective healthcare. Applying principles of KM has become the catalyst for quality healthcare delivery and management.

This chapter provides a detailed understanding of the practice of KM within the healthcare industry. The content includes critical aspects of healthcare operations, knowledge strategies for healthcare operations, knowledge essential elements for healthcare, knowledge mapping and medical informatics, knowledge creation and discovery in medical informatics, applying KM to healthcare, and knowledge tools and techniques for healthcare.

"Show Me the Money!": Knowledge Management for Financial Services (Chapter 10)

The financial services industry is a highly dynamic and competitive marketplace. As the fight for customers intensifies, it is increasingly important to attend to customer needs while ensuring customer information is shared with the right people at the right time across the institution. To this end, the technology supporting the institution is vital to facilitating the movement of information and knowledge to the customer. KM systems will have an increased importance as trends in personal investing move toward broader services and integrated product offerings.

By utilizing a KM system, all employees interacting with a customer will have up-to-date knowledge of that customer's breadth of relationship and experience with the institution. This helps the institution with cross selling, up selling, and reporting on the effectiveness of any new customer initiatives.

Today, organizations are integrating KM into their business philosophies, making it more common practice and therefore less differentiating factor of success, thus creating the need for KM practice to become more and more superior. This is especially true in the light that more and more knowledge is becoming available, while at the same time also being becoming more sophisticated, making KM more complex. This results in the fact that businesses that manage knowledge better within their organization and outside of it addressing the evolving customer needs will improve their overall performance and become the leaders within the industry.

It is well recognized that the financial services business environment is ever changing and is doing so at an ever-increasing rate. The stock market (DOW, NASDAQ, and S&P) swings on the earnings of large corporations, the ever-evolving political climate, the volatility of European and Asian markets, and the price of oil, just to name a few. This presents financial organizations with the challenge of acting and reacting to this volatility and communicating an appropriate value proposition to the market. In addition, having an increasingly sophisticated consumer who is armed with the latest trading technology has added further stress to these companies to deliver the right knowledge, at the right time, in the right way to their customers.

This chapter focuses on the use of KM within the financial industry. Specific attention will be on how KM is being leveraged in the commodity (futures and options) and the stock market, including the mutual funds sector within the United States. Online trading financial companies, the electronic trading applications in the commodities and stock market, and the sophisticated trading tools leveraged by today's financial consumer are the catalyst for the implementation of KM practices, policies, procedures, and applications, all aimed at creating a differential between companies that deliver financial services and the people who are working to build financial stability with them.

"Are You in Good Hands?": Knowledge Management in Insurance (Chapter 11)

In the insurance industry, trade secrets, confidential information, and valuable ideas are part of the workforce knowledge. Recruiting, selecting, training, and managing contact center employees, agents, and other corporate and field office employees present a real challenge for insurance companies. In addition, government and industry laws and regulations as well as ethics present their own unique challenges of understanding, application, and enforcement. These challenges are being addressed through the implementation and execution of KM policies, practices, procedures, and software applications.

In the insurance industry, there are an ample number of factors as stated above to be considered for KM to facilitate decisions within a problem situation. These factors include the sharing and transfer of experiences (tacit knowledge) as well as the sharing and transfer of practices, how-tos, and lessons learned (explicit knowledge). This knowledge can be transferred through sharing, and in some instances, it can be codified (Rhem, 2005). It is very difficult to retain the intellectual capital when a person leaves an organization; moreover, it is difficult to value these intangible assets and is essential to retain them inside the organization in order to take competitive advantage of these assets (Rhem, 2005).

Applying KM will facilitate the insurers' ability to meet these challenges and achieve efficiencies by leveraging the combined knowledge of its workforce and effectively turning it into a competitive advantage. Insurance companies (as well as others) are focusing on providing for their customers and in doing so generating profitable growth. In the face of a demanding economic environment, tight margins, regulations, availability, and quality of people, as well as data, information, and knowledge, all insurance organizations are facing challenges on several fronts. These include talent management (see Chapter 6), organizational responsiveness to the customer, cost control, and compliance.

KM in the insurance industry centers on meeting the customer needs, balancing growth with profit, protecting financial strength, and creating high-performing teams. In this chapter, the focus will be on how insurance companies are leveraging KM to address the needs of the customer through examining customer call centers, agents, decisions supporting underwriting and claims, and use of knowledge of the internal employees.

"Sign Right Here!": Knowledge Management in the Legal Profession (Chapter 12)

KM in law firms has taken off in recent years. Here it's not only a requirement to have KM experience, a KM certification (or formal degree), but most law firms are requiring that future employees also have a *Juris Doctor* (JD). The requirement for a JD may not be as stringent at corporations that are looking for KM resources within their legal departments; they usually look for candidates with KM and/or a library sciences background. All of this is fueled by the fact that KM enables legal organizations to respond quickly, efficiently, and effectively when it comes to servicing its employees and at the end of the day, their clients as well.

KM in law firms is often executed through the following elements: building and fostering CoP around practice specialties and/or areas of responsibility; development and use/reuse of knowledge assets; enabling collaboration beyond the CoP and into extended communities; capturing and validating knowledge produced as a result of collaboration; systematically hosting tacit knowledge; arranging and efficiently presenting knowledge assets to users; and creating/nurturing a culture of knowledge sharing, collaboration, and lifelong learning.

According to Ted Tjaden,

> In a law firm setting, *explicit knowledge* tends to be precedent agreements, checklists, research memos, opinion letters, and "how to" guides. Equally—if not more important—is the *tacit knowledge*, being what lawyers know, their experience and their professional judgment. Capturing and organizing explicit legal knowledge can be relatively straightforward and involves a combination of technologies (internal document management systems, search and tagging technology, and intranets). Capturing and organizing tacit legal knowledge can be more challenging. In most firms, tacit knowledge is transferred through mentoring, training and allowing a knowledge-sharing culture to flourish. (Tjaden, 2010; [my emphasis])

In this chapter, the focus will be on how law firms manage their vast array of explicit and tacit knowledge. In addition this chapter presents an understanding of how explicit and tacit knowledge when used together can provide the law firm with a distinct advantage over its competition. This chapter will specifically examine how law firms are leveraging precedent development, legal research, competitive intelligence, training lawyers (talent management), intranet deployment, project management, and client support, all in relation to instituting KM within their legal institutions.

"A Mind is a Terrible Thing to Waste!": Knowledge Management Education (Chapter 13)

The increased focus on the knowledge economy has heightened interest in KM as a profession, an occupation, and its essential competencies. Many believe that it is time to acknowledge KM as a professional area of practice and it is necessary to begin a formal discussion of the educational foundation needed to support this area of professional practice. Although there is a wealth of published and informal literature, thoughts derived from practice, and dialogs on these topics, a consensus on what constitutes the core elements of KM competencies and KM education is lacking.

A consensus is needed among those who are currently providing KM training, teaching KM via traditional course work, and supporting KM programs and departments within organizations. This consensus needs to be informed and supported by knowledge professionals who are currently working in knowledge roles today. In addition, as with all professional domains, the KM domain needs to be continuously reviewed and refreshed by professional educators and working professionals.

KM education must connect education and strategic learning competencies with skill and ability in knowledge strategy development, implementation, collaboration, and leadership and management skills, in addition to technical competencies. KM continues to be a growing discipline in which organizations are seeking qualified individuals. This is reflected in many institutions of higher education offering an MSc degree in KM. This degree offers students an opportunity to enter the knowledge economy and become an important asset to organizations working to get the right knowledge, to the right people, at the right time.

This chapter will focus on KM education delivery and options within universities and colleges as well as in KM certification organizations. This chapter will cover topics such as strategic roles and responsibilities of KM professionals in organizations today and the educational needs of these professionals, standard KM competencies, KM curriculum development and delivery, and teaching methodologies.

"Big Knowledge!": Knowledge Management and Big Data (Chapter 14)

The proliferation of data, information, and knowledge has created a phenomenon called "Big Data." KM when applied to Big Data will enable the type of analysis that will uncover the complete picture of the organization and be a catalyst for driving decisions. The connection between Big Data and KM brings together the entirety of your organization's structured and unstructured data sources that are spread across a wide variety of repositories, databases, data warehouses, and content sources, in order for your organization to tap into its vast know-how to make better decisions on a multitude of issues and directions on an ongoing basis.

Currently, the ability for an organization to tap into its Big Data sources to gain a competitive edge places a heavy reliance on analytics. Organizations are investigating ways to efficiently and effectively collect and manage the data, information, and knowledge they are exposed to via various internal and external sources (which are typically networked together). KM will bring opportunities—both technical and organizational—when working with Big Data. Organizationally, KM delivers strategy, governance, process-centric approaches, and inter-organizational aspects of decision support as well as technical considerations when incorporating new data sources and new frameworks for Big Data analytics, including KM.

This chapter takes a look into where KM and Big Data are heading toward within the organization. The advancement of search technologies (which play a key role in delivering knowledge within a KM system) impact our ability to access Big Data will be examined here. In addition to search technologies, several other KM technologies are addressing Big Data. These technologies include solutions that mine unstructured data and manage and use/reuse the knowledge found in Big Data. This chapter will examine knowledge classifications, social network analysis, Big Data sources, and information architecture, all aimed at providing details on how KM is and will work with Big Data.

"What Have You Done for the War Fighter Today?": *Knowledge Management in the Military (Chapter 15)*

KM in the US military has been implemented using a top-down approach that is resonated through each branch, command, directorate, division, group, battalion, and so on. The US military has established a culture of KM that leverages its personnel, processes, and systems to facilitate a consistent flow of knowledge and the mechanisms to execute and make decisions from this knowledge.

It is widely acknowledged that KM strategy is a desired precursor to developing specific KM initiatives. The US military has established KM strategies from the top down in every branch. As this strategy is propagated and aligned through the organization, it is often a difficult process due to a variety of influences and constraints. These KM influences and constraints include understanding, conflicts with IT organizations, funding, technology usage and configuration, and outsourcing.

Any discussion of KM in the military should include a discussion of the Army Knowledge Management (AKM) principles, which were signed out by the army chief of staff (General Casey) and the secretary of the army in 2008. The AKM principles still are in effect and have served as a basis for KM efforts in the army and the federal KM arena at large.

Each US military branch works to overcome barriers in KM adoption. To this effort, an establishment of processes and tools, which involves providing approaches and solutions for knowledge sharing, has influenced a change in people's habits. This change will drive values to move US military organization culture to father overall

KM adoption. In support of the US military in its knowledge sharing efforts, CoP have become an integral method of sharing and distributing knowledge across all branches of the military. In addition, enterprise web search capabilities have been implemented to increase "findability" of key content, which is the leverage for decision making at all levels of command.

In my examination of KM in the military, I will take a holistic approach. This approach will not only begin with an examination of the AKM but also look at what each branch is doing from strategy through tactical implementation of KM programs, systems, and initiatives down to the command level. I will look at the synergies between the branches and identify tips, techniques, and best practices. In addition, I will leverage my own experiences as well as the experiences of others whom I have interviewed in the process of understanding the practice and execution of KM within the various military branches.

Drinking the Knowledge Management Kool-Aid: Knowledge Management Adoption (Chapter 16)

Many organizations have begun to understand the value and promise KM can bring to their workforce. Delivering innovation through collaboration and sharing remain the cornerstones of KM. However, once your organization has established its KM strategy and/or rolled out its initial KM offering (i.e., KM system, KM process, and tools) what happens next? What happens next is the adoption process. Whether it's a new process, procedure, or system, getting your workforce to leverage and use it in the course of executing activities and delivering on their task will be essential to your KM program's success. In order to achieve this, there must be processes and vehicles in place to allow, encourage, and reward staff members as they work within this new paradigm. It will not be easy. As with anything new, it will take some time for the adoption to occur. To move this along, there must be KM supporters, mentors, and/or evangelists at all levels of the corporate infrastructure to encourage the workforce to "drink the KM Kool-Aid." In other words, buy in and practice KM in all aspects of performing tasks and activities.

Developing an organizational culture of knowledge sharing, collaboration, and lifelong learning should be the goals of any KM program. Organizations such as the Fluor Corporation, Irving, Texas, have been successful in infusing KM within its culture. From human resource activities to leveraging knowledge for strategic purposes, to engaging with clients, Fluor sets an example of how KM can be leveraged effectively in an organization. Drinking the "KM Kool-Aid" is a slow and deliberate activity grounded in a basic KM process of Connect → Collect → Catalog → Reuse → Learn and Innovate. When practiced effectively, this process will be a cornerstone to enabling the adoption of KM throughout your organization.

Failure Is Not an Option: Why Do Knowledge Management Programs and Projects Fail? (Chapter 17)

Although the lack of or absence of adoption will set your KM efforts on a path for failure, there are many other contributing factors that will also lead you down this road.

The fact is that few KM initiatives are successful. But, why is this the result? What is the cause and effect? Is it because there is a lack of qualified professional? Or is there more to it than these? What about a magic "silver bullet"? Is it a cultural issue?

I believe the reason why KM initiatives fail are varied and can be attributable to many factors. Moreover, I believe one of the main reasons why KM initiatives fail is based on how the organization views KM. KM is viewed just as a function of the call center. It is more than a function of a call center and its benefits are far-reaching as any Lean process or any other initiatives that a corporation may put into practice. KM is mainly viewed by most corporations that have a KM effort as a cost of doing business. This is an error in philosophy. KM is a method of reducing expenses, improving productivity, and enhancing value.

KM will improve efficiencies that will increase a corporation's profitability, and enhance the quality of work, performance, and overall value of the corporation. KM allows tacit knowledge to be leveraged, transferred to increase the quality of work performed across the corporation. This tacit knowledge allows KM to eliminate the "reinvent the wheel" syndrome. This transfer of knowledge is the essence of KM.

Outside of a corporation's philosophy error, there are several reasons for the failure of KM initiatives. Some of those reasons are as follows:

■ Expecting KM technologies to replace KM processes or create processes where none exists
■ Lack of participation from all levels of a corporation
■ Forcing inadequate processes into new technology
■ Lack of maintenance and resources after initial standup
■ Lack of education and understanding of what KM means to the individual
■ KM does not become ingrained into the corporation's work culture
■ Lack of involvement in creating and evolving KM content
■ Lack of metrics to measure the impact of KM on the corporation or insufficient/incorrect metrics being captured
■ Lack of monitoring and controls in place to ensure the knowledge is relevant, and is current and accurate

KM initiatives are essential to a corporation's growth and are more than just the cost of doing business. Successful KM initiatives once completed and funded correctly will increase a corporation's profitability, and enhance the quality of work and overall value of the corporation.

Summary (Chapter 18)

In this book, I have presented details about KM in various industries, where I have had the opportunity to help clients implement KM solutions as well as specific KM topics that are critical in today's KM landscape. These solutions and topics ranged from KM strategies, knowledge transfer planning/execution, implementing KM systems, Big Data search, KM adoption, deploying methods to capture knowledge, and planning and executing on KM governance.

Each chapter includes key learnings as well as tips and techniques for those currently instituting KM in that particular industry and/or topic. Each chapter examines and analyzes the subject matter, and the keys for successfully applying the subject matter in "real-world" situation(s).

Knowledge Management in Practice is intended as a reference for KM practitioners, organizations implementing KM, and those who are studying KM at the various academic and KM certification institutions. This chapter presents a synopsis of what was presented in each chapter, the intended key takeaways, and a peek into the future of individuals and organizations practicing KM.

Outline of the Book

This book will give detailed information on applying KM practices, procedures, and techniques to solve real-world problems. The applications of KM that will be examined include social media; knowledge and content management; search engine optimization; capturing and codifying tacit and explicit knowledge; KM in disaster preparedness, action, and reaction; KM adoption process in an organization; failure of KM projects; and specific industry applications of knowledge management. This publication will contribute to the advancement in application of KM principles, practices, and procedures, as well as the systems that support KM.

Each chapter will include key learnings as well as tips and techniques for those who are currently instituting KM. The following section outlines the structure each chapter.

Structure of Each Chapter

Each chapter will examine and analyze the relevant subject matter, key learnings for successfully applying the subject matter, and tips and techniques for applying the subject matter in "real-world" situation(s).

Lessons learned from each chapter will refer to the knowledge gained through the experience of working within a specific domain(s), which can be negative or positive and can have a significant impact on the organization. Identifying and applying the lessons learned helps eliminate the occurrence of the similar problems in future and/or replicate successes that will establish best practices in future KM initiatives.

Tips and techniques listed in each chapter will refer to points to consider when implementing KM within a particular subject examined in that chapter. It will often take into consideration how to apply a significant lesson learned to improve successful implementation of a particular KM concept(s).

Now we will begin our "real-world" examination of the practice of KM.

Chapter 2

The Case for Implementing Knowledge Management

If your organization is losing valuable knowledge due to staff retirement, staff moving to other departments, or staff dismissed for a variety of reasons, then your organization has a strong case for the implementation of a knowledge management (KM) strategy. Specifically, if your organization is experiencing any of the following scenarios then it has a strong case to implement a KM program or at the very least initiate a KM project to address these needs.

Scenario 1: Customer service representatives respond to customers and/or potential customer inquiries with inconsistent and oftentimes incorrect answers.
  – For interacting with your customers, the information in your organization can be transformed into useful and actionable knowledge to address customer inquiries and provide them with what they need to know at the right time and the right context.
  – Customer-facing activities include
    • Providing knowledge to customer support representatives in response to customer inquiries.
    • Providing FAQs to customers related to the products, services, and other aspects about the organization via self-help options/functionality.
    • Knowledge is also provided through help modules accessed by the customer usually through the organization's website, and/or through web-based chat or click-to-call capabilities.

Scenario 2: Your organization has a need to address employee/associate knowledge needs:

- Knowledge provided here reflects the need for employees to access key knowledge holders in the organization to answer questions, collaborate on problems/issues, and/or provide content.
- The knowledge in this space often resides in the minds of individual workers (tacit knowledge). In addition, there exist a myriad of artifacts, which include but are not limited to, lesson learned, standard operating procedures, guidelines, templates, tips and techniques, spreadsheets, presentation files, videos, and graphics (explicit knowledge) that must be captured to address the individual worker's knowledge needs.

Scenario 3: Your organization has a need to address corporate operations knowledge needs:

- The corporate operations/technical support activities of the firm provide technical solutions to inquiries not only to customers but also to internal knowledge workers (employees) as it pertains to any hardware and/or software being provided by the organization.
- The knowledge in this area is reflected by documenting software "bug" solutions, known errors, software patches, issue resolutions, and other specific data concerning the hardware and software configurations in the organization.

Scenario 4: Your organization has a need to bring new product innovations to the marketplace:

- The need for KM in this area addresses situations where duplication of effort occurs, not having the right team in place to perform the research to bring the product innovation to market successfully and in a timely manner, always reinventing or starting from "square one," difficulty locating current and/or historical corporate information/knowledge on a specific topic(s), and expertise leaving the organization creating a knowledge gap (see Chapter 5).

The business case for KM represents a well-argued and logically structured document that puts forward the business rationale for investing in a KM initiative. The case for implementing KM as with any business case must clearly establish the following:

- The problem or business opportunity addressed by the KM initiative
- Applying/leveraging KM to address the problem
- Detail the options available to implement the KM solution
- Analyze the risk of doing nothing
- Analyze the cost–benefit, risk, and financial assessments (return on investment [ROI]) of the proposed KM solution

KM Business Case Structure

In order to construct a KM business case, understanding its structure is the first step. The KM business case structure (see Appendix A) consists of the following:

Problem statement

The problem statement is the identification of the problem or business opportunity being addressed by the KM initiative. A problem statement is clear, concise, and to the point and is often the compass to keep the team focused on delivering an outcome that solves the intended issue(s)/opportunity being addressed.

Understanding the five "Ws"

The five W's consist of Who, What, Where, When, and Why. Remembering the five Ws will enable you to construct the problem statement in a way that will present pertinent details that are being addressed. The following details the five Ws.

Who: Who does the problem affect? This pertains to specific stakeholders (groups, departments, customers, etc.).

What: What are the boundaries of the problem, for example, organizational, work flow, geographic, customer, and segments—What is the issue?—What is the impact of the issue?—What impact is the issue causing?—What will happen when it is fixed?—What would happen if we didn't solve the problem?

When: When does the issue occur?—When does it need to be resolved?

Where: Where is the issue occurring? Only in certain locations, processes, products, and so on.

Why: Why is it important that we fix the problem?—What impact does it have on the business, employees, or customers?—What impact does it have on all stakeholders, for example, employees, suppliers, customers, and shareholders? Each of the answers will help to zero in on the specific issue(s) and properly articulate the problem statement. Remember that your problem statement should be solvable (a solution should be able to be deployed to resolve the issues presented by the problem statement) (Figure 2.1).

KM Solution Analysis

The KM solution analysis involves analyzing how KM will be leveraged to address the problem or business opportunity.

Needs Analysis

In the needs analysis (also called "requirements definition") phase, one begins documenting the business opportunity (or problem). Any issue can be looked upon as a problem or an opportunity. In writing business cases, I have found that you get a much warmer reception if you frame things in a positive light, that is, as

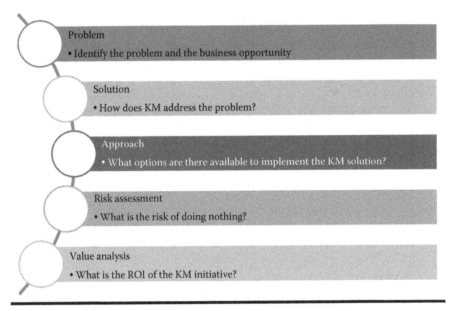

Figure 2.1   KM business case structure.

opportunities, rather than as problems. In defining the opportunity, one needs to first be clear in identifying the objectives. Objectives are the measurable outcomes that one wants to achieve upon the completion of the proposed KM initiatives. Identifying the objectives and being clear on why they make business sense is very important. Objectives should be tied to outcomes from the strategic assessment phase, for example, the current and/or desired states of the business and the current business needs. Objectives are normally classified as first-order (critical), second-order (important), and third-order (nice to have).

KM Solution Implementation Approach

The KM solution implementation approach explores the options that are available to implement the KM solution determined in the solution analysis. The implementation has two possible components: (1) A program level component providing the business case calls for implementing a KM program (2) and/or a KM initiative approach.

The KM program must optimize the organization, exchange, currency, and accessibility of knowledge, so that employees and other stakeholders spend less time looking for what they need in order to make critical decisions and complete specific tasks and activities. Effective workers do not just need to recognize their own knowledge and skills, but they must also recognize and strategically use those of others.

Program management is a method to manage related groups of KM initiatives.

Project Management Institute defines it as

> A group of related KM initiatives managed in a coordinated way to obtain benefits and control not available from managing them individually. Programs may include elements of related work outside scope of the discrete KM initiatives in the program. (PMBOK p. 368)

In summary, a program is a collection of initiatives and KM initiatives that are designed to accomplish a strategic business objective. As stated above in defining the problem statement, it is important to know the business drivers (five Ws) concerned with the work being done. Because of the potential high cost and complexity of some programs and/or KM initiatives, it is essential to sell the benefits and gain support for program and/or KM initiative. To explain the aspects of a program further, a program can include a single product or deliverable, many deliverables, can be a combination of ongoing support activity in addition to deliverables, and usually focuses on business objectives and delivering value. Some characteristics of programs include deliverables with a strategic intent; may initiate a business change; can be a significant change to the organization; success criteria may include growth, productivity gains, and improvement in the market; there could be significant risks; are longer in duration than KM initiatives; and benefits are achieved throughout the duration of program. KM program initiatives include KM strategy, KM governance, KM taxonomy and information architecture development, change management, and KM communications planning and execution.

Software Methodologies

When implementing a KM solution that is driven out by a specific KM initiative within the overall program (or as part of a standalone initiative), a standard software methodology (Iterative, Agile/Scrum, OpenUP, or Knowledge Acquisition Unified Framework [KAUF]) (Rhem, 2011) should be utilized. The following sections briefly describe these methodologies.

Iterative Software Development Methodology

The Iterative software development methodology moves forward in increments called "iterations." The goal of each iteration is to develop a portion of working software that can be demonstrated to all the stakeholders, and that the stakeholders will find meaningful. The software developed by iteration should cut through all or most of the major subsystems of the KM initiative. It should not be concentrated to a single subsystem. Each iteration represents an effort made by each member of the team to build a small part on their behalf of the KM initiative and integrate those parts together (see Figure 2.2). The length of iteration depends upon the kind of KM initiative we

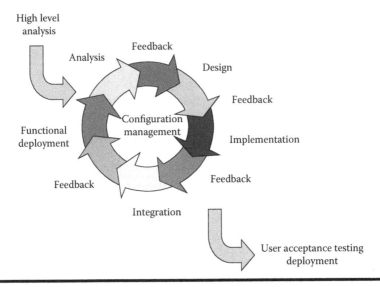

Figure 2.2 Iterative software development process: Project iteration flow (ncicb. nci.nih.gov).

are working with. However, short iterations are to be desired over long ones. The shorter the iteration, the less time passes before the team gets feedback. Iteration lengths of 1 or 2 weeks are not too short for most KM initiatives (Wiley, 2012).

Agile/Scrum

Agile/Scrum KM initiative management is an agile software development process. Scrum models allow KM initiatives to progress via a series of iterations called "agile sprints" (see Figure 2.3). Each sprint is typically 2–4 weeks, and sprint planning in the agile methodology and Scrum process are essential. Although the agile/Scrum methodology can be used for managing any KM initiative, the agile/Scrum process is ideally suited for KM initiatives with rapidly changing or highly emergent requirements such as software (Cohn, 2013).

The agile sprint itself is the main activity of Scrum KM initiative management. The agile methodology and Scrum process is iterative and incremental, so the KM initiative is split into a series of consecutive sprints. Each is timeboxed, usually to between 1 week and a calendar month. One survey found that the most common sprint length of a Scrum agile process is 2 weeks. During this time, the Scrum team does everything to take a small set of features from idea to coded and tested functionality (Cohn, 2013).

OpenUP Methodology

OpenUP is a lean Unified Process that applies iterative and incremental approaches within a structured life cycle (see Figure 2.4). OpenUP embraces a pragmatic, agile

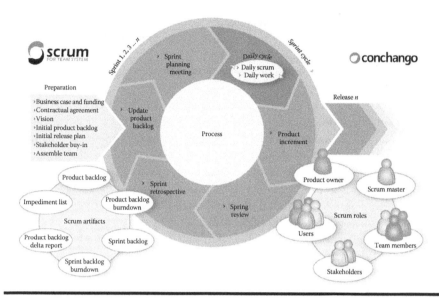

Figure 2.3 Scrum model overview (http://consultingblogs.emc.com/Admin/ ImageGallery/blogs.conchango.com/Colin.Bird/Scrum%20Overview%20 Diagram.png).

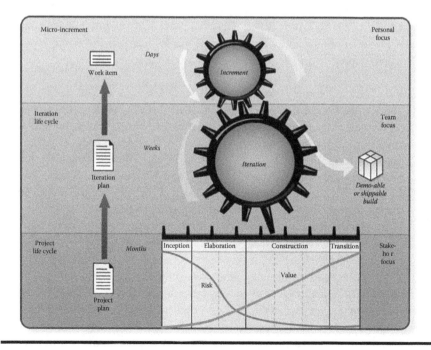

Figure 2.4 OpenUP (http://epf.eclipse.org/wikis/openup/).

philosophy that focuses on the collaborative nature of software development. It is a tools-agnostic, low-ceremony process that can be extended to address a broad variety of KM initiative types.

OpenUP is based on four mutually supporting core principles:

1. Balance competing priorities to maximize stakeholder value
   Promote practices that allow KM initiative participants and stakeholders to develop a solution that maximizes stakeholder benefits and is compliant with constraints placed on the KM initiative.
2. Collaborate to align interests and share understanding
   Promote practices that foster a healthy team environment, enable collaboration, and develop a shared understanding of the KM initiative.
3. Focus on the architecture early to minimize risks and organize development
   Promote practices that allow the team to focus on architecture to minimize risks and organize development.
4. Evolve to continuously obtain feedback and improve
   Promote practices that allow the team to get early and continuous feedback from stakeholders, and demonstrate incremental value to them.

Knowledge Acquisition Unified Framework

When the KM initiative calls for capturing tacit and explicit knowledge of the organization, the KAUF provides a repeatable process for identifying understanding and cataloging knowledge. The following briefly describes the seven steps that outline this framework.

Step 1—Define domain knowledge:
   The first step in the KAUF is to identify what domain (business unit/division/department, etc.) will be the focus of your knowledge elicitation and what knowledge is pertinent to be captured in this domain. In order to determine the knowledge to be captured, key knowledge holders and subject matter experts (SMEs) in the specified domain must be identified. This is typically done through a knowledge mapping exercise. Once this occurs, the KM analyst must ascertain what knowledge is essential to be captured. This can be accomplished through a series of interviews/surveys and analysis working closely with the key knowledge holders and SMEs.

Step 2—Decompose the domain knowledge:
   When attempting to solve any large-scale problem, we would typically break the activity into a number of smaller tasks; to help a domain experts (SMEs, content managers, contributors, etc.) populate the knowledge repository, we should similarly break the activity of knowledge acquisition into a number of smaller tasks. Structuring the task of populating the knowledge repository into a number of distinct sub-steps (typically based on the taxonomy/ontology

that has been established) will ease the process of populating the knowledge repository gradually.

Step 3—Determine interdependency:

Interdependency is when two or more pieces of knowledge/information depend on one another equally (one component depends on another). Finding the interdependency's between different pieces of knowledge (documents/artifacts, and/or expertise) will guide the knowledge analyst and domain expert(s) in completing the knowledge acquisition task. Determining the interdependence between aspects of knowledge/information will facilitate in identifying the missing pieces of knowledge, determining related pieces of knowledge, and determining any inconsistencies with the knowledge gathered for that domain.

Step 4—Recognize knowledge patterns:

When analyzing knowledge/information, the process of connect, collect, catalog, and reuse will uncover patterns of knowledge, and recognizing these patterns will contribute to increase efficiencies in the knowledge/information being captured.

Step 5—Determine judgments in knowledge:

If the knowledge being captured is determined to be judgmental (i.e., uncertain or "fuzzy"), then it must be analyzed to understand if conflicts exist. In addition, consulting with expert resources to come to a consensus as to what represents the "correct" knowledge may also be necessary.

Step 6—Perform conflict resolution:

There are situations in which sufficient expertise and/or documents are unavailable to solve conflicts within the knowledge being gathered. If the knowledge being captured has some uncertainty or is fuzzy, you must first specify preconditions in the context of one or more of the conflicting elements of the knowledge to prevent those conflicting elements from being considered.

Step 7—Capture/catalog the knowledge:

Tacit knowledge is now sufficiently ready to be cataloged and transformed into explicit knowledge to be prepared for inclusion into a KM solution (Figure 2.5).

Risk Assessment

The risk assessment analyzes the risk involved in implementing the agreed upon KM solution as well as the risk of doing nothing.

Value Analysis

The value analysis examines closely the value gained by the organization when implementing the KM solution. An analysis on the achievable ROI, including a timeline for when that would be realized, is also presented.

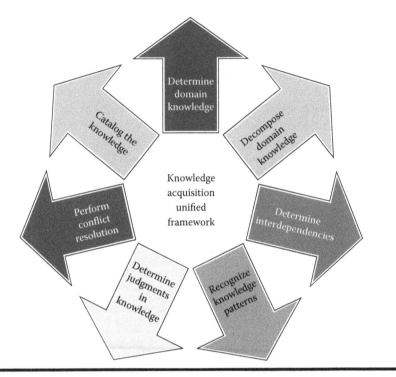

Figure 2.5   Knowledge acquisition unified framework (KAUF).

ROI for KM

From the outset, one must realize that making the case for a KM effort and calculating an ROI is not easy when compared to making the business case for a new piece of equipment, such as new computer color photocopier or office furniture, in a more traditional situation. Investing in a piece of equipment can be directly tied to increases in product quality and/or quantity through multiple metrics (e.g., lower defect rates and finished products per hour). However, calculating the ROI for investments in KM efforts is not that simple or direct.

It is my experience that ROI for KM is measured by how well it supports the mission and/or objectives of the organization. Taking this into account, at the end of the day, what matters is whether the KM initiative increased the performance of its users or how well did it support the strategic mission of the organization.

When we are looking at achieving a return on our KM initiatives historically, it can take a considerable amount of time to show results or visible ROI for an organization. However, there is an approach by Mark Clare to estimate the value of the intangible benefits of KM (Clare, 2002). This approach, the knowledge value equation (KVE), simply states that the value created from managing knowledge is a function of the costs, benefits, and risks of the KM initiative. It can be mathematically stated as follows: KM value = F (cost, benefit, and risk), which equals total discounted cash flow created over the life of the KM investment (Clare, 2002). This formula attempts to quantify the intangible impacts of KM relating it back to cash flow. This includes improved problem solving, enhanced creativity, and improved relationships with customers and other performance-related activities.

The following are the three common indicators of the viability of the KM initiative: net present value (NPV), internal rate of return (IRR), and the payback period. NPV helps us normalize future cash flows (both the cash we intend to spend and the cash we expect to receive) into their present value. As a general rule, if the NPV of a KM initiative is greater than zero, then you invest in the KM initiative. If the NPV is negative, you should not invest in the KM initiative. The reason for this is simple, the future cash flows, do not justify the present investment. The IRR is the discount rate (also called "investment yield rate") for the KM initiative. It is the rate at which the NPV for a KM initiative is equal to zero. When comparing two KM initiatives, the one with the higher IRR is preferred. Another option to the IRR is to present the ROI. This value represents, as the name implies, the savings (benefit) one will derive out of the KM initiative for the investment (cost) outlays.

The payback period helps one estimate how quickly the investment will be recouped. Put in another way, it is the time required for the savings to equal the cost. When comparing two nearly similar alternatives, a rational person will choose the KM initiative with the shorter payback period. The important thing to bear in mind is that no single financial metric will be adequate for evaluating a KM initiative's feasibility or its value proposition in comparison to other uses of the funds. Metrics are best used in conjunction with each other, as each one provides a slightly different value perspective.

Unlike traditional (e.g., manufacturing) KM initiatives, financial analysis for a KM initiative has two more complications. First, much of the benefits derived from a KM initiative will be based on soft facts; that is, KM lead to changes in behaviors, approaches, and methods that, on their own, may not have direct bottom-line impacts. However, when these are mapped and traced to organizational processes, the impacts can be measured and articulated. Needless to say, this is often a more time-consuming and creative effort than simply measuring direct impacts, as in the case of outcomes from a new piece of manufacturing equipment. Equally important is that there is a lag time between when one invests in a KM effort and when one witnesses outcomes that result in payoffs. Accounting for this lag time is not easy, yet it is essential to building an adequate business case.

Investing in KM is akin to a group as a whole investing in a common effort. Consider the case of investing in initiatives such as the prevention of global warming by reducing greenhouse gas emissions or the promotion of fair trade practices. Most people agree that preventing global warming or increasing the adoption of fair trade practices benefits society. The challenge arises when we ask who wants to take responsibility for investing in these efforts. If taxes were raised to support these efforts, would you be happy? Rational individuals often want others to bear the cost of these common efforts and gladly enjoy the benefits, yet hesitate to initiate responsibility. A similar predicament faces KM efforts. Departments within an organization want their peers' units to invest in a common effort. Each department might see KM as an effort someone else should put up resources for and hence defers spending its own resources. In some organizations, KM efforts might be viewed as a "tax" levied.

KM Metrics and Key Performance Indicators

KM strategy will link the best practices to initiatives to expected benefits (Best practice → KM initiative → Benefit). At every phase in KM tactical delivery of initiatives, metrics should provide a valuable means for focusing attention on desired behaviors and results. Each KM initiative and KM activity should have its own set of metrics.

KM performance measures have several objectives:
- Help make a business case for implementation or sustainment and expansion
- Provide targets or goals to drive desired behavior
- Guide and tune the implementation process by providing feedback
- Retrospectively measure the value of the initial investment decision and the lessons learned
- Develop benchmarks for future comparisons and for others to use
- Aid learning from the effort and developing lessons learned

Key performance indicators (KPIs) and metrics to track for the KM strategy include the following:

Customer satisfaction: Customer satisfaction can be improved, specifically in contact centers and agencies, where there is constant interaction with the customer. Customer satisfaction is best measured using standard market research techniques:
- Surveys
- Follow-up telephone calls
- Focus groups

Search engine usage: Search engine logs can be analyzed to produce a range of simple reports, showing usage and a breakdown of search terms.

Knowledge use: A more direct measure of many KM initiatives is whether the information is being "used in practice." As usage normally happens outside of the system, it must be reported by the staff. Provide simple mechanism for notifying when information is used, and implement a rewards mechanism to encourage timely reporting.

Number of users: Directly related to system usage is the total number of staff accessing the system. This should clearly grow as the system is rolled out across the organization. This can be tracked via security login in order to determine accurate staff numbers.

User rankings: This involves asking the readers themselves to rate the relevance and quality of the information being presented. SMEs or other reviewers can directly assess the quality of material in the content management system or KM platform.

Edits required: This can be done by utilizing workflow capability. Audit trails generated by this can be analyzed to determine how many edits or reviews are required for each piece of content. If the original material is of a high quality, it should require little editing.

Links created: A Popular page with useful information will be more frequently linked to from other parts of the system. By measuring the number of links, the effectiveness of individual pages can be determined.

Information Currency

This is a measure of how up to date the information stored within the system is. The importance of this measure will depend on the nature of the information being published, and how it is used. The best way to track this is using the metadata stored within the content management system, such as publishing and review dates. By using this, automated reports showing a number of specific measures can be generated:

- Average age of pages
- Number of pages older than a specific age
- Number of pages past their review date
- Lists of pages due to be reviewed
- Pages to be reviewed, broken down by content owner or business group

The KM system will allow variable review periods (or dates) to be specified, depending on the nature of the content. This metric is a tool for ongoing knowledge article (KA) and FAQ management.

User Feedback

A feedback mechanism will be established for the KM system. Use of such a feedback system is a clear indication that staff is using the knowledge in the knowledge base. Although few feedback messages may indicate the published KA/FAQ to be entirely accurate, it is more likely that the system is not being accessed, or that the feedback mechanism is not recognized as useful. Alternatively, although many feedback messages may indicate poor-quality information, it does indicate strong staff use. It also shows they have sufficient trust in the system to commit the time needed to send in feedback.

Distributed Authoring

The extent to which the business as a whole takes responsibility for keeping content up to date is a metric in itself. At the most basic level, the number of KM system authors can be tracked against a target. A more rigorous approach uses statistics from the workflow capabilities to determine the level of activity of each author.

Transaction Costs

A process analysis activity can also determine costs involved in completing tasks. This allows direct cost savings made by implementing and leveraging the KM system. Multiplied out by the number of times the activity is completed in a year, the whole-of-business savings can be determined. This could be substantial in a large organization such as state farm.

Strategic Look at the KM Business Case

A KM strategy entails a collective visioning as to how sharing knowledge can enhance organizational performance, and the reaching of a consensus among the senior management of the organization that the course of action involved in sharing knowledge will in fact be pursued. It is implied in such a process a set of decisions about the particular variety of KM activities that the organization intends to pursue, including the leverage of the organization's knowledge assets (human capital being the number one asset), and the execution of the process and tools that will enable sharing of knowledge and innovation to occur.

When developing a KM business case, it is important to identify, in terms of the strategic assessment, the critical initiatives that the organization is currently engaged in, and/or those it is planning to embark on. These initiatives need to be thoroughly examined from a KM perspective. What will be the role of KM in these efforts? KM efforts should support and facilitate ongoing strategic initiatives, and it is very important that a proposed KM effort be tied to these initiatives in as direct a manner as possible.

A KM effort that is disconnected from the strategic initiatives of the organization has limited, if any, chance of being well received by the organization. Normally, any strategic initiative will have a number of tactical and operational objectives. These are good elements into which the KM efforts should be tied.

As with any KM initiative, it is important to find an executive sponsor for the KM effort. It is vital to communicate the value proposition of the KM effort to the strategic initiative. You should present KM not for the sake of doing KM, but as a means to further the strategic objectives in which the executives are interested.

Examine your organization carefully and determine if any of the above scenarios is something you are dealing with. Take necessary steps to keep your organization viable by initially crafting a business case to present to the senior management, and once it is approved, develop a KM strategy that will define the roadmap for executing the various aspects of the KM business case.

The KM effort needs to be communicated from its strategic value proposition rather than its technical intricacies. Getting executives to believe and visualize the overall value of the KM perspective and expertise is the critical outcome of getting approval of the KM business case and to start your KM initiative.

Key Learnings

The following are some key lessons learned from this chapter:

- For any KM business case to be approved and successfully implemented, there must be strong executive sponsorship and leadership.
- KPIs and metrics to track the KM strategy must be measurable.

Tips and Techniques

The following are some of the tips and techniques deduced after reading this chapter:

- To provide a roadmap and to communicate the direction, vision, and mission of KM in your organization when completing a KM strategy as part of any KM program is necessary.
- When developing the KM business case, minimize the number of options available by conducting a detailed feasibility study beforehand.
- When the KM initiative calls for capturing tacit and explicit knowledge of the organization, follow the KAUF.

Chapter 3

Being Social: Knowledge Management and Social Media

Social media brings the power of sharing and collaboration to the masses. Whether it's Facebook, Twitter, or YouTube and leveraging any of the myriad of mobile devices, knowledge sharing and collaboration have become a way of life. At the core of knowledge management (KM) is knowledge sharing and collaboration, and social media tools have business and government taking notice.

Social media offers organizations the opportunity of connecting with potential customers at virtually no cost. It is possible to set goals and get return on investments (ROI); however, you have to know where you're going and what you want to achieve. Once you have this information, you can allocate your resources wisely. Typically, a social media strategy will enable the organization to know where to start and what social sites to concentrate. When you know the lay of the land, it's much easier to plot a path to your destination. A social media strategy will be your organization's roadmap to plot this destination.

To reach your public successfully, you need to start telling your stories directly, and do it in a way that sparks conversations, interest, and action. The value proposition of social media is sustained conversations that shape perceptions and attract customers to purchase your products and services, and participate in the activities (blog, Twitter, forums, surveys, etc.).

The use of social media does not represent a onetime application, but a holistic environment to promote programs, events, communicate ideas, solicit thought, and to connect the institution to its customers (and potential customers) within the

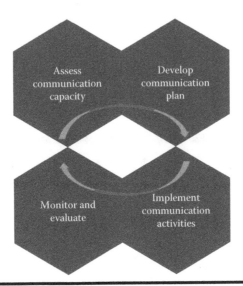

Figure 3.1 Participatory communication cycle.

community. These customers represent our constituents and partners to engage in communication and feedback. Including a participatory communication cycle (see Figure 3.1) in your overall social media strategy will give you a clear direction and knowledge of your communication capacity, communication activities, which will be of most benefit, as well as the communities, which should be monitored and evaluated.

Participatory Communication Cycle

The participatory communication cycle is leveraged to enhance the capacity of individuals and communities to sustain communication activities (Corbett 2010). The participatory communication cycle consists of assessing your communication capacity, developing a communication plan, implementing communication activities, and monitoring and evaluating the results.

Assessment of communication capacity as it pertains to implementing social media is to understand the potential constraints of the proposed medium being utilized (Twitter, LinkedIn, Facebook, etc.), and to ascertain the staff needed to produce, send, and respond to communication within the perspective channel(s). This assessment should include an analysis of your organization's legal and political constraints to social media, conventional sources, and types of messages, as well as communication style and scope (Corbett 2010).

The development of the communication plan can occur once the assessment is completed. This includes developing an overall strategy that provides a set of objectives and an action plan to execute these objectives (Corbett 2010). This communication plan will include the following components: key communication objectives, key stakeholders and audience, messages to be crafted, identification of activities and determination of timelines, identification of roles and responsibilities for the planning and execution, budget, and key performance indicators (KPIs) to monitor and evaluate the results (Corbett 2010).

Once the communication strategy and action plan have been identified, implementation of communication activities can begin. When the communication activities are clearly conveyed, associated resources and funding are put in place and the objectives of the strategy and its associated action plan are carried out, Corbett (2010).

As the participatory communication cycle moves into the monitor and evaluation (M&E) stage, it is at this point when your organization can begin to analyze and assess the impact of its communication cycle, as it pertains to the use of social media. However, this is a continuing cycle and as the organization moves back into assessing communication capacity, M&E should not only occur toward the end of the project but also at the beginning, and should be directly linked to each of the communication activities identified in the action plan (Corbett 2010).

KM and the Participatory Communication Cycle

KM within the participatory communication cycle occurs as the organization assesses and learns from the impacts of communication within the various social media outlets as dictated by the action plan. Through interaction with customers, suppliers, and partners your organization will gain valuable knowledge regarding issues, opinions, and perception of your product and services as well as the company as a whole. In responding to the various comments within social media concerning your organization, with an attempt to answer/respond in the correct way, company representatives must have access to the right knowledge. This knowledge will facilitate representatives respond in a consistent manner and take control of your company's voice within social media.

Social Media, KM, and the Enterprise

Social media takes knowledge and makes it highly iterative. It creates content as a social object. That is, content is no longer a point in time, but something that is part of a social interaction, such as a discussion. It easily disassembles the pillars of structure as it evolves. For example, content in a microblogging service can shift meaning as a discussion unfolds; conversations in enterprise social networks that link people and customer data can defy categorization; and internal blogs and their comments don't lend themselves to obvious taxonomy.

Social media in the enterprise has gotten the attention of KM scholars and practitioners. It should mean that many of the benefits we experience in the consumer web space, which include effective searching, grouping of associated unstructured data sources, and ranking of relevance, will become basic features of enterprise solutions. In the enterprise, for example, when looking to staff a project with a certain skill set, the social capabilities that will be leveraged would include role, primary skill sets, secondary skill sets, number of years of experience, and rating on efficiency of each skill. Social media's impact on KM will bring about more time by analyzing the knowledge that is being created through social interactions.

The objective of social media in a company is always to streamline the processes and leverage technology as an enabler. April Allen states in her blog (November 28, 2012) that "Rather than killing off KM, I think social media has brought it to life. It's less about dusty tomes on bookshelves not being updated and more about connecting the dots in real time. It's nimble and adaptable" (Allen, 2012). Christopher Palmert presents a perspective from the systems/tool side of social media and KM. Palmert states

> It is not a problem to find social media applications that can be used for knowledge management. The basic version of applications like "Yammer" are even available for free. However, the axe cannot replace the carpenter, if one does not know how to use it. In addition to technical know-how, a strategy is required for successful knowledge management. The technology plays only a secondary role and there are enough systems. The success or failure depends on the organizational structure, which is challenged by implementing the social media tools. (Palmert, 2012, p. 1)

As the evolution of social media and KM expands to a global perspective within the enterprise, it presents challenges that are currently not fully understood. Global social KM as depicted in Figure 3.2 describes the cross-cultural knowledge exchange and collaboration that exist among individuals and organizations (Pirkkalainen and Pawlowski, 2013). Pirkkalainen and Pawlowski (2013) state that the KM component identifies a more specific view on the organizational and individual challenges coming from a collaborative distributed setting, which include where knowledge is being created, shared, and adopted by organizations and individuals.

As social software is being deployed for KM and collaboration, adoption toward this functionality in the enterprise has been limited. Furthermore, it has been indicated that it is not yet clear that social software tools will be able to globally support distributed KM. Figure 3.2 depicts the key components of global KM and social software that must be considered for adoption (Pirkkalainen and Pawlowski, 2013).

Social Media Policies, Procedures, and Guidelines

Social media policies, procedures, and guidelines ensure a consistent and uniform way in which we can leverage social media platforms. Expanding social media beyond the corporate walls and including sites such as LinkedIn, Twitter, and

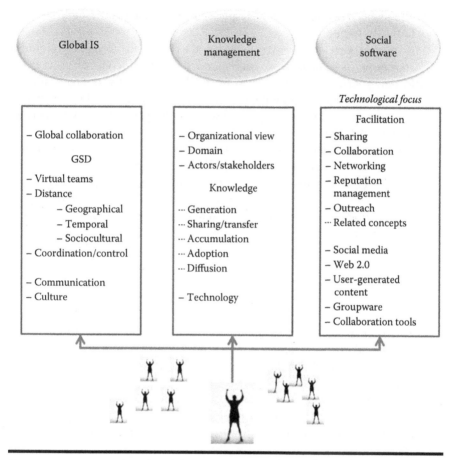

Figure 3.2   Focus points for global social knowledge management.

Facebook to be accessed, monitored, and leveraged will play a key role in executing your social media strategy.

LinkedIn

LinkedIn is the premier business-oriented social networking site. The LinkedIn Group is the organization's environment where we can collaborate to exchange ideas and points of interest with our current students, faculty, alumni, employees, and other interested parties. LinkedIn has more than 75 million registered users in 200 countries and territories worldwide and provides an excellent platform to educate the business community about the value that the institution brings to the communities it serves. The following are the guidelines for posting and interacting in the LinkedIn Group.

1. Group members are personally responsible for the content they publish in the LinkedIn Group.
2. Be mindful that whatever you publish will be public for a long time—protect your privacy and take care to understand the terms of service of a site.
3. Identify yourself—your name and, when relevant, role at your organization—when you discuss your organization-related matters, such as products or services.
4. You must make it clear that you are speaking for yourself and not on behalf of your organization.
5. If you publish content online relevant to your organization in your personal capacity, use a disclaimer such as this: "The postings on this site are my own and don't necessarily represent the organization's positions, strategies or opinions."
6. Respect copyright, fair use, and financial disclosure laws. Don't provide your organization's or another's confidential or other proprietary information and never discuss business or other sensitive matters publicly.
7. Don't cite or reference clients, partners, or suppliers without their approval.
8. When you do make a reference, link back to the source.
9. Don't publish anything that might allow inferences to be drawn, which could embarrass or damage you or anyone.
10. Respect your audience. Don't use ethnic slurs, personal insults, obscenity, or engage in any conduct that would not be acceptable in any situation.
11. You should also show proper consideration for others' privacy and for topics that may be considered objectionable or inflammatory—such as politics and religion.
12. Be aware of your association with online social networks. If you identify yourself as a student, employee, or alumni, then ensure that your profile and related content is consistent with how you wish to present yourself with colleagues.
13. Don't pick fights, be the first to correct your own mistakes.
14. Try to add value. Provide worthwhile information and perspective. Your organization's brand is best represented by its people and what you publish may reflect on your organization's brand.
15. Don't use logos or trademarks unless you are approved to do so.

Twitter

Twitter is the premier microblogging service enabling its users to send and read other users' messages called "tweets." Tweets are text-based posts of up to 140 characters displayed on the user's profile page. Tweets are publicly visible by default; however, senders can restrict message delivery to their friends' list. Users may subscribe to other author tweets, this is known as "following," and such subscribers are known as "followers." As of late 2009, users can follow lists of authors instead of just following individual authors. Twitter has gained popularity worldwide and currently has more than 100 million users.

Twitter has the ability to call into action a massive amount of people in a limited amount of time for any cause or purpose. It can also be harmful by propagating negative and erroneous information that is difficult to recover from. Information dissemination on this platform must be used wisely. This power to share must be handled with a sense of privilege and responsibility. From a negative perspective, we have seen more and more often that our tweets have caused loss of jobs, lawsuits, and some cases public outrage. However, the positive aspects such as increased awareness, promoting ideas, launching careers, entertaining, and bringing people together for a cause have outweighed the negative impacts of Twitter, and it has become a major part of many organizations social media strategy.

Twitter is and always shall be a means to listen to your customers, clients, colleagues, industry leaders, and anyone else who might comment on your product or business. It is about networking and knowledge sharing. The uses for Twitter are limitless. You just have to find your niche. You have to ask, "What are the benefits of being on Twitter?" Some will share knowledge, whereas others will just use Twitter as a way of being available to customers. Either way, as long as you are actually listening and staying engaged, you will benefit.

One of the best things Twitter can do for a company is simply to humanize it. Allowing a real person to put a voice to an otherwise impersonal entity can give a new dimension to your organization's relationships with clients, which is otherwise not possible. Some of the more successful brands on Twitter allow and encourage a multitude of voices from within the corporate walls to twitter, not only engaging clients but also each other.

Before you actively try to build an audience, post a few tweets to familiarize yourself with the process, and spend some time reading what others in your industry are talking about on Twitter. Use the "Find People" search function at the top of your Twitter page to look for people you know will want to follow you back: people within your company, current clients, and colleagues. Send a few @ replies out to people who are following you. Respond to things they are talking about. When they in turn respond to you with and @ reply, the people following them will take notice of you and may choose to follow as well.

It's also a good idea to look at whom the people you know are following. That can give you ideas about whom you want to search for. Use the Twitter search function to find subjects relative to your industry and see who's talking about them. Remember that conversation is very important. If all you do is post your thoughts and ideas without engaging anyone in conversation, you're just a broadcaster. Eventually, if you are a well-known brand, and if you do things right on Twitter, new people will start following you every day.

Be personable: Too many companies represent themselves on Twitter by spewing automated and static information, or authorized quotes from the public relations department. These only serve to keep the brand parked neatly in a dry dock, gathering dust. Most people who twitter do it for the human connection.

Stay away from discussing politics and religion: Your mother told you this a long time ago, and it's still good advice, unless, of course, your business is politics or religion. In that case, go for it. Otherwise, you are just going to alienate half your followers, maybe more. People are passionate about their political and religious beliefs; if you are representing a brand, you will do it a great disservice by taking a position on either subject.

Be aware of your voice: Think of Twitter as a ship we are all traveling on. You have to play nice with others or you'll be shoved aside and ignored—or, worse, made to walk the plank. Besides, you never know when you might end up doing business with someone you now consider a competitor.

Don't be a complainer: No one wants to listen to someone who keeps whining or pointing out all the things that are going wrong in the industry or the world. If you want people to follow you and listen, look for the positive. Sure, there will be times when you have to talk about things that aren't encouraging or upbeat; some situations demand a solemn tone. But don't make this a theme. Don't make it what you are about. Remember, anyone can whine and complain, but a leader offers solutions.

Facebook

Facebook has become the world's leading social media site for individuals, groups, and families (businesses are beginning to see its value) to share their world with their friends and followers and to keep in touch with extended family members. Now, more than ever, organizations are creating a presence on Facebook to extend their reach to the growing number of potential (and younger) customers. Facebook users can share news stories, videos, and other files with friends. Personal notes can also be written and shared with friends. When sharing an item, users can attach the item to their Wall for all to see, or can tag individual people that they think would be most interested in seeing the item. When a user is tagged, they receive an e-mail notification.

These options for sharing and collaborating are what makes Facebook a powerful tool for your organization. Here are some numbers to support this: 1.15 billion users, 700 million daily users, average time per Facebook visit is 20 min and 8.3 h is the average amount of time each user spends per month, 70% of monthly active Facebook users in the United States are engaged and connected to a local business (Wallace, 2013).

Although many businesses are yet to experience the full potential of Facebook, the capabilities are finding their way into many organizations.

Social Media Strategy

A social media strategy is your organization's roadmap to guide you through the social media maze. To reach your customers and potential customers successfully, you need to start telling your stories directly, and do it in a way that sparks conversations, interest, and action. The value proposition of social media is for sustained conversations that shape perceptions and attract students to enroll in programs and participate in its activities.

The following sections describe more specifically the aspects of a social media strategy. This strategy will identify specific activities and initiatives that must be executed to ensure that the components of the strategy are made actionable and contribute to the success of meeting the goals, objectives, and mission of the Knowledge Systems Institute.

Listen to Conversations

Social media will allow tapping into various synergistic communities to get an understanding of what their educational needs are, how programs align with those needs, and how to position programs to meet those needs. Specifically, to execute this, part of the strategy must focus on:

■ Where do the conversations take place that are synergistic to your organization's objectives and mission, and does it make sense for to have a presence?
■ What are these communities talking about, and should they have a voice?
■ What are your organization's competitors doing in social media, and can they present a competitive advantage?
■ What's the buzz about our competitors?
■ What content resonates with this audience?
■ Are there subjects of interest that could provide content for?
■ What social sites have the most conversation?
■ Whom the "fire-starters" need to connect with?
■ Who are the influencers in these blogs or communities?
■ Where are the opportunities and threats?

Establish a Share of the Voice

There are millions of conversations on social media sites every day. Every organization needs to monitor for conversations about the programs and activities that are synergistic to what it offers and becomes part of the conversation. Share of voice is described as the percentage of mentions about your brand/company/organization in the particular niche or market you're active in.

Some of the questions we must answer to achieve an active voice in our selected social media sites are as follows:

■ Do people use a generic description of what we do, or do they talk about our course offerings or activities specifically?
■ Are the comments positive or negative? What is the ratio of positive to negative?

- Are key messages appearing in these conversations? If not, what content is trending?
- How are our competitors faring in these conversations?

The context of your organization's content in a competitive set shows how your brand stacks up against your competitors online. Your organization's share of voice leads to an increase in the market share. This increased market share will be supported by an increase in student enrollment. Establishing and tracking of share of voice is becoming an important part of social media. A gain in share of voice is an important measurement for social media programs.

Set Goals and Benchmarks

It is important to measure the progress and success of the social media strategy against the goals and objectives identified by your organization. At every phase of executing this strategy, metrics will provide a valuable means for focusing attention on desired behaviors and results.

Listening to the online conversation allows you to tap into what people are interested in right now, what they talk about, and what they like and dislike. This information will give the insights that lead to achieving your strategic goals.

The aim is to achieve the following targets.

Find and Establish Communities   Every day a blog, social network, or social media site seems to pop up. Understand to participate in the places that make sense. Part of your research should include listening to what's being said online, which includes "who" is talking about you, and "where" the conversations are taking place. Once you know where the majority of the conversations take place you can sensibly allocate resources for best ROI. Some of the activities that have been identified are as follows:

- Identify the bloggers who talk about our industry, courses, and/or activities.
- Monitor blog posts (i.e., Google Blog Search) to see who is writing on a certain key topic.
- Track mentions of your brand and generic keywords that describe what your organization does in social news sites such as Digg, Newsvine, Kirtsy, and StumbleUpon.
- Track content about your industry, courses, and/or activities in social network sites (i.e., Facebook and Twitter).

Identify Influencers   What is influence? It can be defined as *implicit or explicit effect of one thing (or person) on another.* What influences people online has changed dramatically in the past few years. The idea that the person with the most followers or subscribers has the biggest influence is no longer valid. Today, influence is about accuracy and trust. If you want to reach the bloggers and social networkers who have influence, you will need to influence their perception and/or their behavior. They're the ones who send a flood of traffic to our website, because when they link to or recommend our courses and/or activities, their followers take action.

Some of the parameters we should use to determine which blogger and networkers to focus on are as follows:

- *Traffic*: Unique visitors, page views, and RSS subscribers
- *Inbound links*: Primarily contextual links from well-ranked sites and blogs
- *Reader engagement*: Time spent on site, comments
- *Recommendations*: Retweets, bookmarking, tagging, and sharing of content
- *Connections*: Number of followers/mutual connections across multiple social sites
- *Track record*: Age of domain, number of blog posts, and length of engagement
- *Web traffic to your site or blog*: Analytics tell which sites are sending users to your site
- *Conversion rate of those visitors*: What is the rate of conversion for each referring site?

Identify and Select Tools   There's a wide array of social media tools to choose from and the task can be confusing. However, our content strategy will guide us in identifying where to start. If the majority of the conversation about our industry, courses, and/or activities is on Twitter, then we will need a custom-designed Twitter account.

Here's the list of social media tools:

- Search optimized press releases
- Social media news release format—with multimedia and social bookmarks
- Search optimized articles
- News feeds (RSS) to syndicate all your content
- Socializing your news content—"share this" buttons, tagging, and bookmarking
- Blogs
- Microblogging (Twitter)
- Podcasts
- Images
- Video
- Social networks (i.e., Facebook and LinkedIn)
- Social media news sites
- Widgets
- Social media news room—gather and present all your social media content on your website

Create and Develop Content   Once the content strategy, based on solid research is developed, bright ideas will naturally flow about what to create and how to deliver this content. Experimenting with a Facebook page and a Twitter feed isn't enough. You will need to create supporting content, for example, a company blog, an interactive website, interesting articles, images, and videos.

Good content not only sparks conversations, but it also builds links. People will share the content, and they'll link to it from blog posts and tweets. This can raise search visibility and drive a lot of traffic to our content.

Engage and Facilitate Conversations   Content should be created with a view to inspire and allow participants to engage in conversations. Social media is about a two-way flow of conversation. People are no longer willing to be passive bystanders—they want to take active part in the conversation. Customer engagement can get you through the toughest of times—it's both a customer acquisition and retention strategy.

Engaging Your Audience   Followers and traffic are good and well, but are they engaging with you? Ninety-three percent of the Internet users active in social media say that they expect a company to have a social media presence to be able to actively engage with that company. The Forrester Research report "Social Media Playtime Is Over" clearly shows that dabbling or experimenting is not enough. You have to deliver genuinely interesting and valuable content that meets the needs of your audience and actively engages them.

Facilitate the Conversations   Word of mouth has long been the "holy grail" of marketing. Peer reviews, opinions, and comments are now the number one influencer prior to purchase or decision online. Not only do you want them to be engaged with you, but you also want them to be talking positively about you to each other. Facilitating these conversations should be our ultimate goal. An organization must make things easy for visitors or users of your website by providing excellent content, which they desire to share and discuss. And then give them tools to make it easy to do this—send to a friend button, share this, bookmark this, subscribe, discuss, and comment.

Measure Results

Why measure?
   If you can't measure it, you can't manage it. It's that simple. You need to know where you are when you start, what needs to be achieved, and as you move along the path, you have to have tools to measure your progress. This way you can see if you are on track and adapt fast if things go awry. Your measurement has to be based on business objectives—and those objectives have to be set as measurable goals. Just setting up attributes to track on a dashboard is not enough.

What to measure?

What you are going to measure will depend on what goals you have set in the initial part of your strategy. Based on listening and research, you should have determined what actions you need to focus on in social media. Measure what you did and what impact it had, and then you can see what result it had.

Return on engagement

There are many tools available today to track engagement—how many people clicked a link in a blog post? How many times was the message retweeted? How many followers does the person who retweeted you have?

Track the growth of your share of voice

Compare the number of articles, posts, tweets, videos, or images where a brand and its competitors are mentioned. Calculate how many times brand is mentioned the most, relative to its competitors, and by what margin. Track your growth in the share of voice.

Track your share of conversation

Share of conversation is the degree to which a brand is associated with the problem or need that it is setting out to help with.

Sample Social Media Strategy—Roles and Responsibilities

The following represents an organization's social media roles and responsibilities:

Social strategist:
- *Responsibilities*:
  - Development of the overall strategy/program, including ROI
  - Executing initial identified initiatives
  - Developing social media roadmap and project plan
  - Interacting with agreed upon social media sites (Twitter, LinkedIn, and Digg)

Community manager:
- *Responsibilities*:
  - Customer facing role—interacting with social media participants
  - Manage content to be leveraged on social media sites
  - Manage presence on social media sites (Twitter, LinkedIn, and Digg)

Content manager:
- *Responsibilities*:
  - Development of the overall content (look-n-feel) of social media sites
  - Manage content to be leveraged on social media sites
  - Interacting with agreed upon social media sites (Twitter, LinkedIn, and Digg)

Develop a Content Strategy

Success in social media depends on the quality of your content. It's about engaging people, and the key to engagement is good content. In social media, people are creating, reading, saving, tagging, and sharing content. Your organization must produce the kind of content they value and desire to share. Telling your story online in the right place to the right people will give you your intended results, and establishing a well-thought-out content strategy, which leverages existing content and builds new content when needed based on solid research, will deliver these results.

Measuring Results

When measuring results, it is important to evaluate the data and conclude if you need to tweak or expand your program. You need to tell your story to customers, potential customers, employees, potential employees, business partners, and specifically to all those whom you interact with and who you wish to interact with.

Key Learnings

Establish your organization's roles and responsibilities to handle your social media presence and monitor and respond (if necessary) to the communication about your organization. The following is a sample of the roles and responsibilities you should consider for you social media strategy.

Tips and Techniques

Brand reputation: By communicating with your alumni, students, perspective students, and friends through social media (LinkedIn, Twitter, and Digg), you will begin to build a positive brand as the innovative, state-of-the-art, and cost-effective leader in computer science graduate and certificate programs.

Increased brand awareness: The social media sites being leveraged will facilitate getting the word out about your organization's curriculum, events, and activities. By posting news articles in Digg, and interacting with our constituents via Twitter and the professional community through LinkedIn, you will begin to build our brand and associate it with programs such as healthcare informatics, KM, digital art, and software programming education at the master's level.

Increase share of voice: By getting the word out about your curriculum in the degreed and certificate programs, communicating with other thought leaders and constituents, and interlinking our Twitter, LinkedIn, and Digg presence with our website, you will increase its share of communication and interaction in the areas in which you specialize.

Thought leadership: Your organization's specific use of social media through LinkedIn, Twitter, and Digg will provide an outlet for your content manager(s) to post information, respond to other participants, and make cutting-edge research available. This will demonstrate your organization's thought leadership in the areas of healthcare informatics, KM, digital art, and software programming education at the master's level.

Chapter 4

Dude, "Where's My Car?": Utilizing Search in Knowledge Management

Have you ever experienced a situation when you just could not find that document on your content management system or a specific job aid, standard operating procedure, or knowledge article in your knowledge repository? You may have known part of the title or what some of the contents were, but you couldn't put your finger on it. You executed the latest search mechanisms on the site, and you had to weed through several pages of content searching for that elusive piece of information or knowledge. Then, finally after a period of time (who knows how long) you either find it (OH Yea!) or give up in frustration (Arrrg!!). A contributing cure for your dilemma, as well as mine and countless others, is to implement an information architecture (IA) that will drive a user-centric taxonomy, metadata, and associated keywords to enable the "findability" of your content (information and knowledge).

Information Architecture

Has been described in many ways by many scholars and practitioners alike. Usability. Gov states that "Information architecture (IA) focuses on organizing, structuring, and labeling content in an effective and sustainable way." Downey and Banerjee offer another definition of IA which states "IA is the art and science of organizing information so that it is findable, manageable and useful" (Downey and Banerjee, 2011, p. 25). Finally, I offer my definition of IA: IA connects people to their content (information and knowledge) that includes the high-level rules that govern the manner in which information concepts are defined, related, realized, and managed by the enterprise.

IA focuses on everything you can define about a solution without specifying the underlying system (the raw plumbing) or specifying the particular user interface that will be employed to deliver and manipulate the information. IA is implementation and system independent. It is concerned about the architecture of how information is used, how it flows, and how it fits within the user's world (its context). This leads to developing systems that will be intuitive to its users.

The outcome of a comprehensive IA implementation is a systematic description of the content of a given product, service, or environment. This type of detail contributes to the understanding and documenting of the complexities of system design to enable intricate solutions to be functional, transparent, and user-friendly. IA also forces clarity upward into the user interface and downward into the system architecture, contributing to simplifying design, development, and implementation. The IA in essence creates a common ground between designers and developers by bridging the gap between the user interface and underlying systems or technologies.

A well-defined IA not only helps you expand the function of your designs, but it can also inform consistent experiences and paths for the evolution of future designs across many variants within a family of products, services, or environments.

IA consists of several elements. The elements of focus here include information organization (information or content model, taxonomy, and metadata schema), information access, governance, and user experience. These items work hand-in-hand to deliver the following benefits of IA:

- User-centric identification of categories of content
- Single source of structure and meaning
- Increases ability to find content
- Intuitive navigation of systems
- Increases the ability to keep content fresh and relevant
- Enables a better search experience
- Improves content quality ("one source of truth" or "authoritative source")
- Reduces data reconciliation efforts ("location of data")
- Improves sourcing options for content (identifies source of record)
- Reduces storage volume (decreases the proliferation and duplication of content)

IA has become an essential ingredient to ensure a competitive advantage for organizations of all sizes. Organizations continue to search for practical ways to create business value by getting their arms around the content of the enterprise to enable its employees to take action not only to perform their day-to-day activities but also to service the customer. Organizational benefits of IA include unlocking content to let it flow rapidly and easily to people and processes that need it; cost-effectively store, archive, and retrieve the right content, in the right context, at the right time; protect and secure that content to meet compliance requirements, and make it accessible for business insight where and when necessary; and finally mitigating risks inherent in business decision making by providing knowledge assets when and where necessary and in its proper context.

To prepare your organization to develop an IA, you must consider the structure and composition of a repository (or website), the information collection and individual document intelligence, accessing content (search and retrieval), as well as being able to locate and/or navigate to the content. In developing the IA structure, Downey and Banerjee (2011) describe a checklist in order to provide a consistent method in constructing the IA. The IA checklist presented (see Figure 4.1) evolved over a few iterations before a final IA checklist was formed. The checklist focuses on the essential areas of the IA such as the model, taxonomy, and metadata. It also

Original IA checklist	Revised IA checklist	Final IA checklist
Information organization • Modeling • Composition • Classification Information access • Search • Navigation • Findability • Search analytics • Security Information governance User experience	Information organization • Taxonomy • Modeling • Structure • Semantics Information generation • EIA alignment • Content • User experience • System interface • Scalability • Standards Information integration • Analytics • Search • Composition Information consumption • Search • Metrics • Monitoring Information governance • Stewardship • MDM • Reuse • Policy Information quality of service • Security • Availability • Reliability • Usefulness	Information consumption • General • Availability • Metrics Information generation • General • Extraction • Characteristics • Metrics Information organization • Modeling • Classification • Semantics • Structure • User experience Information access • Search • Discovery • Analytics • User experience • Navigation • System interface • Metrics Information governance • Information Stewardship • Information Classification Stewardship • Policy Information quality of service • Security • Availability • Reliability • Scalability • Usefulness

Figure 4.1 Information architecture checklist. (From Downey, L. and Banerjee, S., *J. Inform. Architect.*, 2(2), Available at http://journalofia.org/volume2/issue2/ 03-downey/, 2011.)

identifies significant supporting areas such as information access, governance, and quality of service (security, availability, and reliability). Downey and Banerjee indicate that

> These IA checklists either cover the process of performing IA activities on a project or are specific to actually designing or reviewing the design of IA. The identified checklists focus more on process, design, and design review—and do not include issues of infrastructure, platform, services, technology, policy, and standards. Our goal in designing the IA checklist as part of the architectural review process was to create a set of questions that gets people thinking about and discussing IA in terms of infrastructure, existing technology, services, and platform across the enterprise as well as information generation, delivery, consumption and governance in order to lay the foundation that can then be fully exploited and realized at the user interface level. This broad perspective encourages a collaborative approach to an IA solution. (Downey and Banerjee, 2011, p. 27)

Content Model

A content model provides the framework for organizing your content, so that it can be delivered and reused in a variety of innovative ways. Once you have created the content model (sometimes referred to as an "ontology") for your content repository, you will be able to label information in ways that will enhance search and retrieval, making it possible for authors and users to find the information resources they need quickly and easily (see Figure 4.2). The content model shows the content types ("Car in Service"), it's metadata fields (Car ID, Date Entered, and Service) as well as relationships to other content types ("is a" → Unpowered Car, "is a" → Powered Car).

Creating your content model requires analysis, careful planning, and a lot of feedback from your user community. The analysis takes you into the world of those who need and use information resources every day. The planning means talking to a wide range of stakeholders, including both individuals and groups who have information needs and who would profit from collaboration in the development of information resources. Getting feedback requires that you test your content model with members of your user community to ensure that you have not missed any content types, domains, relationships, or other perspectives.

The content model is typically developed from working with your business/content subject matter experts (SMEs). In working with your SMEs, business rules about the information relationships are established, and this greatly contributes to the construction of the content model. The content model will support the search process through establishing relationships between the content and describing how this information behaves (via metadata).

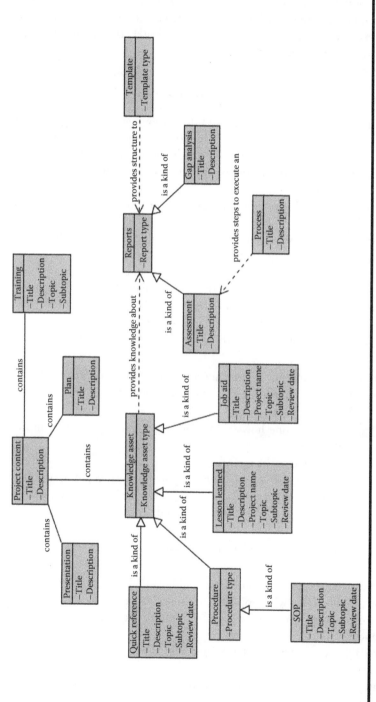

Figure 4.2 Example of a content model.

The information displayed represents a sharable, stable, and organized structure of information requirements for your system (i.e., content management system, knowledge management [KM] system, and/or website). The following are the steps necessary in constructing the content model.

Steps Involved in Constructing the Content Model

1. Identify/document the domains of information within the organization.
2. Identify/document each of the content types within the domain.
3. Identify/document the relationships between the domains.
4. Identify/document the relationships between the content types within each of the domains.
5. Identify/document the relationships between the content types located in other domains.
6. Document the business rules that support all relationships (Note: Capture business rules as you determine relationships).
7. Identify/document the metadata within each content type.
8. Define user roles/access within the content model (Note: This is done by analyzing and including user profiles within the model structure).
9. Describe (define) all domains and content types.
10. Describe (define) user roles within the information structure.

To determine if a system such as a website and/or content/knowledge repository has no underlying content model, the following are some signs:

- Difficult to determine how to get from the home page to the information you're looking for.
- Links do not retrieve the intended page.
- Navigating to what you need brings you further away rather than closer.
- Scrolling through a long alphabetic list of all the articles ever written on a particular subject with only the title to guide you.

A well-conceived content model has the following characteristics:

- Links to pertinent information are readily available.
- You are able to get what you need in three clicks or less.
- The content retrieve is tailored for you and in a way you can quickly consume it and use it.
- Available cross-references (associated and related content) are in the right places.
- Categories right away look familiar to you and navigation seems more intuitive.

When a content model is clearly defined and established, the users of the various systems who implement the content model will be on track to finding, retrieving, and using the content they need. A great method for flushing out and validating your content model is to perform a card sort exercise (you more than likely will have to conduct several card sorts). For more information, review the section on card sorts as well as the box "How to Conduct a Card Sort."

Taxonomy

Taxonomy is a hierarchical classification or framework for information retrieval. Taxonomies represent an agreed vocabulary of topics arranged around a particular theme. Taxonomies can have either a hierarchical or nonhierarchical structure. However, typically taxonomies are presented in a hierarchical fashion as illustrated with taxonomies such as in libraries, biology, or military organizations (see Figure 4.3).

Hierarchical taxonomies are a tree-like structure with nodes branching into sub-nodes, where each node represents a topic with a few descriptive words. This way of classifying information becomes more important as the number of items increases and people have more trouble remembering what they have and where to find it. This is critical as we move into Big Data, which represents the immense volume of information available to organization and the public through the vast array of social media sites and throughout the Internet.

Content types and metadata along with a solid taxonomy will greatly enhance your search to return to what you are looking for. Taxonomies are the basis of classification schemes and indexing systems in information management (see Figure 4.4). Information professionals and librarians rely on classification and controlled vocabularies to aid precision search; abstract and index publishers make investments in indexing and thesauri to add value to their products. Many organizations are experimenting with semantic technologies, hoping to automatically extract the meaning inherent in documents and supplementing, or even replacing, the human editorial process.

Taxonomies of entities for search engines are designed to improve relevance in vertical search. Vertical search content area may be based on topicality, media type, or genre of the content. Common verticals include shopping, the automotive industry, legal information, medical information, scholarly literature, and travel. Examples of vertical search engines include Trulia.com and Yelp. However, general web search engines attempt to index large portions of the web's content by using a web crawler, whereas vertical search engines typically use a focused crawler that

```
600 Technology (Applied sciences)
    630 Agriculture and related technologies
        636 Animal husbandry
            636.7 Dogs
            636.8 Cats
```

Figure 4.3   Example of Dewey decimal hierarchical structure.

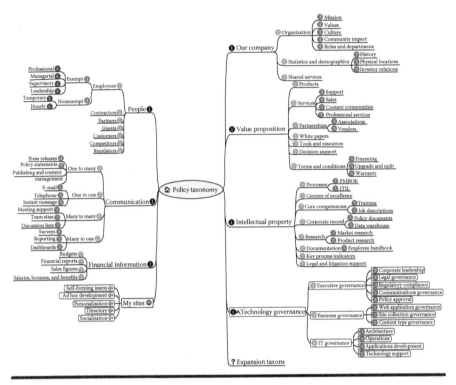

Figure 4.4 Example of a taxonomy of policy information.

attempts to index only web pages that are relevant to a topic or set of topics. Vertical search can be viewed as similar to enterprise search where the domain of focus is the enterprise, such as a company, government, or other organization.

Taxonomies, thesauri, and concept hierarchies are crucial components for many applications of content and KM systems as well as information retrieval and natural language systems. Building, tuning, and managing taxonomies are important factors in approving the search experience that should not be overlooked.

Metadata

Metadata is an important aspect of the IA and in particular the content model. Metadata is primarily used for labeling, tagging, or cataloging information or structuring descriptive records. Metadata (fields and attributes) are assigned to a content type to provide a means to describe it and provide the means in which to find content once it becomes part of a system. The metadata attributes and values that are embedded in each content type (sometimes referred to as an "object") within the content model make it possible for the person searching for a flight reservation, a vehicle to purchase, and a multitude of other items within a system to find what they are looking for.

The creation of metadata has generally been approached in two ways: professional creation and author creation. In libraries and other organizations, creating metadata, primarily in the form of catalog records, has traditionally been the domain of dedicated professionals working with complex, detailed set of rules and vocabularies. The primary problem with this approach is scalability and its impracticality for the vast amounts of content being produced and used, especially on the World Wide Web. The apparatus and tools built around professional cataloging systems are generally too complicated for anyone without specialized training and knowledge. A second approach is for metadata to be created by authors.

Metadata Fields

The metadata fields describe the primary dimensions of a content type. Metadata fields are the individual items of metadata stored within a content type. There are two types of metadata fields:

- *Required metadata*: This includes fields that are required to describe the content type.
- *Custom metadata*: This can be configured by an administrator to any values required by the site or installation.

It is important to note that the same metadata fields can be used in multiple metadata groups and each metadata field has a setting associated with it. The following settings are common to most metadata fields:

Name: Enter the name of the metadata field
Data type:
- *Boolean*: A true or false value
- *Date*: A date/time field
- *Floating point number*: A floating point number
- *Integer*: An integer field that supports up to 32-bit numbers
- *Large integer*: An integer field that supports up to 64-bit numbers (not normally required for custom metadata)
- Text
- *Unicode string*: An alphanumeric Unicode string

Specialized Settings

The following settings apply only to certain data types:

- *Default value*: Enter an optional default value for the field. Depending on the data type, this can be a checkbox or a specialized value entry such as a date, a time code value, or even two values.

■ *Lookup values*: Choose a lookup from this list to display the metadata field as a pop-up menu with a set of values. Only the lookups with the same data type are displayed. See for details on creating lookups.
■ *Date only*: This is a checkbox that forces only dates to be entered.
■ *Scale numbers*: This is a checkbox that scales numbers to three digits (999 maximum) with the appropriate suffix. For example, 1000 becomes 1K.
■ *Don't format numbers*: This is a checkbox that forces the metadata field to use raw numbers without formatting, such as commas separating groups of thousands.
■ *Multiline*: This is a checkbox that allows multiple lines of text to be entered in the metadata field.

Metadata Attributes

The metadata attributes describe the individual instances of a content type. Metadata attributes further define the behavior of content by describing their accessibility to other content. Since search engines are explicitly designed to recognize predefined keywords, metadata values are extremely important. Once you determine the information a user will want to look for within a document and what data should be extracted, you will need to assign those values as metadata attributes. Whenever possible, standard metadata attributes should be used. These attributes provide a wide range of options for storing your document's metadata. Users can restrict searching to specific attributes, and so it is important that you use standard metadata attributes whenever possible.

Simple attributes: Simple attributes are those whose values can be stored in a single database column.
List attributes: A list attribute is one that can have a set of values, where each value is a simple one and all the values are of the same type.

Metadata Schema

A metadata schema establishes and defines data elements and the rules governing the use of data elements to describe a resource. A metadata schema is used to define the metadata fields that need to be filled out on particular content type. Each schema defines the fields and their type, whether it is required, the default value of the field, whether it can be edited (see Figure 4.5). You can create as many metadata schemas as you may need for the system. Metadata will not only enable designers to gather and rearrange the information to suit their requirements, but the information developers would also have many ways to organize the information.

Content type:		Corporate artifact				
Order	Column name	Description	Type	Re-quired	Default value	Choice fields
1	Business area	The area of the business in which the content belongs.	Choice	Yes		Corporate, retail, institutional, brokerage operations
2	Division	The division within the business unit that this artifact is associated with.	Choice	No	Blank	
3	Department	The department within the business unit thet this artifact is associated with.	Choice	No	Blank	
4	Artifact type	The group of artifacts in which this one belongs or is assigned to. (i.e., product)	Choice	Yes		Policy, procedure, product, form, service
5	Description	An abstract describing what the content is about	Text	Yes		
6	Owner	The content author, SME, or primary contact in regards to the information presented in this artifact.	Lookup	Yes		
7	Published date	The data the artifact was published to the EKMS	Date	Yes		
8	Review period	The period desig-nated in months indicating the freq-uency a review must take place.	Numeric	Yes		
9	Security level	The level at which this artifact can be accessed and viewed.	Choice	Yes	Shared	Shared, controlled restricted
10	Keywords	Any special terms identidying this artifact.	Text	Yes		

Figure 4.5 Example of a metadata schema.

Card Sort

Card sorting is a method used to help design or evaluate the *IA*. In a card sorting session, participants organize topics into categories that are sensible to them and reflect the categorizations of content that they work and communicate with. To conduct a card sort, you can use actual cards, pieces of paper, or one of several online card-sorting software tools (see box "How to Conduct a Card Sort").

Card sorting will help you understand your users' expectations and understanding of your topics. It is often most useful once you have done some homework to find out about your users and understand your content. Knowing how your users group information can help you:

- Build the structure for your systems that handle content.
- Decide what to put on the main page and landing pages of the system.
- Label categories and navigation.

Depending on your needs, you may choose to do an open or closed card sort:

Open card sort: Participants are asked to organize topics from content within your website/repository into groups that make sense to them and then name each group they created in a way that they feel accurately describes the content. Use an open card sort to learn how users group content and the terms or labels they give each category.

Closed card sort: Participants are asked to sort topics from content within your website/repository into predefined categories. A closed card sort works best when you are working with a predefined set of categories, and you want to learn how users sort content items into each category.

Card sorting will not provide you with all of the answers to develop the final structure of your IA and user-experience design, it can help you answer many questions you will need to tackle throughout the information design phase. In many cases, there will likely be some areas that users disagree on regarding groupings or labels. In these cases, card sorting can help identify the following trends:

- Do the users want to see the information grouped by subject, process, business group, or information type?
- How similar are the needs of the different user groups?
- How different are their needs?
- How many potential main categories within a certain navigation are there?
- What should those groups be called?

You may find yourself conducting several card sorts with a varying degree of scope. This will better equip you to come to an agreement to the questions stated above as well as enable you to better address the information design phase.

Search Facets

Faceted search offers remarkable potential for putting the search experience in the hands of the user. It provides a flexible framework by which users can satisfy a wide variety of information needs, ranging from simple lookup and fact retrieval to complex exploratory search and discovery scenarios.

With faceting, search results are grouped under useful headings, using tags you apply ahead of time to the documents in your index. For example, the results of a

HOW TO CONDUCT A CARD SORT

Prepare the Cards
1. Create your list of content topics. Topics can be phrases or words, very specific or more general. As a suggestion, limit yourself to 50–60 topics or less. This means there might not be a card to sort for every page on the site.
   For a new site, list the content topics for the categories of information that you are likely to have on the site.
   For an existing site, list the most important/popular types of content.
   To create this list:
      Review the content listed in your content inventory.
      Identify the most important or most frequently used content.
2. Decide whether you will be doing a physical card sort or using online card-sorting software.
   If you are using online card-sorting software, consult the software instructions.
   If you will be conducting a card sort using physical cards, write each topic on a separate index card.
      Use self-adhesive labels and a word processor. The cards will be neat, legible, and consistent. You'll have the list of topics in the computer for later analysis.
      Number the cards in the bottom corner or on the back. This helps you when you begin to analyze the cards.
      Have blank cards available for participants to add topics and to name the groups they make when they sort the cards.
      Consider using a different colored card for having participants name the groups.

Set-Up the Session
1. Plan about 1 h for each session, or longer if you have many cards.
2. Arrange the space.
   For paper card sorts, ensure the participant has enough room to spread the cards out on a table or tack/tape them up on a wall. A conference room works well.
   For online card sorts, ensure there is a computer with an Internet connection available as well as room for both the participant(s) and facilitator to sit comfortably.
3. Plan to have the facilitator or another usability team member take notes as the participant works and thinks aloud.
4. As with other techniques, arrange for payment or other incentives to thank the participant for spending the time and effort helping you.

(*Continued*)

Lead the Session

1. Show the participant the set of cards. Explain that you are asking for help to find what categories of information should be on the site's home page and what those categories should be called.

   In an open card sort, explain that you want to see what groupings of cards make sense to the participant, and that you will ask for a name for each group of cards once the participant has grouped them.

   If you are conducting a closed card sort, explain that you want to see how the participant thinks the cards fit within the defined groups.

2. Ask the participant to talk out loud while working. You want to understand the participant's thoughts, rationale, and frustrations.

3. Let the participant work. Minimize interruptions but encourage the participant to think aloud. Allow the participant to:

   Add cards—for example, to indicate lateral hyperlinks or additional topics.

   Put cards aside to indicate topics the participant would not want on the site.

4. If, at the end, the participant has too many groups for the home page, ask if some of the groups could be combined.

5. Ask the participant to name each category.

   In an open card sort, give the participant a stack of different colored cards. Ask the participant to use the colored card to name each group. Ask what words the participant would expect to see on the home page or second-level page that would lead the participant to that particular group of content items.

   In a closed card sort, asking about word expectations, their final card organization, and other follow-up questions can provide valuable insight and observations for your research.

6. At the end, thank the participant and give the payment or gift if promised.

Remote Sorting Sessions

1. Create your list of content topics. Topics can be phrases or words, and can be very specific or more general. It might be tempting to have a card for every topic on your site, but in this case, more might not be better. Consider the cognitive load on the participant. You want them to be as on task for your first card as your last. As a suggestion, limit yourself to 50–60 topics or less.

2. Prepare the cards according to the software instructions.

3. Email your participants a link to the study. Provide instructions for the sort (whether open or closed) and let them know approximately how long the session should take to complete.

(Continued)

4. If a comment box is available, urge participants to use the field to record any observations or questions. Although you will not be able to answer them in real time for the participant, these comments can be useful for your analysis.
5. Thank the participant for his or her time and provide instructions for receiving payment or gift (if promised).

Analyze Your Data
1. Prepare your data for analysis.
   If you used online card-sorting software, consult the software instructions. The software will analyze participant data in a variety of ways.
   If you used physical cards for the test, either photograph the sort or use the numbers on the cards to quickly record what the participant did. Photograph or write down the names the participant gave to each grouping and the numbers of the cards the participant included under that name. Then you can reshuffle the cards for the next session.
   Create a computer file for each session to gather a complete picture of the detailed site map each user creates.
   Work from your original list of topics and move topics around to recreate each participant's groupings and enter that participant's name for the groupings.
   If you used a physical card sort, you can also take a photograph of the finished card sort for reference later.
2. Analyze qualitative information based on user comments.
3. Analyze quantitative information based on:
   Which cards appeared together most often
   How often cards appeared in specific categories
4. For a less detailed analysis of the results, use your notes and recordings of the participants' names and card numbers under each person's name to find commonalities from different sessions.
5. For a more detailed analysis, consider using an Excel spreadsheet to show the relationship between the cards or use one of the available software programs to analyze your data.
6. Pull together your findings in a report to share with your team and stakeholders.

After you analyze the data from card sorting, you should have useful information for structuring the information architecture of the site. You should use the results of your card sort to help you define the navigation of your site.

Source: http://www.usability.gov/

shopping query for books might be grouped according to the type of book and the price.

Each time the user clicks a facet value, the set of results is reduced to only the items that have that value. Additional clicks continue to narrow down the search—the previous facet values are remembered and applied again.

Faceted search results provide an easy-to-scan, browsable display that helps users quickly narrow down each search. The faceting tags that you store with your documents provide a way to add your own taxonomy to directly control the presentation of search results. In the end, it's about helping the user find the right information. Faceted search gives a user the power to create an individualized navigation path, drilling down through successive refinements to reach the right document. This more effectively mirrors the intuitive thought patterns of most users. Faceted search has become an expected feature, particularly for commerce sites.

Faceted search is performed in several parts:

- *Index*: To each document in the index, add tags to specify a value for each facet. For example, for each book in the index, tag it with the type of material and the price range.
- *Search results*: For every search, the server returns a count of how many matching documents were tagged with each value within each facet. For example, if the query was for "books," you might find out that in the facet "type of material," your index contains 13 science fiction books, 15 romance novels, and 10 cookbooks; and in the price facet, there are 5 books under $10,200 books from $10–$19.99, and so on.
- *Query*: You can include facet values as query criteria. For example, you can write a query that returns only the romance novels under $10.
- *Web page*: Use the facets and document counts returned by the server to create a set of facet links on your web page. Then construct queries to be activated by each facet link, passing in the appropriate values.

Store the facets and facet values as metadata by adding tags to documents in your system.

After you have tagged documents, the server will start to show faceting data in the results it returns for search requests. For example, if you search for books about France, you might get results like the following:

French History
France Travel
French Art

You can filter a search by using facet values. This is similar to using document variables. Before you start implementing faceting, take some time to decide on the facets and values that make sense for your index. When you consider how to categorize information, all sorts of interesting questions can arise. Depending on the size of your index and whether you are working in a large enterprise, you might need to hold a few meetings involving key people such as website designers, product managers, information architects, and others. The goal of your design phase is to arrive at a scheme, which will define the facets and their values.

The Role of the Information Architect

The information architect is the essential person(s) who will ensure user input is incorporated into the design and construction of your content and KM systems. The information architect ensures that the categorizations of content (information and knowledge) correctly reflect how the user views and works with their content as well as ensure application configuration that will facilitate a search experience, which in turn will yield the right results to users. These individuals incorporate techniques such as developing the content model(s), taxonomy, and metadata schema. Specifically, the information architect assumes the responsibility for the following (see Figure 4.6):

- Investigating the requirements of the customers for the content and structure of information deliverables.
- Understanding the underlying content structure of the information categories that authors must produce and developing standards based on these structures.

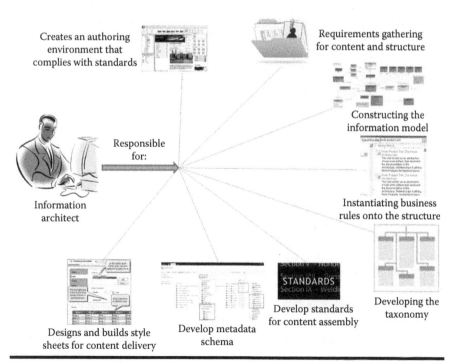

Figure 4.6 The role of the information architect.

- Instantiating business rules into the structures to support authors and encourage compliance.
- Creating structures that promote finding and reusing content in multiple contexts, including metadata schemes, to label content appropriately for delivery to customers.
- Creating an authoring environment that accommodates both the preferences of authors and the needs of the business for compliance with standards.
- Developing standards for content assembly in multiple media that meet customer and business requirements.
- Building style sheets that apply appropriate formatting to content for each type of deliverable.

Instead of focusing on typical IT problems, the information architect approaches the project with a threefold focus: user of the information, the information itself, and the business/organization.

The information architect typically begins to organize information according to three interrelated primary dimensions: workflow, product model, and information type.

He or she begins by analyzing the types of work done by the end users of their products or services and begin to construct the content model. The developed content model begins with a dimension that enables the information architect to label information topics among their content types with relationships that represents the end user's workflow. This is typically followed by understanding the metadata that will describe each of the content types. The information architect represents a key individual (or team) who will incorporate the users' content representation and navigation requirements into the final application as well as provide the design to ensure accurate search and retrieval of the content.

Search Intent

The search intent is another aspect of search where the IA is very valuable. Using the IA's user-provided metadata and keywords, the intent of the search being performed by the user can be determined. Search queries are informational, navigational, or transactional. As part of this process, characteristics are defined for the different types of queries. For example, use of question words (i.e., "ways to," "how to," and "what is"), queries containing informational terms (e.g., list and playlist), and queries where the searcher viewed multiple results pages. Some of the steps to determine search intent include: the selection of keywords, capturing a list of the top site URLs that return from each search, identifying the best search terms and keywords, leveraging the meta keywords identified in the keywords metadata field, and sorting the keywords and phrases in descending order of their perceived importance.

Your environment should be modeled based on the taxonomy to provide functionalities to the end users in form of site navigation, branding, and search. Taxonomy planning is important for the long-term adoption of any system because it provides the framework by which users find the content (information and knowledge).

Tools

There are many tools and possible solutions available to solve our search dilemma. The following are a few tools to consider if we ever hope to not only find information on our knowledge repositories but also to provide solutions to our inquiries.

Knowledge Management Suite for SharePoint 2010 from Layer2 is focused on improved content tagging and discovery. Although this product has not been rated with any reviews, it promises to deliver many features that a taxonomy structure will be able to take advantage of. These features include the following:

- *Tag Suggester*: While tagging an item or document, display a suggestion list based on term store taxonomies, tagging rules, item properties, context, and document content.
- *Auto Tagger*: Tag items and documents in background without any user interaction, based on Term Store taxonomies, tagging rules, item properties, context and document content. Auto Tagger could be helpful for initial tagging, for example, after content migration from any system to SharePoint 2010, as well as for daily background operation.
- *Taxonomy Manager*: Manage the Term Store with additional metadata properties (e.g., tagging rules and related tags), export and import, change management, workflows.
- *Tag Navigation Web Part*: It provides collaborative tagging by using the SharePoint 2010 managed metadata taxonomy tree directly for content discovery and navigation.
- *Tag Directory Web Part*: Render the SharePoint 2010 managed metadata taxonomy tree as flat A–Z directory category index directly for content discovery and navigation.
- *Tag Cloud Web Part*: Navigate the content by its importance using a familiar taxonomy-based tag cloud.
- *Related Content Web Part*: Automatically display related content in a given context using managed metadata.

By the way, Layer2 provides shareware (free) version of their Knowledge Management Suite.

Wordmap Taxonomy Management Software

Wordmap's software enables organizations to develop classification schemes or taxonomies, upload and store documents by reference to them, and then to publish rich information resources for their users to search and navigate. Using taxonomies and classification schemes enables the Taxonomy Management Software to provide structure to content, enabling precise and relevant answers to searches quickly. Some Wordmap Taxonomy Management Software clients include AstraZeneca and the Harvard Business School. The complete product set can be deployed standalone—or easily integrated to improve the performance and consistency of existing systems. Learn more about the Wordmap Search Integration Framework, and how it connects enterprise applications such as SharePoint and Endeca to centralized taxonomy management.

Data Harmony: Expert Knowledge Management with Powerful Semantic Tools and Intelligent Design

Data Harmony software indicates that it provides KM solutions to organize your information resources by applying a taxonomy/thesaurus structure. Data Harmony's software tools enable you to construct a logical framework of topics, reflecting the vocabulary of your business or subject area—and then apply these topic terms to your resources precisely and consistently. Data Harmony tools include the following:

- Thesaurus Master—Taxonomy and thesaurus construction and management.
- Machine Aided Indexer (M.A.I)—Automatic indexing or editorial aid in indexing.
- Maistro™—Combine Thesaurus Master and M.A.I. for maximum efficiency in both automatic indexing and taxonomy construction.
- Additional KM tools—supplement the abilities of these primary products for even greater power in KM.
- Integrates with numerous content management systems, including Microsoft SharePoint.
- Exports taxonomy files in XML, OWL, SKOS, and 11 other formats.
- Handles taxonomies in virtually all languages.
- Uses concept categorization for precise tagging and smarter search.

Smart Logic provides an ontology software tool to build and manage complex ontologies. This software package is their Ontology Manager: The tool is designed for anyone with a basic knowledge of taxonomies and information science to develop "models." A business analyst can use the tool to assist in the process of building a model. For information scientists and information architects, the tool conforms to industry standards and has the flexibility and functionality they need to develop complex models. Some of the features are as follows:

- Creates the model of links and structure between language elements that can drive a new user experience.
- Holds any term "metadata" to drive or enhance connected applications.
- Ontology Manager is designed to allow multiple users to create, enhance, and browse several types of semantic model, which include Lists, Controlled vocabularies, Taxonomies, Thesauri, and Ontologies.

Key Learnings

The following are some key learnings gathered from this chapter:

- It is not just the search tool that will enable users to find content, but a well-formed IA along with the search tool will also render the best search results.
- When developing an IA, it is best to leverage a checklist (see Figure 4.1; Downey and Banerjee, 2011). This checklist ensures all aspects of the IA are covered.
- When constructing a content model follow the steps in order to provide a consistent structure and approach.

Tips and Techniques

The following are some of the tips and techniques deduced after reading this chapter. *Best practices for card sorts.*

- Limit the number of cards. Do not attempt to sort "ALL" of your content, and be mindful of participant fatigue. It's recommend that 30–40 cards at the absolute outside be used, especially for an open sort.
- Randomize the order of presentation, so that each piece of content has a chance to be sorted earlier in the session.
- Provide the participants with a time box of how long the card sort will take before beginning the session to help them better gauge the required time and effort.
- For an open sort, consider requiring users to sort the cards, and not to label them, since that might be the more challenging part of the task, provided that you have limited your items as suggested in point 1.
- Consider an open sort as part 1 and a closed sort as part 2 of your process. Part 1 allows you to learn what goes together, whereas part 2 allows you to really test out your labels to see if they are intuitive to your participants.

Chapter 5

The Age of Discovery: Knowledge Management in Research Institutions

Research institutions are critical to innovation and new product creation. The speed to market for new products is essential to stay ahead of the competition. Knowledge Management (KM) plays a central role not only from the perspective of knowing what has been done and/or what is being done in other areas of research, but also from the collaboration and knowledge sharing among researchers contributing to new ideas that produce innovative products for the marketplace.

Research institutions and research departments that use KM effectively have an advantage over their peers who do not use KM by developing better products, having improved processes to deliver products to market more efficiently, increasing the level of innovation at their organizations, and establishing an environment of empowerment through collaboration for research professionals. KM adoption and effectively using KM are challenging, and this chapter addresses the challenge of equipping research professionals with the necessary tips, tools, and techniques that will accelerate the use of KM. This accelerated use of KM will enable research institutions to realize the benefits KM offers to compete effectively in their respective industries.

Five Challenges Faced When Implementing KM in Research Institutions

There are challenges (I would like to call "opportunities") in implementing KM in all organizations. However, research institutions present a unique challenge of what knowledge should be shared and at what time. On account of the nature of clinical trials for pharmaceutical researchers, the technology and engineering studies and proof of concepts for software, and engineering and manufacturing companies, sharing tacit and explicit knowledge in a timely manner could be the difference between success and failure, producing groundbreaking innovation, or delivering just another product. The following are five challenges/opportunities in implementing KM within a research organization:

1. Integrating KM into the everyday operations
2. Building effective communication strategies
3. The need to create a conducive environment for the adoption of KM practices
4. Understanding the required knowledge to be shared
5. Determining the necessary tools to be used to facilitate KM

As identified from the above challenges, KM adoption (see Chapter 16 for more details concerning KM adoption) and effectively using KM are the primary challenges. This chapter addresses the challenge of equipping research professionals with the necessary tips, tools, and techniques that will help accelerate innovation through the use of KM. Specifically, there will be five key take-away items that the research professional will be able to gleam from this chapter, and they are as follows:

1. Establish the case for implementing a KM strategy
2. KM strategy (specifically for research organizations)
3. Techniques for knowledge sharing
4. Techniques to stimulate innovation
5. Methods/tools for capturing, cataloging, and reusing research, and locating research knowledge/expertise

The Case for Implementing a KM Strategy

Chapter 2 addressed the case for implementing KM. This chapter specifically identifies scenario 4. This scenario specifically addresses to those organizations that have a need to bring new product innovations to the marketplace. It states

■ The case for KM in this area addresses situations where duplication of effort occurs, not having the right team in place to perform the research to bring the product innovation to market successfully and in a timely manner, always reinventing or starting from "square one," difficulty in locating current and/or historical corporate information/knowledge on a specific topic(s), and expertise leaving the organization, thereby creating a knowledge gap.

The major purpose of research organizations is to bring innovative ideas to the marketplace. If your research organization is experiencing what is being described in scenario 4 in Chapter 2, then your organization has a case for implementing KM.

To articulate the case for implementing KM at your research institution, the following questions must be answered:

1. What incentive do I present to my research professionals to encourage them to share their knowledge?
2. What is the return on investments (ROI) for research institutions/departments using KM?
3. How important is it to receive executive leadership buy-in on leveraging KM?
4. What is the key challenge facing research professionals using KM?

In order to implement KM into your research department or institution, you must present a case by identifying problem(s) that need to be addressed, which can be as follows:

- Duplication of effort
- Nonavailability of an appropriate team to perform the research
- Always reinventing or starting from "square one"
- Difficulty in locating current and/or historical corporate information/ knowledge on a specific topic
- Expertise leaving the organization, thereby creating a knowledge gap

Developing Your KM Strategy

The KM strategy presented here specifically applies to research institutions and the unique challenges they face. The vision, mission, and subsequent initiatives that address specific problems of your research organization should be identified and detailed within this strategy. Aligning KM initiatives to address a specific research problem is identified in Table 5.1. This table, although not an exhaustive list, will give you some perspective on where to start.

Components of a Research Organization's KM Strategy

The following represents the categories and details that must be included in your KM strategy, which will be leveraged to address research problems that KM can effectively solve.

Table 5.1 Research Problems Aligned to KM Initiatives

Research Problem	KM Initiative
Duplication of effort	Creating a knowledge map of key knowledge holders and their research
Research team expertise alignment	Expertise locator to align the experts and their experience to the right research effort
Always reinventing or starting over from "square one" whenever a new research initiative is started	KM system (knowledge base, knowledge map, collaboration, and knowledge sharing environment) to locate content, expertise, and share knowledge on similar previous or current research being conducted
Difficulty locating current and/or historical content on specific research topics	Knowledge repository containing research specific content (information and knowledge)
Difficulty finding expertise within the organization	Incorporating an expertise locator as part of KM
Capturing the expertise of experts before they leave the organization	Knowledge capture process for both tacit and explicit knowledge and a knowledge base to capture and catalog the knowledge

Executive Summary

This section briefly reveals to your reader the present situation of your company, the likely future of the organization, and the need to implement a KM strategy. The executive summary should highlight the strengths of your overall plan and therefore be the final section you write.

KM Vision Statement

The KM vision statement takes into account the current status of the organization and serves to point the direction of where KM in the organization is heading toward. As a means of setting a central goal that the organization will aspire to reach, the vision statement helps to provide a focus for the mission.

KM Mission Statement

The KM mission statement serves as a guide to the actions of the organization as it pertains to KM, spell out its overall goal, provide a path, and guide decision-making. It provides the framework or context within which the company's KM Strategy is formulated and aligns with the KM vision (Note: the KM Vision and Mission are often combined).

Current KM Environment (Include If One Exist)

This section details the current knowledge environment. Any KM activities and experience will be detailed here. This section will also outline any benefits that have been gained, and how they can be built upon or leverage in future initiatives.

Challenges and Knowledge Needs

The key issues and knowledge needs of the organization will be summarized here and will include any knowledge resources, processes, and tools that will be needed to effectively execute the KM strategy.

Strategy Details and Key Initiatives

The key activities to implement the KM strategy (knowledge capture, knowledge transfer, knowledge sharing, innovation strategies/initiatives)

Key Performance Indicators and ROI

A key performance indicator (KPI) is a selected indicator that is considered key for monitoring the performance of a strategic objective, outcome, or key result area important to the success of an activity and growth of the organization overall.

R&D sums up the activities centered around research and development, with the purpose of improving current situations and performance within the organization. According to the Organization for Economic Co-operation and Development, R&D refers to creative work undertaken on a systematic basis in order to increase the stock of knowledge, including knowledge of man, culture and society, and the use of this stock of knowledge to devise new applications. There are 82 KPIs for R&D published within knowledge and innovation as part of the KPI Compendium.

Some of the KPIs related to KM within R&D include the following:

Cost savings due to R&D
Cost per R&D laboratory surface
Percentage of staff with PhD degrees
Number of new products per researcher
Cost per researcher
Number of first to market products
Number of products/services co-developed in partnership with customers
Percentage of product development projects completed
Number of patents per million dollars of R&D investment
Number of payback period of new products

Presented in more detail in Chapter 8, the knowledge value equation, by Mark Clare (2002) presents a way to measure the value that KM will bring to your research organization. This equation examines the use of discounted cash flow (DCF) and presents an equation: KM value = F (cost, benefit, and risk) = Total DCF created over life of KM investment. The equation states that the value created from managing knowledge is a function of the costs, benefits, and risks of the KM investment (project or strategy) in leveraging and protecting the knowledge (Clare, 2002). This equation can be applied to the cost/benefit of the innovation that leads to new products being introduced to the marketplace.

An important concept identified in determining the knowledge value equation is to build a knowledge value tree (see Figure 5.1). A knowledge value tree makes the connection between knowledge and value in an organization, which is more visible by understanding the relationship and connection of KM functionality, business impact, and financial impact (Clare, 2002). When applied to research, the business and financial impact of the innovation have to be analyzed. One could also take into account the societal impacts/benefits as another dimension/extension of the equation.

Dependencies

This section will detail critical dependencies such as the availability of key personnel, approval of budgets, and available technologies to initiate the KM strategy. This section will also analyze the effect of not executing the KM strategy at all.

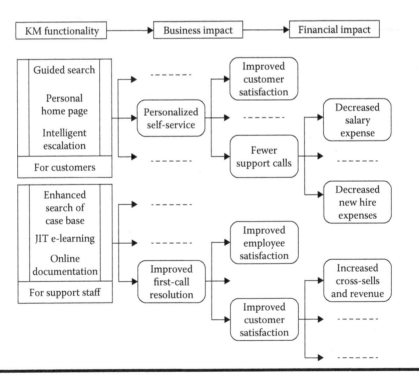

Figure 5.1 Knowledge value tree.

On-Going KM

On-going support, which describes the on-going execution of the KM strategy, includes:

Identifying the key knowledge holders within the organization
Creating an environment that motivates researchers to share
Creating opportunities and utilizing tools to harvest knowledge
Creating opportunities to foster innovation
Designing mechanisms for governance and maintainability of knowledge
Measuring the effects of executing the research knowledge strategy

Establish a Research KM Office

The Research Knowledge Management Office (RKMO) is comprised of senior management and core team members and is the vehicle for implementing and keeping under review the KM program and the on-going KM initiatives that will be championed by the organization. This office will serve as the organizational component that will operationalize the KM program, executing the initiatives that align with the vision and mission of the KM strategy.

Tools

This section details the necessary tools and how they will be used to deliver the KM research strategy.

Knowledge Sharing Techniques

Knowledge sharing is an essential part of the KM research strategy. The following represents techniques for knowledge sharing:

- Conducting after action reviews (AARs) (capturing lessons learned)
- Identifying/participating in communities of practice (CoPs)
- Working in collaborative settings

After Action Reviews

An AAR is a facilitated session that is conducted with a team or a group after completion of a piece of work or project. The objective of an AAR is to capture the knowledge gained by the team as a result of the performing/executing the work.

An AAR
- Makes learning conscious and explicit.
- Identifies valuable lessons that may be helpful to future teams.

- Enhances team openness and cooperation.
- Allows closure at the end of the project.

Some AAR facts include the following:

Participants: An AAR is conducted by the persons who participated in the activity being reviewed. Formal AARs may be conducted by a facilitator, but the participants should be those persons who were actually involved, not their representatives or off-site supervisors

The AAR is conducted

- At the end of a project.
- At the end of a particular phase in a project.
- At the end of a conference.
- At the end of a procurement action.
- Immediately following a significant event or action.

The *types of AARs include the following*:

Formal: Formal AARs are generally conducted at a more extended break in the activity being reviewed; they may take a full day and result in a detailed report.

Informal: While an activity is in progress, or for an activity of short duration, most of the AARs in which our associates are likely to participate will be informal, consisting perhaps of an hour-long discussion at the end of a day. More likely to result in a mid-course correction than a policy shift, informal AARs enable teams to identify what is working—and what needs work.

AAR steps: These describe the general steps in conducting an AAR and their significance. The specific steps taken in conducting an AAR will depend on how much time you have allotted, outside resources needed and/or available, the complexity of your operation, and what is expected to be accomplished (Table 5.2).

Communities of practice: CoPs are groups of people who share a common interest in a particular domain area, and who interact regularly to learn how perform aspects of the discipline better. CoPs are formed by people who are engaged in a collective learning experience, who usually interact often to learn, share, and to better perform their craft.

A CoP

- Can exist online via discussion boards, wiki's, news groups or in real life via meet-ups or other group settings.
- CoPs consist first and foremost of practitioners; specialists who perform the same job or collaborate on a shared task.
- CoPs often form spontaneously, driven by the need of the members for operational knowledge.
- CoPs are also deliberately encouraged where knowledge transfer is necessary.

Table 5.2 After Action Review Steps

After Action Review Steps	Comments
1. Assemble participants as soon after the event(s) as practicable.	
2. Establish rules and explain objectives.	
3. Summarize events as they were planned to occur, with work and time estimates, as appropriate.	
4. Elicit discussion on how the events actually took place. Strategies to make this happen include:	
• Identify mistakes, but don't assign blame. The focus should be on the actions, not on the actors	The AAR discussion is a process of discovery, as all team members share their perspectives on what happened and why. The shared observations of the newest interns through the senior-most associates are essential to piece together how and why some objectives were met and others were not.
• Articulate assumptions	The explicit statement of previously overlooked assumptions often leads to better solutions.
• Address objective and subjective dimensions of the events	Discussion subjects, including attitudes, expectations, fatigue, and stress, may help to explain outcomes in addition to more objective information.
• Ask open-ended questions, not questions that have one-word answers	Open-ended questions encourage discussion and exploration of a topic. They are also less likely to make participants defensive. Compare, "Describe your trip to the court house," with "Why did it take you so long to get to the court house?"

(*Continued*)

Table 5.2 (*Continued*)   After Action Review Steps

After Action Review Steps	Comments
Big picture questions include: • *What* went well, and by what standard? • *What* could have gone better? • More detailed questions may address: • *Why* actions were taken? • *How* associates responded to situations? • *When* actions were taken relative to other events? • *What* alternative actions might have achieved better results? • *What* is required to replicate good performance?	To follow up on what went well/what could have gone better, ask participants to assign a numerical rating to an action. Subsequent discussion on how to improve the rating may lead to the kinds of details that will enable the team to improve overall performance.
5. *Record results*: List the associates who participated, what learning was achieved, what changes are planned, and what practices will be strengthened.	Some of the observations of the AAR will need to be shared with higher and lower levels of the organization.
6. Establish the expectation of AARs as a regular, re-occurring feature of your organization's operations. They should not be considered a sign of failure.	As a group activity, the AAR can promote group cohesiveness and identity. Through repetition, it makes individuals more reflective practitioners.
7. AAR pitfalls that must be avoided: • Allowing performance critiques • Lecturing • Over-analyzing minutiae • Griping, complaining, and general negativity • Allowing stronger personalities to dominate the review, keeping others from participating	

In cultivating CoPs, Etienne Wenger points out three characteristics that make a CoP:

Domain: The domain represents a shared membership of interest. "Membership therefore implies a commitment to the domain and therefore a shared competence that distinguishes members from other people."

Community: The community is represented by members engaging in joint activities and discussions, helping each other, and sharing information. They build relationships that enable them to learn from each other.

Practice: A CoP is not merely a community of interest, for example, people who like certain kind of dog. Members of a community of practice are practitioners. They develop a shared repertoire of resources: experiences, stories, tools, and ways of addressing problems. A Practice takes time and sustained interaction.

For CoPs, see Figure 5.2.

Working in Collaborative Settings

Working in collaborative settings encourages the sharing and exchanging of ideas. Having spent many years as a KM consultant, working in this type of environment, I can attest first hand to the effectiveness this type of workspace provides when it comes to collaborating. According to my experience, collaborative workspaces are ideal for a maximum of 12 people. Too many people and there will be an abundance of "side bar" conversations going on that the whole group could, but will not benefit from.

On the "Office Snapshots Blog—Pixar Headquarters and the Legacy of Steve Jobs," It is indicated that Steve Jobs redesigned the offices of Pixar to suit a more collaborative and diverse thinking environment. At Pixar, these offices originally housed computer scientists in one building, animators in a second building, and executives and editors in a third. Jobs recognized that separating these groups, each with its own culture and approach to problem-solving, discouraged them from sharing ideas and solutions. This environment encouraged animators to introduce fresh perspectives when perhaps the computer scientists became stagnant; and maybe the executives would learn more about what animators and scientist are doing. Jobs ultimately succeeded in creating a single cavernous office that housed the entire Pixar team, and John Lasseter (2012), Pixar's chief creative officer, indicated that he'd "never seen a building that promoted collaboration and creativity as well as this one."

The key features that make for a collaborative office space:

■ An open plan and other design features (e.g., high-traffic staircases) that encourage accidental interactions.
■ More common areas than are strictly necessary—multiple cafeterias and other places to read and work that encourage workers to leave confined offices.
■ Emphasis should be laid on areas that hold two or more people, rather than single-occupancy offices.
■ Creation of purpose-free generic "thinking" areas in open-plan spaces, which will encourage workers think in the presence of other people, rather than thinking alone.

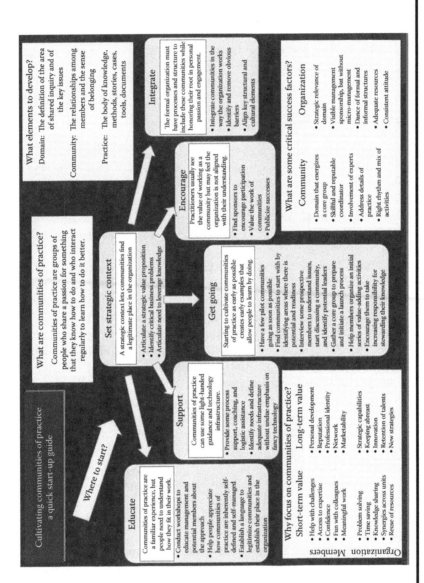

Figure 5.2 Cultivating communities of practice: A quick reference guide. (Courtesy of Etienne Wenger.)

Innovation Techniques

Having initiatives that stimulate innovation is another key ingredient of the KM research strategy. The following represents techniques to stimulate innovation:

Creating diversified teams
Conducting the knowledge café
Conducting root cause analysis sessions
Creating opportunities for brainstorming

Creating Diversified Teams

In my blog post in 2010, I wrote about the need for diversity in order to stimulate innovation.

> The power that Knowledge Management (KM) brings to an organization is its ability to leverage the power of diversity. I am not speaking of just diversity of race, gender and/or religion, but diversity of thought. Through collaboration, knowledge sharing and knowledge reuse it is important to leverage different points of view, different experiences and different cultural backgrounds to stimulate diversity of thought. This diversity of thought leads to innovation. This innovation will enable organizations to deliver unique and or improved products and services to its customers as well as improve the way the organization does business.

Diversity of thought has to be encouraged and used in our organizations today. From a research perspective, by bringing a diverse mindset and experiences to the table, we can begin to understand that diversity of thought will stimulate innovation; we must realize that diversity in our collective thought is a must if an organization wants to stay ahead of its competitors.

The Medici Effect

The Medici effect (see Figure 5.3) is the ultimate environment to stimulate innovation. According to Frans Johansson, the author of *The Medici Effect*, the Medici effect is

> The place where different cultures, domains, and disciplines stream together toward a single point. They connect, allowing for establish concepts to clash and combine, ultimately forming a multitude of new groundbreaking ideas. This intersection where all of these fields meet and the explosion of remarkable innovations that are found there is called…. (Johansson, 2014)

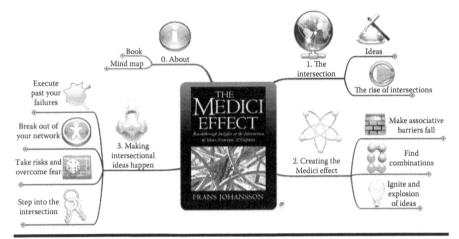

Figure 5.3 Medici effect components. (Data from Luciano Passuello, 2008. The Medici Effect Mind Map, http://www.biggerplate.com/mindmaps/d182919/ the-medici-effect.)

The Medici effect utilizes the diversity of thought and brings those different cultural, intellectual, and life experiences together to increase the level and opportunity for innovation.

Creating the Medici Effect

To utilize the diversity of thought our organizations bring to research and to innovations that occur, an environment to stimulate this innovation must be created. The innovation techniques mentioned earlier are those activities that build an environment to create innovation and your own Medici effect. To create the Medici effect, Frans Johansson states

> We can ignite this explosion of extraordinary ideas and take advantage of it as individuals, as teams, and as organizations. We can do it by bringing together different disciplines, cultures and searching for the places where they connect.

Applying the Medici effect will enable intersectional ideas to flourish once you step into that intersection of different disciplines and cultures.

Conducting the Knowledge Café

"Knowledge cafés" is a term used for group sessions where a number of people (from a small number to several hundred) are assembled to discuss implications of some topic that affects them and their organization.

Typically, the knowledge café is conducted by presenting the topic and its background to the group. This presentation is followed by brief (5–15 min) discussions small groups (five or fewer persons) of the implications and what they may mean for the participants.

The groups are then scrambled and discussions are repeated—often for four or five cycles before summaries are collected. Knowledge café's solicit input and obtain buy-in for a new product, project, or initiative, as a stimulus to innovation: Knowledge cafés connect people to people, people to ideas, and ideas to ideas; they challenge people to reflect on their thinking, surface new ideas, and make new connections. It also breaks down organizational silos and encourage knowledge sharing and creation of a knowledge sharing culture.

Creating Root Cause Analysis Sessions

Root cause analysis is typically a result of a brainstorming session. In Surviving Root Cause Analysis (Robitaille 2014), the Chartered Quality Institute indicates that root cause analysis creates the input to corrective action planning by establishing requirements. Without thorough and well-controlled investigation of the root cause of a given problem, any attempt at corrective action is doomed. It would be like manufacturing a product without fully developing the specifications needed to fulfill the design requirements.

The first step in this process is to evaluate the situation—the inputs—and arrive at a conclusion in order to initiate root cause analysis. The second is to select the members of the team who will conduct the root cause analysis. Giving thoughtful deliberation to the assignment of team members is as important as it is for any other process. It's important to assign tasks to competent individuals, to communicate expectations, and to ensure their availability for the project.

As you begin to select participants, it's important to communicate the distinction between evaluation and root cause analysis. Otherwise, there will be the predictable confusion, with individuals assuming that once they've told you that the bore is undersized, or the battery needed to be replaced, or a test wasn't correctly scheduled, their job is done. What they need to understand is that root cause analysis has just begun.

There are two simple tools that help to generate ideas about what could have happened. They are brainstorming and the "five whys." The overwhelming benefit of both of these is that they stimulate our creativity; they get us out of our habitual narrow focus, so that we can explore other possibilities.

Creating Opportunities for Brainstorming

In a 2010 *Fast Company* article by Gina Trapani she indicated that, "Coming up with good ideas is a major part of your job, so you want to have the right tools on hand to generate as many ideas as possible during a brainstorming session." Here are some tools and techniques for doing just that.

When you want to perform free-form thinking and gather ideas and tasks around a central concept, try a mind map. In the middle of the page, write down your topic. Then, all around the topic, jot down tasks, words, ideas, and connect them by drawing lines between them and branching similar ideas off of them. The most effective offline tool for mind mapping is probably a classic whiteboard, wet marker, and eraser. To mind map online, check out www.mindmeister.com, a free Web app where you can create, share, and publish your maps. The advantage of mind mapping is that it's not linear bullet points, and because it's unstructured, it can encourage more free thinking.

When you're brainstorming, create the environment your brain needs to get creative. Give yourself plenty of writing space and utensils; get everything out of your head and onto paper to make room for new insights. When you can, get yourself out of your normal workspace—go outside, or to the conference room with the great view, or to the coffee shop—to get the creative juices flowing. When you can, choose an open space with high ceilings. A 2007 study showed that people in rooms with high or vaulted ceilings tended to think more freely and abstractly.

If generating ideas is a regular part of your job, make sure you have tools you love to use on hand all the time. Splurge on a fancy pen or notebook, something that you love to write with, and take it with you on the train or to the dentist, and write whenever you have a chance, capturing any thought that might be useful.

Methods/Tools for Capturing, Cataloging, Reusing, and Locating Research Knowledge/Expertise

The proposed model is based on the principle that a research center has a "knowledge reservoir" of its own. This knowledge base is much more than the sum of individual knowledge of employees, and it is capitalized, more or less over time, through information products (documents, databases, software, etc.) or by knowledge exchanges/transfers, individual or collective. The knowledge is created by the research actors (which are the principal "knowledge workers" of a research centers), most of time by interaction with the various information systems available in the center (databases, search engines, document management systems, software, etc.). Some knowledge is exchanged in an informal or semi-formal way (discussions, communities, seminars, etc.); it produces tacit knowledge. Some knowledge is codified in new records (publications, reports, documents, etc.); it is explicit knowledge. It accumulates in the firm during its history, and forms what is called a "knowledge capital."

The research center has the vocation to produce knowledge, an immaterial product. The development of the knowledge map started from a conceptual classification of domains, which organizes the information around subjects, objects, or finalities. The process has several steps.

Location of Knowledge Domains

This step consists (from reference documentation and eventually from interviews) in highlighting knowledge domains by the successive analysis of research departments, their activities, projects, and products. The necessary reference documentation consists of the following:

- Documents of an organization (missions, organizational charts, descriptions of activity, portfolio of activities, etc.)
- Documents concerning production (publications, studies, activity statements, etc.)
- Strategic documents (mid-term plans and summaries of previous mid-term plans)
- Quality documents

Construction of the Representation of the Knowledge Capital by a Knowledge Map

The former step is a deep analysis of the activities of the firm. The next step aims at making it accessible and more usable. The representation must be adapted to the operational vision of the people concerned. The main idea of the cartography is to distribute the different knowledge domains on strategic axes. The definition of strategic axes is conditioned by the strategic orientation given to the business process. One may use the missions of the firm as they are defined in the basic strategy, but it may also integrate new axes concerning strategic development. The map was built following a considerable number of discussions with different actors and numerous cross-validations. First, the cartography was carried out on the research domains of the institute. It was then extended to the whole portfolio of activities, including the support activities. The map is now available on the intranet with an online form, which allows employees of the institute to "self-declare" regarding a certain number of their skills.

Knowledge Map

A knowledge map is a graphic representation of interconnected knowledge sources. This organized knowledge involves large bodies of interconnected facts. It is useful for organizing related knowledge/knowledge holders in a structured manner that facilitates comprehension by showing the connections between the various pieces.

A knowledge map is usually the results of a knowledge audit. The knowledge audit is an investigation into the organizations knowledge assets, where they are, who interacts with them, and how to access them. A typical knowledge audit looks at the following:

- The organization's knowledge needs
- The knowledge assets or resources it currently has and where they are
- The knowledge gaps
- The knowledge flow within the organization
- The existing knowledge blockages

The knowledge map example shown here is the result of a knowledge audit for A.J. Rhem & Associates, Inc., a small management and software development consulting firm (see Figure 5.4). The A.J. Rhem & Associates' Corporate Knowledge Map is a visualization representing the flow of knowledge within the organization. An analysis of the knowledge map indicates the following:

- All of the corporate knowledge flows in and out of the president.
- There is no interaction with others in the senior management team but through the president.
- The president, managing director, and training director are all interacting with the marketing/sales staff and training staff.
- The president and training director are both interacting with the consulting staff.
- There is some cross-training/interaction between the consulting staff and training staff.
- The president is the only one interfacing with the finance/accounting department.

The following indicates the initial knowledge needs of the organization as specified by the knowledge audit:

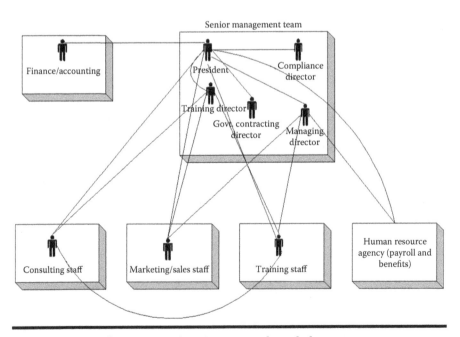

Figure 5.4   A.J. Rhem & Associates' corporate knowledge map.

- Knowledge sharing program is necessary between the president and the senior management staff, in order to distribute the corporate knowledge from the president to other senior management staff members.
- Foster an atmosphere of knowledge sharing among all members of the senior management staff through weekly stand-up meetings.
- Realign senior management team and the communication between the consulting staff, marketing/sales staff, training staff, and human resource agency to have communication and receive direction from one senior management and have all senior management report to the president.
- Formalize program to provide cross-training between the consulting staff and the training staff. This will facilitate increasing the skill and knowledge level of consultants and trainers in order for each to fill the other's role when necessary.
- Formulate knowledge transfer plan to share and cultivate knowledge between management staff as well as consultant and training staff members.

This presents a typical example of using a knowledge audit/knowledge map as a tool for understanding knowledge and expertise within your organization.

Knowledge Portal/Repository/Knowledge Base

A knowledge portal/repository is a technology used to capture, catalog, store, and retrieve content and knowledge. The knowledge portal/repository also provides organizations with a rich and complex shared information workspace for the generation, exchange, and use/reuse of knowledge.

Similar to a knowledge repository, a knowledge base is a collection of role-specific knowledge. This knowledge includes tips, techniques, procedures, guidelines, and work products related to performing activities and tasks for a specific role (i.e., research administrator, research analyst, data analyst, and principle investigator).

A knowledge base typically contains a representation of explicit knowledge to solve some of the most common problems facing the organization. The intent of the knowledge base is to accumulate this knowledge and make it available to its users.

In order to make a knowledge base more effective, there are many points to be considered. In my experience in developing a knowledge base, I have determined the following five aspects of a proficient knowledge base:

1. Quickly search, retrieve, add, and update content (information and knowledge) to the knowledge base. This allows for users to contribute to the knowledge base more effectively.
2. Designed for collaborative use. A real-time collaborative environment and knowledge capture facility creates a lively free exchange of ideas.

3. Provide guided participation (via a blogging structure as an example) that will lead to new learning. In this environment, someone acts as a "moderator," creating structure and topics to stimulate conversations and to capture the knowledge/solutions being addressed.
4. Integrate a variety of media (i.e., video, voice, and text). Incorporating video and voice will add richness to the interaction and to the knowledge/solutions being captured.
5. Help in the decision-making process. Enable the knowledge base to recognize where key knowledge holders exist, their core competencies, and the content that they author, access, and share.

Key Learnings

The following are some key learnings from this chapter:

- Some key points to consider implementation KM in your research organization:
  - Get executive buy in
  - Align KM research strategy with the enterprise's KM strategy and the organizational strategy
  - To begin the adoption process execute no or low budget KM
  - Conduct the knowledge audit (first major initiative)
  - Construct an (interactive) knowledge map (outcome of the knowledge audit)
- Facts about—no or low budget KM consists of executing the following activities:
  - Bringing back notes and other materials from KM classes and/or KM conferences
  - Meetings—make decisions and be intentional about transferring/sharing knowledge and documenting outcomes and next steps
  - Performing knowledge cafés where appropriate (see section on "Innovation Techniques")
  - Informational brown bags—lunch and learn
  - After action reviews and lessons learned
  - Training—mentoring and cross-training, e-learning
  - Knowledge sharing—alerts, organizational awareness, and quick tips

Tips and Techniques

The following are some of the tips and techniques deduced after reading this chapter:

Tip regarding conducting a knowledge audit

■ The knowledge audit is usually the first major step of a KM initiative. It's used to provide a sound investigation into the company or organization's knowledge "health."
■ A knowledge audit looks at problems and puts the information in the context of the problem. The reason a knowledge audit is so vital is because it gives an organization a comprehensive picture of its strengths and weakness, allowing it to focus its efforts in the right direction.

To get quickly started using KM in your research efforts follow these quick tips:

1. Start with a list of the roles in your organization.
   You must have a clear understanding of how your organization creates value for your users (both internally and externally). Make sure you can answer these questions:
   • What are the major activities and processes that take place?
   • Who carries out each of these activities?
   • Where are the decisions made?
   This information is probably already available to you, as part of your organizational governance. If it isn't, then have a think about governance before you get started on KM.
2. Identify activities that would benefit from improved knowledge (Note: Expansion of the scope of your KM program should take place after your high-priority activities have been started and/or completed):
   − Prioritize these activities that
   • Use a lot of resources.
   • Have a major impact on internal and external knowledge users.
   • Are not currently performed well due to a lack of knowledge.
   Look in some detail at how these activities are performed. Talk to the people actually doing the work and making the decisions and identify how knowledge supports them:
   − What knowledge is available now?
   − What knowledge could improve the activity?
   − Does someone else in the organization have the knowledge that is needed?
   This should result in a list of activities that could benefit from improved knowledge, and some idea of where that knowledge could be found.
3. Identify tools and techniques to help with knowledge transfer.
   There are many different tools and techniques that can be used to help acquire knowledge in the right place. Consider creation, storage, and management of content identifying all the different approaches you might use based on your organization's culture and preferences, as well as on the type of knowledge you need to manage.

The following is an initial list of things that you might want to include:

- Searchable document repository
- Knowledge base integrated into your internal and external knowledge customers (including service management and customer facing toolsets)
- Mentoring and coaching
- Webinars and podcasts
- Discussion forums and social media platforms
- Instant messaging, click-to-e-mail, and click-to-call features

When you have a comprehensive list of possible techniques, you can consider which of them might be suitable for each of the activities and types of knowledge that you identified in the previous step.

4. Motivate people to share the knowledge that is needed.

Most of the knowledge you need probably already exists within your organization, but you will need to motivate the people who have this knowledge to share with those who need to use it. This will depend on your organizational culture, and on the tools and techniques that you have selected.

You will probably want to identify a small number of KM champions to model the behavior you want, and to encourage other people. It can also be very effective to publish the names of people who make useful knowledge contributions, and to provide reward and encouragement for the desired behaviors.

5. Motivate people to use the knowledge that has been shared.

Remember that knowledge can only create value when it is used by someone to make decisions or deliver services. You need to think about incorporating the knowledge that is being created into the activities that you identified earlier.

Use techniques to identify and acknowledge the authors of the most reused pieces of knowledge, and the people who make the most use of shared knowledge. When you know what knowledge is being reused, you can also use this to justify further investment in KM and to plan future improvements.

6. Manage your knowledge to ensure it remains relevant and helpful.

Don't forget that KM isn't a one-off project; it has to include a change in the culture of your organization. This means applying all the management of change techniques that you would use for any other organizational change.

Leverage a comprehensive governance plan for your knowledge assets. You will need to constantly review the sources of knowledge, to ensure that they remain relevant and helpful, and purge anything that is out of date.

Chapter 6

"Where Have All My Experts Gone?": Knowledge Management in Human Resources and Talent Management

If your organization is losing valuable knowledge due to staff retirement, staff moving to other departments, or staff dismissed for a variety of reasons, then your organization has a strong case for the implementation of a human capital/talent management strategy. Managing your human capital when your staff enters the organization through employee orientation; mapping their roles, responsibilities, and their work products as they perform their duties; and executing a comprehensive exit interview are all aspects of a knowledge management (KM) strategy aimed at moving your human capital to corporate capital. Specifically, I want to address leveraging KM to manage your human capital.

Infusing a human capital management (HCM) strategy with KM such as knowledge capture, knowledge cataloging and reuse, knowledge sharing, and connecting expertise throughout your organization will improve the talents of your people and increase the organizational competency.

Some time ago, I had a conversation with one of my colleagues regarding his organization's loss of critical expertise. As people started to move in and out of the company valuable knowledge gaps appeared. In a statement of exasperation he asked,

"Where have my experts gone?" To address these gaps, the organization began to seek short-term (6 months or less) expertise to perform specific duties. When these resources moved on the organization was back to square one. This led him to ask the following questions: "How can we address this in the long term?" "Where can we find experts to fill these positions long term?" "How would you address this issue?"

These are indeed, given the situation, the questions that we must seek to address. I informed him that the first task would be to prioritize the areas that have experienced knowledge loss, and based on that perform a knowledge audit of the area that has been identified as the higher priority. In addition, further knowledge audits should be scheduled for the remaining areas as his organization became more comfortable with executing knowledge audits. I also informed him that the knowledge audit will reveal to him what specific knowledge gaps exist, who are the current knowledge holders, and what percentage of knowledge is tacit, explicit, or both.

If the knowledge gap is tacit, then understanding the specifics of this tacit knowledge would help you determine the type of expertise you need to hire and the duration for the same. If the knowledge is explicit, then your key knowledge holders may have access to this knowledge somewhere in the organization (knowledge repository/portal, network folders, on the shelf, etc.). You may also have the ability to purchase this knowledge or perform research to document this knowledge. I also believe that engaging the key knowledge holders when it comes to identifying the "right" personnel to bring in to fill key positions will start to address his concerns about where to find the experts he needs.

A KM strategy entails a collective visioning as to how sharing knowledge can enhance organizational performance, and the reaching of a consensus among the senior management of the organization that the course of action involved in sharing knowledge will in fact be pursued. Implicit in such a process is a set of decisions about the particular variety of KM activities that the organization intends to pursue, including how the knowledge assets of the organization will be leveraged (with human capital being the primary asset), and the execution of the process and tools that will enable sharing of knowledge and innovation to occur.

As part of applying KM to a comprehensive human capital/talent management strategy, an understanding of the roles, work products (artifacts), and tasks (activities) are key for a person's onboarding and/or gaining understanding of what is required for a particular job (see Figure 6.1). It is important for any organization

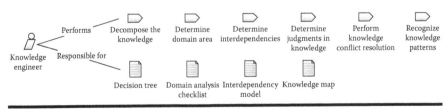

Figure 6.1   Example of knowledge captured for the knowledge engineer role.

to not only identify the corporate roles, tasks, and work products but also to provide the necessary guidance around this aspect of the corporate structure. In doing so, creating an environment in which all employees can seek to achieve knowledge in specific roles is essential to infusing corporate knowledge and managing human talent within the organization.

One way to accomplish this is to build a knowledge base of corporate roles, the tasks that each role performs, and the work products that are produced along with the guidance (i.e., whitepapers, templates, FAQs, key contacts, PowerPoint presentations, video, and audio).

Role-Based Knowledge

Role-based knowledge focuses on the specific knowledge needed to perform in a given role. It identifies the activities that are needed to be performed as well as the work products that are needed to be produced.

Role Knowledge Base

A role knowledge base is a repository of worker knowledge, which is aligned directly to roles that are leveraged by the organization. This knowledge is specifically captured for a role (analyst, staff assistant, project manager, marketing specialist, etc.) and is aimed at performing tasks related to activities that produce work products.

The Knowledge Acquisition Unified Framework (KAUF)™ is an example of a role knowledge base geared toward capturing and cataloging role-based worker knowledge. The KAUF is utilized to capture explicit as well as tacit knowledge and transition this knowledge into an environment in which it can be harvested into a KM repository, knowledge-based system, knowledge map, or other KM tool. The KAUF provides a repeatable process for identifying, understanding, and cataloging the tacit and explicit knowledge of the organization during the knowledge elicitation process.

Knowledge Map to Identify Experts

To assist in establishing the knowledge repository (or "library," as it is sometimes called), producing a knowledge map of your organization will be greatly beneficial. A knowledge map is an excellent tool to facilitate the identification of the key knowledge holders and knowledge gaps; it identifies areas to leverage existing knowledge and where knowledge is eroding. However, performing a knowledge mapping exercise should focus on a particular department, functional area, or specific organizational domain and gradually built upon until an entire knowledge map of your organization exists.

Knowledge mapping is an essential component of conducting a knowledge audit and overall KM strategy. The knowledge map serves as a navigation aid to identify and locate explicit and tacit knowledge. This mapping directly leads to identifying candidates for tacit knowledge capture within the organization. The knowledge map should be an interactive knowledge map with accessibility through the organization's information system infrastructure (intranet, SharePoint, etc.).

In order to properly manage your organization's human capital assets, it is important to identify knowledge and content managers and knowledge architects who can facilitate in capturing, codifying, organizing, and maintaining your corporate knowledge assets. Furthermore, these resources will be the principle staff involved in the creation of your knowledge repositories, knowledge mapping, and strategy and audit activities.

For a moment, consider the value of having such an environment and its many uses. Some of them that immediately come to mind include being able to quickly have a new person filling a role to come up to speed and create assigned deliverables. Or, perhaps having a repository of "knowledge nuggets" supplied by experienced people in that role, which can serve as the repository of worker knowledge that can be accessed by anyone in the organization, which will lead to performing that role more effectively and efficiently. This will lead to increased performance within the workforce and will transition your organization to compete in these challenging economic times and well into the future.

Human Capital Management

Human capital is the stock of competencies, knowledge, habits, and social and personality attributes (including creativity and cognitive abilities) embodied in the ability to perform labor so as to produce economic value. HCM is an approach to employee staffing that perceives people as assets (human capital) whose current value can be measured and whose future value can be enhanced through investment.

HCM contains a set of practices that are focused on the organizational need to provide specific competencies and are implemented in the following three categories: talent acquisition and planning, workforce management (WFM), and workforce optimization.

Talent acquisition and planning: Today's knowledge-driven economy requires workforce planning to attain and retain talent, regardless of the size of your organization and industry. Your strategy must deliver high-quality talent at the right time to address the right knowledge gaps to improve/continue operational efficiency.

Talent acquisition and workforce planning must be linked to gain perspective on opportunities for collaboration. The merging of the two groups is identified as a way to link the talent planning (strategic) and execution (tactical) aspects of talent management. This enables better line of sight into the current and future talent requirements for their areas of responsibilities.

In order to source, identify, recruit, and select talent that meet the long-term workforce, the plan is use multiple strategies for attraction and recruitment of talent. The amount of resources deployed to a vacancy is dependent on both the quantity and the difficulty.

The majority of vacancies require a multi-pronged approach using internal and external resources. This will include using the services of some search firms for strategic recruiting services to assist in the identification of the passive candidate.

A process for designing effective advertising campaigns that enhance the initial buy-in with key potential talent is a key component to attract new talent into the organization. There is a direct linkage to align talent to corporate objectives. A focus on key occupations and geographic locations with a tailor message will enhance the ability to attract the "right" talent.

Workforce management: WFM is all about assigning the right employees with the right skills to the right job at the right time. WFM is basically all the activities needed to maintain a productive workforce, including payments and benefits, human resources (HR) planning, training and development, time-keeping and attendance, recruitment, performance management, and forecasting and scheduling. Our focus for WFM includes career and succession planning/talent acquisition, talent management and/or applicant tracking, learning management and/or training management, and performance management.

Workforce optimization: Workforce optimization is concerned with enabling businesses to take control of all aspects of their staffing, and helps staff understand how they affect the business's performance, with an emphasis on improving this incrementally over time.

Workforce optimization, in addition, takes this one step further by using analytics to tie WFM to key business concepts such as growth, profit, and customer experience. Workforce optimization is best viewed as the next logical step in the move to optimize the performance of staff and to understand and manage the overarching impacts of staff based on both operational efficiency and the customer experience.

Workforce optimization is closely related to and an evolution of WFM by encompassing all aspects of managing the complete workforce life cycle (see Figure 6.2). KM infused within workforce life cycle management will include knowledge transfer activities during the onboarding process facilitated by HR; access to specific role-based knowledge geared to quickly get

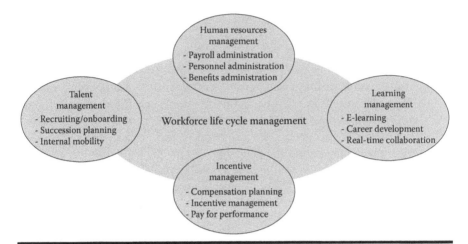

Figure 6.2   Workforce life cycle management.

the new employee up to speed and to provide key knowledge throughout the employee's evolution in the organization will be facilitated through talent management; to incentify the employee to share knowledge to increase performance will be initiated through specific incentive programs facilitated by incentive management; and learning management will facilitate filling gaps in knowledge and/or needed expertise to perform current and future organizational functions.

HCM within an organization provides employees with clearly defined and consistently communicated performance expectations. Managers are responsible for rating, rewarding, and holding employees accountable for achieving specific business goals, and as identified earlier, KM will play a key role in creating innovation and supporting continuous employee growth and performance.

Talent Management

Talent management is a set of integrated organizational HR processes designed to attract, develop, motivate, and retain productive, high-performing employees. As opposed to HCM where there is an emphasis on the management of employees. Susan Heathfield (2016) in her article "What Is Talent Management—Really?" states "Talent management is an organization's commitment to recruit, retain, and develop the most talented and superior employees available in the job market."

Talent management (from John Hopkins University, Office of Talent Management and Organization Development)—includes the following:

Workforce planning: The intentional and strategic projection and planning of access to talent (either internal or external) with the skills, knowledge, and behaviors essential for the achievement of the organization's strategic objectives and/or demands.

Recruiting: The ability to successfully attract and hire key talent for current and future organizational needs through competency-based advertising and interviewing efforts.

Onboarding: The process of acclimating new hires and ensuring that they quickly feel welcomed, and valued by the organization. This process enables new employees to become productive members of the organization, who understand expectations for their job roles. Onboarding goes beyond traditional "orientation" programs, which focus mainly on managing policies, forms, and procedures.

Strategic plan/goal alignment: The process of developing and implementing plans to reach an organization's long-term goals and objectives. It is the roadmap to lead an organization from where it is now to where it would like to be in 3–5 years.

Performance management: An ongoing process of communicating and clarifying job responsibilities, priorities, performance expectations, and development planning that optimize an individual's performance and aligns with organizational strategic goals.

360-degree assessments: 360-degree feedback is an assessment tool that provides faculty and staff leaders with feedback on their performance. Supervisors, peers, and direct reports answer questions based on their perceptions and observations of the leader's skills and attributes.

Executive coaching: "A helping relationship between a client and a consultant, who uses a wide variety of behavioral techniques and methods, to assist the client to achieve mutually identified goals to improve professional performance and personal satisfaction in an effort to improve the effectiveness of the client's organization Kilburg, 2000.

Leadership development: Intentional goal-driven activities that enhance the quality of leadership abilities or attitudes within an individual or an organization.

Professional development: Process of establishing training goals and plans that link to individual goal attainment, career planning, and possible succession planning.

Career path/Career development: This includes structuring the career progression of the organization's employees and an individual's process for identifying job opportunities within an organization's structure, and the sequential steps in education, skills, and experience-building needed to attain specific career goals.

Recognition programs: A method of acknowledging, honoring, encouraging, and supporting individuals and teams who contribute, through behaviors and actions, to the success of the organization.

Compensation: A way to reward individuals for important work accomplishments, contributions to the goals of the organization, and increased skills and competencies in their jobs.

Succession management: Succession management is a process for identifying and developing internal personnel with the potential to fill key or critical organizational positions. Succession management ensures the availability of experienced and capable employees that are prepared to assume these roles as they become available.

Diversity/inclusion: Diversity represents a group consisting of individuals with similar and different experiences and backgrounds. Some of these differences include race, color, religion, gender, national origin, sexual orientation, age, disability, veteran status, and ethnicity, but there are many other dimensions of diversity. "Diversity" does not address how people with different backgrounds and experiences function or work together.

Engagement: The extent to which employees are committed to their organization's goals and values, motivated to contribute to organizational success, and at the same time are able to enhance their own sense of well-being.

Competencies: Those measurable behaviors, characteristics, abilities, and personality traits that identify successful employees against defined roles within an organization.

Retention: A systematic effort focused not only on retaining an organization's talented performers but also on creating and fostering a welcoming work environment and high-retention culture. The end result is an organization that operates more effectively and efficiently, while becoming a great place to work.

KM Influence on Talent Management

KM will directly influence the following aspects of talent management by

Workforce planning: Providing guidance on knowledge gaps (either internal or external) and the long- and short-term needs of the organization to address it.

Recruiting: Providing an understanding of the competencies needed for talent to be successful in the position/role you are recruiting for.

Onboarding: Providing and ensuring that new hires have access to knowledge of the company, their specific department, and role(s) they will be filling for the organization. This enables new employees to become productive members of the organization, who understand expectations for their job roles.

Strategic plan/goal alignment: Influencing the process of developing and implementing plans (with specific projections of knowledge needs and the alignment of that knowledge) to reach an organization's long-term goals and objectives. It is the roadmap to lead an organization from where it is at present to where it would likely be in 3–5 years.

Performance management: Ensuring that employees have access to critical knowledge and expertise to perform well in their designated role(s). It is an ongoing process of communicating and clarifying knowledge that optimizes an individual's performance and aligns with the organization's strategic goals.

Leadership development: Providing the right knowledge and expertise that will enhance the quality of leadership abilities or attitudes within an individual or organization.

Professional development: Providing access to knowledge and expertise (both internal and external), and plans that link to individual's goal attainment, career planning, and possible succession planning.

Career path/career development: Providing individual's knowledge of the competencies, role-based knowledge (tasks, activities, and work products being produced), and access to fill knowledge gaps will give an understanding of what is needed to attain specific career goals.

Recognition programs: Enhancing the method of acknowledging, honoring, encouraging, and supporting individuals and teams who contribute to include knowledge sharing activities, which contribute to the success of the organization.

Compensation: A way to reward individuals for important work accomplishments, contributions (including knowledge contributions) to the organizational goals, and increased skills and competencies in their jobs.

Succession management: Providing access to knowledge and expertise (both internal and external) to ensure the availability of experienced and capable employees who are prepared to assume roles as they become available.

Talent management focuses on all of the employees from planning, recruitment, onboarding to exit interview. In this chapter both HCM and talent management have been combined because KM will have an influence on the entire workforce life cycle and many aspects of talent management. The goal of both HCM and talent management is to create a high-performance, sustainable organization that meets its strategic and operational goals and objectives, and having the right knowledge at the right time in the right context is key in achieving this goal.

High-Impact Talent Management Framework

One final word on talent management! To begin infusing KM within talent management, your organization must start with a talent management model. Building a talent management model to suit an often volatile and transformational business landscape requires taking a detailed look at talent management. Bersin & Associates' Talent Management Framework® takes this detailed approach. In developing this framework, they examined hundreds of organizations and intended to show a graphical depiction of how the various talent management processes come together (see Figure 6.3) (Bersin et al., 2010).

The framework begins by defining a talent strategy in the context of the business strategy. In this case, Bersin indicates that the talent strategy should help the company to achieve its business goals. Alignment to the business strategy is critical for the next area, workforce planning. In workforce planning, the organizations will define their talent segments, identify critical roles, and analyze organizational skills gaps. This information will be leveraged to drive succession plans, recruitment strategies, and learning agendas. It is then that the company enters into the solution phase of talent management (Bersin et al., 2010).

"Capability and competency management" is next; it is this information (skills, competencies, and experiences) that will enable organizations to answer the following questions: For what do we hire? Against what do we assess? Toward what do we develop? (Bersin et al., 2010).

Job profiles capture this critical information, and should be developed and managed for all critical roles, which should have been defined in the previous area of workforce planning. The largest section of the framework, in the center, includes those processes that directly touch the employees at different stages of the employment cycle (recruiting, assessing, developing, and rewarding) (Bersin et al., 2010). One role of talent acquisition is to fulfill the workforce plan. Whether filling positions with internal or external candidates, it is at this stage that a new 'cycle' begins. The next four areas are integral to developing and mobilizing talent to where it is needed (Bersin et al., 2010).

Leadership development: Ensures that companies have high-performing leaders to run the company.

Succession management: Defines the kind of bench strength that is necessary for succession (top down—position-driven).

Career management: Creates awareness of employees' career goals (bottom up—employee-driven).

Performance management: Provides a vehicle for assessing talent.

"Total rewards" is capped on the end of this center section. Throughout the employee life cycle, it is critical that employees are rewarded appropriately.

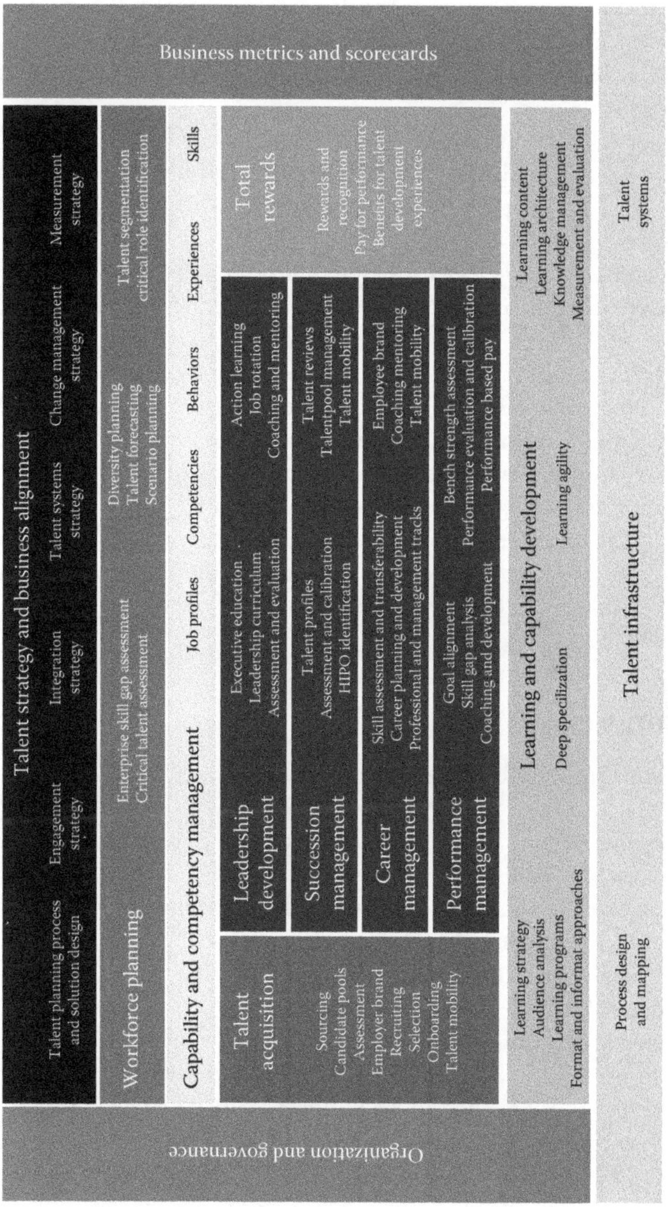

Figure 6.3 New high-impact talent management framework. (From Bersin, J., A new talent management framework, http://www.bersin.com/blog/post/2010/05/A-New-Talent-Management-Framework.aspx. With permission.)

"Learning and capability development" was placed toward the bottom of our framework, across the entire employee life cycle, because it is truly an enabler for talent management strategies to be realized. Without learning, a company and its talent become stagnant. It is essential that talent continues to learn and develop as the business evolves and grows, and the workforce needs change. The learning and capability development function is, in turn, driven by gaps defined:

- Once an employee is hired or moved into a new role (the learning curve)
- By the data from performance management reviews (strengths and weaknesses)
- As a result of an employee's career aspirations (progression)
- As necessary to fulfill a succession plan in some period (readiness)

The pillars or bookends of the framework are essential for keeping all of the moving parts connected. "Organization and governance" ensure alignment, oversight, accountability, and follow-through, whereas "business metrics and analytics" are defined to determine how effective the talent programs are, collectively. As an essential piece of the framework, the "talent infrastructure" ensures that data and processes are aligned, integrated, and accessible. The infrastructure "maps" the processes, so that integration points are clear and provide the systems for enhancing the processes (Bersin et al., 2010).

Key Learnings

The following are some key learnings from this chapter:

Workforce optimization solutions: When selecting a workforce automation solution look for solutions that:
  - Tie together vertical WFM systems and provide bridges HR, operations, and IT.
  - This should be a business-driven approach that automates the entire workforce life cycle (see Figure 6.2).
  - Make key data more visible at more levels in order to support better decision making. This will ensure compliance with a wide range of relevant legislation, and solving business problems related to staff.

When incorporating KM within the HCM/TM strategy:
  - Link KM activities along with learning activities to the employees' developmental goals identified in the performance management process. Organizations depend on learning to skill-up not only their employees but also their customers and channel partners.

Role-specific knowledge:
- Be intentional on describing each role within your organization with the appropriate corresponding set of competencies and a roadmap on the skills and demonstrated knowledge to achieve them.
- Understand that someone's title can be different from the role they are performing at that time (i.e., a financial analyst could have a role of a manager when they have junior analyst reporting to them).
- Distinguishing between roles are important for system access (role-based security).

Tips and Techniques

The following are some of the tips and techniques deduced after reading this chapter:

- Differences between learning, training, and KM
  - It is important to understand the difference between learning, training, and KM. These differences are identified here:
    - Training is a systematic approach to improving employees' knowledge, skills, and attitudes in order to hone their ability to perform today's job responsibilities. Training is an intervention that is delivered by an instructor or facilitator.
    - Learning, on the other hand, is the systematic process of preparing employees and leaders for future responsibilities. Learning is the process of acquiring knowledge or skill in the context of organizational goals by discovering information via tools and mechanisms the organization has made available to learners.
    - KM is distinguished between learning and training in that it provides guidance and ac cess to expertise to address immediate situations where decisions need to be made. Explicit knowledge can take the form of (among other things) job aids, knowledge articles, guidelines, operating procedures, and lessons learned. Tacit knowledge access can be facilitated through (among other things) communities of practice, collaboration environments, and expertise locators. KM methods and knowledge repositories/knowledge bases can supplement and support learning and training events when it comes to applying what someone has recently learned or been trained in.
- *KM needs analysis*: A knowledge needs analysis should be conducted to understand what skills, knowledge, gaps, and attitudes need to be changed or

improved to produce better business results more quickly. A quick assessment can be done in four steps:

- Collect existing performance data on the behaviors to be improved.
- Analyze the data isolating knowledge gap areas.
- Identify the causes for the gaps.
- Recommend and implement knowledge solutions to close the gaps.

Chapter 7

"Sound the Alarm!": Knowledge Management in Emergency and Disaster Preparedness

Introduction

During a time of crisis (such as national disasters, pandemics, and acts of terrorism), relevant information is usually not received by the individuals or group of individuals that need it the most. For instance, many times first responders are not able to respond quickly and effectively without the right information during a crisis situation. The lack of timely and correct information increases level of confusion, resulting in their ineffectiveness that may cause a loss of life.

Our current emergency broadcast systems are ineffective. This ineffectiveness is due to the lack of timely accurate and meaningful information delivered to the correct recipient during emergencies. This prevents first responders, key leadership, and the public from preparing for imminent danger, compromises the ability to make informed decisions, and enacts the proper emergency preparedness operations.

There is a problem delivering first responders the appropriate data, information, and knowledge in a timely manner to effectively execute during an emergency/ crisis event. So what are the contributing factors? The following table outlines the contributing factors related to the lack of available knowledge and the effect on what knowledge management (KM) would bring to first responders.

A summary of contributing factors

#	Contributing Factors	Effect on Users
1	Current alert systems do not align with a cohesive strategy for preparedness, response, and recovery activities during an emergency/crisis event	Lack of planning and execution around preparedness, response, and recovery activities will lead to a lack of injured being treated in a timely manner and prolong timeline and cost associated with response and recovery
2	Many alert systems do not integrate with national, state, and local alert systems	Collaborative alert systems will enable pertinent and comprehensive alert information to be received down to the local level and enable local authorities to respond quickly to a crisis event preventing additional injuries and lose of life
3	Current alert systems do not leverage information services such as weather, geospatial, and intelligence services	Alert systems that leverage services such as weather, geospatial, and intelligence services will potentially be able to provide information on impending emergency/crisis events that will lead to improved preparedness, response, and recover activities, contributing to saving lives and decreasing the amount of injured people
4	Many alerting systems do not enable two-way communication between all relevant emergency officials and first responders	Emergency officials and first responders are unable to make informed decisions concerning emergency preparations and responses
5	Current alerting systems do not enable two-way communication between emergency officials and the public	During emergencies affected individuals are unable to request and obtain immediate assistance
6	Current alerting systems require dedicated hardware, software, and interfaces to the telecommunication providers in order to send emergency messages	Alert volume and speeds are limited to the capacity of dedicated resources provided

(Continued)

#	Contributing Factors	Effect on Users
7	Ineffective information feeds to broadcast alerting systems (television and radio) delays the dissemination of critical information to the public	The public does not receive effective warnings during emergencies
8	Current alerting systems do not have the ability to provide targeted alerts by identifying an ad hoc geographical area	Segments of the public in a geographical area affected by a crisis do not receive critical warnings.

This chapter will focus on a first-responder KM strategy that will provide a holistic approach to leveraging knowledge and implementing technology in order to increase the effectiveness of first responders.

First-Responder KM Strategy

Creating a KM strategy presents a holistic approach to leveraging knowledge and implementing technology to increase the effectiveness of first responders (see Figure 7.1). The KM strategy reflects several key aspects in delivering

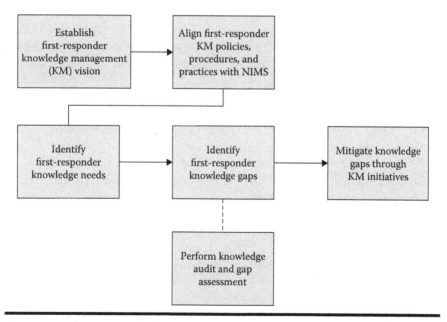

Figure 7.1   First-responder knowledge management strategy process.

knowledge throughout an organization. The KM strategy suitable for execution by first responders should align with the National Incident Management System (NIMS), which according to NIMS (2008, p. 3)) "provides a consistent nation-wide template to enable federal, state, tribal, local governments, nongovernmental organizations (NGOs), and the private sector to work together to prevent, protect against, respond to, recover from, and mitigate the effects of incidents, regardless of cause, size, location, or complexity." The KM strategy for first responders will specifically address disaster preparedness, response, and recovery including the technology that must be leveraged to support this strategy.

In order for any technology initiative to be successful, it must address a need for the organization. The KM strategy will identify the knowledge needs of first responders and determine the communication needs between national, state, and local entities and their corresponding first-responder organizations (such as Fire, police, Emergency Medical Service [EMS], National Guard, and Coast Guard). Our preliminary research has determined that establishing a national alert system is a high-priority initiative for the Department of Homeland Security. This initial system will incorporate the knowledge needs identified in the KM strategy as well as technologies that will enable federal, state, and local governments to support first responders more effectively and efficiently.

Knowledge Shared, Captured, and Reused

In examining the types of knowledge that must be shared, captured, and available for reuse, Nonaka and Takeuchi (as cited by Haggie and Kingston, 2003) have classified knowledge as either tacit or explicit, individual or collective, and have identified knowledge processes that transform knowledge from one form to another (i.e., socialization: tacit to tacit, externalization: tacit to explicit, combination: explicit to explicit, and internalization: explicit to tacit) see Figure 7.2.

In Figure 7.2, socialization refers to the sharing of individual tacit knowledge, and this can happen through collaborative methods such as meetings individuals and/or groups, in person and/or online. Externalization refers to the exchange of tacit knowledge to explicit knowledge, which consists of codifying the tacit knowledge into stories (best practices, SOPs, and tips and techniques), graphically through designs, and/or through the implementation of software (i.e., expert systems or knowledge base systems). Internalization refers to learning by doing, taking in explicit knowledge and creating new tacit knowledge. Combination refers to extracting explicit knowledge, combining it, and presenting it in a form to incorporate it into the organization. This can be in the form of a knowledge base, electronic library, and/or knowledge repository. Combination or explicit to explicit is used for transferring best practice knowledge (Nonaka and Takeuchi, 1995).

The Socialization, Externalization, Combination, and Internalization (SECI) model, as it is commonly referred to, provides the conversion process that transitions

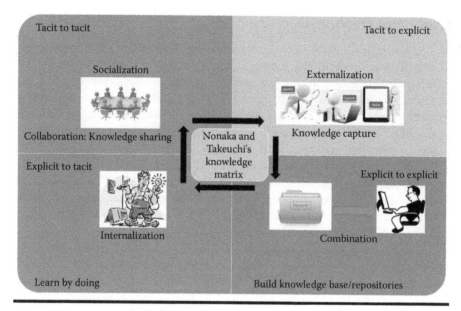

Figure 7.2 Nonaka and Takeuchi's knowledge matrix.

individual knowledge into corporate or organizational knowledge. This knowledge is then leveraged to achieve organizational vision, strategic objectives, and performance expectations (Nonaka and Takeuchi, 1995). This model will serve as the basis to perform knowledge sharing within the first responders when they are deployed to a crisis/emergency event.

In determining the components of a suitable KM strategy for first responders, a determination must be made on the way they serve their clients; the types of knowledge that must be shared, captured, and available for reuse; and should align with the strategic direction of the organization.

The analysis documented in this chapter indicates the way in which first responders serve their clients. Besides the factors influencing the selection of a KM strategy, as indicated by Haggie and Kingston, this information will also drive the formation of a KM strategy for first responders. First responders must have a KM strategy that supports the following:

■ Quick and decisive decision making, collaborative communication, and situational analysis (Balogun et al., 2006)
■ Acquiring EMS-specific knowledge (Coleman, 2007)
■ Knowledge recognition, needs assessment and allocation, and feedback and evaluation (Lesson and Sobel, 2007)
■ Expertise coordination practices (Faraj and Xiao, 2006)
■ Command and control structure (Balogun et al., 2006)
■ Learning and knowledge transfer (Balogun et al., 2006)

Quick and Decisive Decision Making

To support quick and decisive decision making, collaborative communication, and situational analysis, there has to be an incident command structure that disseminates integrated information and knowledge by using real-time communications (National Incident Management System, 2008). During an emergency, firefighters are operating in an atmosphere of panic fear and confusion (Balogun et al., 2006) as well as being under pressure to absorb information rapidly, and judge its meaning, relevance, and reliability (Carver and Turoff, 2007). This information and knowledge of the crisis event is being passed along from individual to individual, team to team, and agency to agency. As this communication escalates, there is a need to incorporate technology to facilitate the rapid flow of information and knowledge that will enable quick and decisive decision making and situational analysis.

The KM strategy for first responders will facilitate quick and decisive decision making through the implementation of an incident command structure and will be further supported by integrating the NIMS protocols, procedures, and policies as indicated by the communications and information management, and the command and management components of NIMS. The communications and information management component will provide common communications planning and process standardization, whereas the command and management component will provide incident command; multiagency coordination; and public information protocols, procedures, and policies in support of the KM strategy.

Acquiring EMS Knowledge

EMSs has emerged as an important part of what services Fire Departments and first responders provide to the public. As Fire Departments evolve to include EMS. EMS personnel are being hired within Fire Departments, and these personnel have to be trained on how to deliver firefighting tasks, which include confining and extinguishing fires, forcible entry, search and rescue, ventilation, salvage and overhaul, and aerial ladder execution (Baker, 2008). This emergence has also increased the need for traditional first responders to acquire EMS knowledge, which includes basic to advance life support. In order to facilitate the acquisition of the appropriate knowledge for all firefighter personnel, a plan for cross-training within the Fire Department to efficiently and effectively deliver its services should be included within the KM strategy. The establishment of knowledge transfer activities is supported by the NIMS preparedness component, which includes protocols for planning, training and exercises, personnel qualifications, and licensure and certification, including equipment certification (National Incident Management System, 2008).

Knowledge Recognition, Needs Assessment and Allocation Feedback, and Evaluation

First responders are operating under pressure as well as in an atmosphere of panic fear and confusion. During an emergency event, the firefighter first responder has to know details about the event as it is happening, what is needed to address the event, who needs specific information and knowledge, and what action(s) have to be taken. This course of action happens in a continuous cycle and is supported by the details within the human computer interface section of the emergency management process. In addition, the NIMS protocols, procedures, and policies as indicated by the communications and information management, and the command and management components support the knowledge recognition, needs assessment and allocation feedback, and evaluation mechanisms needed in a KM strategy for first responders.

Expertise Coordination Practices

During an emergency event, knowledge is being exchanged in a rapid nature. Expertise coordination will establish the process to enable the management of this knowledge and skill interdependencies. Expertise coordination practices (ECP) as part of the Fire Department KM strategy for its first responders will support knowledge sharing and expertise vetting during emergency events (Faraj and Xiao, 2006).

The ECP protocols supported by the KM strategy as identified by Faraj and Xiao will be as follows:

■ Protocols to streamline work and reduce process uncertainty
■ Plug-n-play teaming arrangements, which allow for flexibility of personnel
■ Communities of Practice (CoP) for operational responsibility and training
■ Knowledge externalization to increase knowledge sharing

Expertise coordination activities are supported by the NIMS's resource management component, which includes protocols, procedures, and policies to support the facilitation and coordination of resources throughout every phase of the emergency event (National Incident Management System, 2008). It also addresses the coordination of knowledge among individuals, teams, and agencies.

Command and Control Structure

Command and control address the management of information and knowledge at the tactical level (Balogun et al., 2006). At the tactical level, the KM strategy will address functional (tacit) knowledge at the operation level, which includes task planning (what tasks to do, when to do, and how to execute the task) (Coleman, 2007), event monitoring (monitoring the actions taken and executed during an emergency event)

(Coleman, 2007), understanding the time and place of emergency events, location and nature of the emergency event, reasoning about the cause and effect of the incident, and lessons learned (Balogun et al., 2006). Command and control has been identified as an integral part of any KM system (Balogun et al., 2006), and the Fire Department KM strategy for first responders should establish the protocols, processes, and procedures to address command and control. The KM strategy should specifically establish protocols, processes, and procedures for planning, monitoring, and learning; distributed knowledge framework to support teams; and support critical decision making (Balogun et al., 2006). The establishment command and control activities are supported by the NIMS's command and management component, which includes protocols to support incident command, multiagency coordination, and public information (National Incident Management System, 2008).

Learning and Knowledge Transfer

Because information and knowledge of the crisis event is being passed along from individual to individual, team to team, and agency to agency, there is a need to incorporate policies, procedures, and protocols to facilitate an atmosphere of learning and knowledge transfer. The learning and knowledge transfer must not only take place between the various factions during an emergency but also between the firefighter personnel, traditional firefighters, and EMS personnel. The management and transfer of knowledge as identified by Burstein et al. facilitates organizational learning, instills a culture of learning that contribute to creativity, and the transfer and reuse of knowledge contributes to increasing overall organizational knowledge (Burstein et al., 2004). They state that organizational learning is the "capacity or process within an organization to maintain or improve performance based on experience" (Burstein et al., 2004, p. 318). Learning and knowledge transfer will be a key ingredient in the KM strategy for Fire Departments and for the first responders they deploy on emergency events.

Types of KM Strategies

Three types of KM strategies, namely Codification (Technological) (Haggie and Kingston, 2003; Nicolas, 2004; Smith, 2004), Personalization (Nicolas, 2004; Smith, 2004), and Socialization (Nicolas, 2004), as identified in the literature, will be examined further to ascertain the best-suited KM strategy for first responders.

Codification (Technological) KM Strategy

A Codification or Technological KM strategy focuses on collecting tacit and explicit knowledge, storing it in a knowledge repository, knowledge base, and/or electronic library, and providing it in an explicit codified form (Haggie and Kingston, 2003; Nicolas, 2004; Smith, 2004). This strategy is designed to transition individual knowledge to organizational knowledge. This type of KM strategy is supported by individuals making their tacit knowledge explicit in order for it to be transferred and codified. Furthermore, this strategy is associated with the externalization aspects of Nonaka and Takeuchi's SECI model to transition knowledge from tacit to explicit and also includes Nonaka and Takeuchi's combination aspects of the SECI model to transition the explicit knowledge into an electronic format (as mentioned earlier), which can be accessed and reused by anyone in the organization.

Personalization KM Strategy

A Personalization KM strategy uses technology to assist in the process of people communicating sharing their knowledge (Nicolas, 2004; Smith, 2004). This type of KM strategy manages knowledge that is tied to or associated with a person and is commonly shared directly via person-to-person contact (Smith, 2004). In addition, this KM strategy facilitates and manages knowledge that is centered on learning through shared experience (Nicolas, 2004). The technology leveraged in this strategy consist of CoP, Web 2.0 technologies (i.e., Facebook, Twitter, and LinkedIn), and other knowledge networks and discussion boards, with the objective to transfer, communicate, and exchange knowledge (Nicolas, 2004; Smith, 2004). This strategy is associated with the socialization aspects of Nonaka and Takeuchi's SECI model, which details tacit-to-tacit knowledge exchange.

Socialization KM Strategy

A Socialization KM strategy combines both the Codification or Technological KM strategy and the Personalization KM strategy (Nicolas, 2004). This strategy manages knowledge generated by individuals and groups. Nicolas states that these groups inhabit the same knowledge space and interact through relationships both individual and within and between groups (Nicolas, 2004). This strategy is designed to exchange and pool knowledge (Nicolas, 2004). In combining both the Codification and the Personalization KM strategies, the Socialization KM strategy combines the externalization aspects of Nonaka and Takeuchi's SECI model to transition knowledge from tacit to explicit; the combination aspects of the SECI model to transition explicit to explicit forms of knowledge for electronic storage and reuse; and the socialization aspects of Nonaka and Takeuchi's SECI model, to facilitate individual and group tacit to tacit knowledge exchange.

Factors Influencing the Selection of a KM Strategy

Having an understanding of the essential aspects of an effective KM strategy for first responders will serve as the building blocks in creating a KM strategy template. However, an examination of the factors that may influence these aspects is warranted. These factors could determine what will and will not be included in the final KM strategy.

A KM strategy for firefighter first-responder organizations as indicated by Haggie and Kingston can be influenced by several factors, such as current/planned KM strategy, business sector characteristics, strengths, weaknesses, opportunities, and threats (SWOT), value focus, organizational structure, organizational culture, and nature of knowledge (see Table 7.1) (Haggie and Kingston, 2003).

Based on the factors influencing the selection of a KM strategy, Haggie and Kingston recommend performing the following activities to identify the appropriate KM strategy and initiatives

> identifying the business drivers for your organization, performing an organizational Strengths, Weaknesses, Opportunities and Threats (SWOT) analysis to clearly identify the product and/or service, identify the primary organizational value to its market, use findings to identify primary KM area(s) to consider, identify knowledge intensive activities, prioritize and make an assessment of the high priority activities to be addressed by the KM strategy, and perform feasibility checks on the proposed KM approach. (Haggie and Kingston, 2003, p. 18)

These influencers will be examined when developing a KM strategy template to be adopted by the Fire Department for first responders.

Table 7.1   Factors Influencing the Selection of a KM Strategy

Factor	Examples
Current/planned knowledge management strategy	Goals, desired applications, technology capabilities, and analytic/synthetic approach
Business sector characteristics	Highly regulated, innovative, risk factors, competitiveness, globalization, etc.
Strengths, weaknesses, opportunities, and threats (SWOT)	Reputation, leading product, changing regulations, acquisitions and mergers, globalization, etc.
Value focus	Operational excellence, product leadership, or customer intimacy
Organizational structure	Hierarchical and loose
Organizational culture	Team spirit, individualistic, sharing, and learning
Nature of knowledge	Explicit, implicit, or tacit; task type: symbolic/numeric/geometric/perceptual

Source: Adapted from Haggie and Kingston (2003).

Aligning the KM Strategy with the Business Strategy

Knowledge is viewed as the most valuable resource by an organization. Because of the importance of knowledge to the organization, it is viewed as making a difference in organizational performance. It is my experience more often than not knowledge is poorly managed and that in order to capture the benefits of managing knowledge, an organizational KM strategy is necessary. It is also my experience that a KM strategy must align with the organization's business strategy to be effective. In order to align the firefighter first-responder KM strategy with the overall Fire Department business strategy and examination of how to align both strategies must take place.

To understand how to align the KM strategy with the business strategy, Ekionea and Swain have identified three types of business strategies: defender, prospector, and analyzer (Ekionea and Swain, 2008). The defender business strategy does not seek new opportunities beyond its competence, seldom carries out major adjustments in business structure or technology, is the most stable of the three business strategies, offers high quality products, provides service at an low price, and retains customers by improving business processes (Ekionea and Swain, 2008). The prospector business strategy prefers to research without interruption looking for new products or market opportunities, serves as change agents, invests in innovation through R&D, and seeks flexible technology options (Ekionea and Swain, 2008). The analyzer business strategy shares characteristics of the both the defender and prospector business strategies as well as seeks to reduce risks, maximize opportunities for growth and change while improving business performance (Ekionea and Swain, 2008).

In addition, Ekionea and Swain (2008) have identified three types of KM strategy focus areas of efficiency (improving business efficiency), flexibility (supporting flexibility in business opportunities), and comprehensive (supporting both efficiency and flexibility). The characteristics of their KM strategy focus areas align with Haggie and Kingston, Nicolas, and Smith's KM strategies of Codification, Personalization, and Socialization. Codification aligns with the efficiency focus area through the influence of technology to capture knowledge and improve the efficiency of decision making. Personalization aligns with the flexibility focus area supporting inter-organizational capabilities and processes. Socialization aligns with the comprehensive focus area through its combination of both KM strategies and focus areas. Given this alignment, we can extrapolate the KM strategy and business strategy alignment based on Ekionea and Swain's analysis to be Codification/Efficiency KM strategy aligning knowledge activities with the defender business strategy to improve business processes; Personalization/Flexibility KM strategy aligning knowledge activities with the prospector business strategy to achieve new business opportunities; and Socialization/Comprehensive KM strategy aligning knowledge activities with the analyzer business strategy to reduce business risk and maximize business growth.

Firefighter First-Responder KM Strategy

The key areas stated earlier that an effective firefighter first-responder KM strategy must include quick and decisive decision making, collaborative communication, and situational analysis, acquiring EMS-specific knowledge, being able to quickly act to change, perform task planning, event monitoring, distribute knowledge, perform knowledge recognition, needs assessment and allocation, feedback and evaluation, ECP, command and control, and learning and knowledge transfer. The adoption of NIMS policies, procedures, and protocols can be adopted to support and guide the execution of the KM strategy. Leveraging the NIMS protocols within the KM strategy would provide the basis for all firefighter first-responder organizations to adopt a common KM strategy template.

The KM strategy components that correspond to the key areas of an effective firefighter first-responder KM strategy include incident command structure, knowledge acquisition, knowledge transfer, knowledge recognition, needs assessment and Allocation, KM feedback and evaluation, ECP, and command and control structure. The incident command structure will leverage the policies, procedures, and protocols established by the NIMS's communications and information management as well as the command and management components. These protocols will facilitate quick and decisive decision making, collaborative communication, and situational analysis identified as key areas for the firefighter first-responder KM strategy. The knowledge acquisition and knowledge transfer (see section on Knowledge Transfer Planning for further details) areas of the KM strategy will address the need to acquire EMS-specific knowledge and provide cross-training between EMS and standard firefighting personnel. This area of the KM strategy will leverage the NIMS policy, procedures, and protocols identified in the preparedness component. Knowledge recognition, needs assessment, and allocation will incorporate the design and execution of a knowledge audit (KA) (see section on Knowledge Audit for further details). This area of the KM strategy will leverage the NIMS policy, procedures, and protocols identified in the communication and information management component.

The KM feedback and evaluation area of the KM strategy will incorporate the delivery and execution of an after action review (AAR); see Appendix B, and the section on AARs for further details. This area of the KM strategy will leverage the NIMS policy, procedures, and protocols identified in the command and management component. The ECP area of the KM strategy will address the need to manage knowledge and skill interdependencies and support knowledge sharing of personnel that are deployed to an emergency/crisis event. This area of the KM strategy will leverage the NIMS policy, procedures, and protocols identified in the resource management component. The command and control structure area of the KM strategy is addressing the management of information and knowledge at the tactical level. This includes task planning, event monitoring, time/place of emergency events, nature of the event, cause and effect of the incident, and lessons learned. This area of the KM strategy is also supported by the NIMS policy, procedures, and protocols identified in the command and management component, in addition to the execution of AARs to capture lessons learned.

Knowledge Transfer Planning

Knowledge transfer planning facilitates an organization's capability to encourage and allow learning to occur. Essentially, knowledge transfer is a culture-based process by which adaptive organizational knowledge that lies in people's heads is exchanged with others. Formal knowledge transfer is another basic process by which documents, data, or other types of resources is captured and stored in formats and media that allows for retrieval by others when needed. The objective of a knowledge transfer is to detail the methods, tools, and activities involved in successfully imparting knowledge to the workers of the enterprise.

To foster an atmosphere of knowledge sharing and knowledge transfer within an organization, the process of knowledge transfer should include the following:

- Identifying the key knowledge holders within the organization
- Creating an environment that motivates people to share
- Designing a sharing mechanism to facilitate the transfer
- Executing the knowledge transfer plan
- Measuring to ensure the transfer of knowledge
- Applying the knowledge transferred

Knowledge Audit

A is usually conducted as a precursor to introducing a KM strategy (Crilly et al., 2005). The KA typically has three components: an examination of the sources of data, information, and knowledge that are available, how they are used, and what are the gaps that exist, if any (Crilly et al., 2005). A complete KA will examine the key knowledge holders and existing knowledge systems, and determine how they support the functions and needs of the organization. The KA will examine the knowledge gaps and determine whether the intellectual capital exist currently in the organization to fill the gap or if new knowledge has to be acquired (Crilly et al., 2005).

Action Plan—After Action Reviews

In order to determine the success of initial KM initiatives, it is important to conduct reviews after the completion of each initiative. The use of AAR is an excellent tool to accomplish this. An AAR is a facilitated session conducted with a team or group after completion of a KM initiative (United States Agency International

Development [USAID], 2006). The objective of an AAR is to capture the new knowledge gained from the execution of the initiative and to have it become part of the corporate knowledge culture. Specifically, AARs

- Make learning conscious and explicit.
- Identify valuable lessons that may be helpful to future teams.
- Enhance team openness and cooperation.
- Allow closure at the end of an initiative.

The steps involved in completing/conducting an AAR are described below. This information is summarized from the USAID *After-Action Review Technical Guide*.

1. Assemble participants as soon as practicable after the event(s).
2. Establish rules and explain objectives.
3. Summarize events as they were planned to occur, with work and time estimates, as appropriate.
4. Elicit discussion on how the events actually took place. Strategies to make this happen include the following:
   - Identify mistakes, but don't assign blame. The focus should be on the actions, not on the actors.
   - Articulate assumptions (the explicit statement of previously overlooked assumptions often leads to better solutions).
   - Address objective and subjective dimensions of the events (discussion subjects, including attitudes, expectations, fatigue, and stress, may help to explain outcomes in addition to more objective information).
5. Record results. List the associates who participated, what learning was achieved, what changes are planned, and what practices will be strengthened (some of the observations of the AAR will need to be shared with higher and lower levels of the organization).
6. Establish the expectation of AARs as a regular, reoccurring feature of your organization's operations. They should not be considered a sign of failure (as a group activity, the AAR can promote group cohesiveness and identity. Through repetition, it makes individuals more reflective practitioners).
7. The following AAR pitfalls must be avoided:
   - Allowing performance critiques
   - Lecturing
   - Overanalyzing minutiae
   - Griping, complaining, and general negativity
   - Allowing stronger personalities to dominate the review, keeping others from participating

The AAR discussion is a process of discovery, as all team members share their perspectives on what happened and why. The shared observations of the newest interns through the senior-most associates are essential to piece together how and why some objectives were met and others were not (United States Agency International Development [USAID], 2006).

Additional KM Strategy Template Elements

In addition, the KM strategy will include an executive summary, KM mission statement, KM vision, KM roles and responsibilities, initial KM initiatives, dependencies, and ongoing KM support. The KM mission statement encapsulates the KM mission of the organization and sets the definition of knowledge and KM for the organization to follow. The KM vision is specific to the organization choosing to implement a KM strategy. The KM vision will provide a roadmap for integrating the KM strategy with the strategy of the organization (Bohmann et al., 2007). The firefighter first-responder KM strategy template (see Appendix B) is one that can be leveraged by firefighter first-responder organizations to develop a KM strategy. This template represents the results of the research completed in this section.

Conclusion

Knowledge is an organization's most valuable resource. Although people, process, and technology can give an organization a competitive edge, the improper management of that knowledge to build, organize, and leverage its people, process, and technology will be to the detriment of that organization (Smith, 2004).

Constructing a KM strategy for the Fire Department and the first responders they deploy must be consistent from station to station, whether the station serves urban or rural areas, and the demographics of the community in which it serves. The KM strategy must contain elements of, codification, personalization and socialization. Based on this research and understanding the complexities of the KM strategy for Fire Department first responders, a KM strategy that incorporates the key areas of quick and decisive decision making, collaborative communication, and situational analysis, acquiring EMS-specific knowledge, being able to quickly act to change, perform task planning, event monitoring, distribute knowledge, perform knowledge recognition, needs assessment and allocation, feedback and evaluation, ECP, command and control, and learning and knowledge transfer; understanding the types of knowledge that must be captured; and the associated NIMS policies, procedures, and protocols will be successful.

In addition, the research that contributed to this chapter has uncovered that the KM strategy must align with the business strategy of the organization. Although the focus of this research is on developing and delivering a KM strategy for Fire Departments and the first responders they deploy, an in-depth study of the business strategies deployed by Fire Departments are warranted.

Furthermore, the alignment of those business strategies with Fire Department KM strategies will facilitate the process of institutionalizing KM, thereby making it a part of the culture of the Fire Department and the first responders they deploy. This alignment will also provide insight on the methods, technologies, policies, procedures, and protocols that should be used to provide a holistic strategic approach that will bring for the people who deliver services to the various communities, the Fire Department as a business to improve its overall operations and increase business value to its communities, and the people of the communities who depend on a timely, efficient, and effective service to be delivered by the Fire Department no matter where they live or the situation that may arise.

Key Learnings

The following are some key learnings from this chapter:

■ A way to mitigate the contributing factors related to the lack of available knowledge during an emergency or crisis situation must be taken into consideration when developing a KM strategy for first responders.
■ All first-responder agencies must implement and operationalize a comprehensive KM strategy in order to deliver the right knowledge to the right people and in the right way.
■ Leveraging the SECI model will provide the basis for sharing knowledge during an emergency/crisis situation.
■ When developing a KM strategy for first responders, consider the factors that influence the selection of a KM strategy as depicted in Table 7.1 (Haggie and Kingston, 2003).

Tips and Techniques

The following are some of the tips and techniques deduced after reading this chapter:

■ As communication escalates during an emergency/crisis, technology must be incorporated to facilitate the rapid flow of information and knowledge that will enable quick and decisive decision making and situational analysis.
■ It is extremely important to conduct AARs upon the conclusion (or periods during) and during the execution of KM initiatives. The learning gained from these AARs must be reviewed and taken into consideration when other KM initiatives are launched to ensure success.
■ In order to increase the adoption rate and socialize the KM strategy for first-responder organizations and the systems that are deployed, examine the information presented in Chapter 17.

Chapter 8

Happily Ever After: Knowledge Management in Mergers and Acquisitions

During these challenging economic times, many corporations are facing the prospect of merging with other firms to not only survive but also to have a sustainable and viable business in the future.

According to a November 2015 CNBC article by Catherine Boyle, mergers and acquisitions (M&A) have hit the US$4 trillion mark and could reach record highs. Recent mergers include leading microchip maker Intel agreeing to buy Altera in a deal worth US$16.7 billion; pharmaceutical giant Pfizer agreeing to buy Hospira in a deal worth approximately US$17 billion; and telecommunications giant Charter Communications agreeing to merge with Time Warner Cable for US$78.7 billion, creating one of the largest cable television and broadband Internet providers in existence. In these cases and in all M&A, there is a need to identify the key knowledge holders in order to ensure the success of the merger and/or acquisition.

The effect of these mergers will and often leads to a loss of valuable knowledge from both sides of the merger/acquisition equation. This loss of knowledge is due to positions being consolidated and/or eliminated, other personnel taking early retirement package or other financial incentives. The question is how do we identify who the key knowledge holders are and what knowledge do they hold? Also, has it been determined that this is viable knowledge to the "new" organization going forward and what is our plan to retain, capture, or acquire this knowledge?

All of these questions can be answered with a comprehensive knowledge management (KM) strategy that includes a human capital management component, geared to identify viable initiatives that will address these questions. One such initiative will be to develop a knowledge map of the organization to be acquired. A knowledge map is a mechanism used to identify key knowledge and the knowledge holders of the organization. Once these maps are completed, further analysis is needed to determine the process, procedures, and initiatives necessary to prioritize, retain, and/or acquire knowledge that may leave. Often, organizational knowledge is the reason certain mergers happen. KM is the mechanism to transit individual knowledge to corporate knowledge and facilitates its availability for all employees.

People are at the core of any merger and acquisition, and these transactions thrive and survive on the strength of how corporate cultures and its people can be meshed together. Understanding who the critical knowledge holders are and their relationships as well as their roles, responsibilities, and work products are all components of sound human capital management.

This understanding will lead to determining which positions and personnel perform duplicate functions, which will lead to an understanding of the employees that should be terminated (better yet receive a package and convinced to leave!). Not only do you have to determine which personnel perform duplicate functions, but also who is more valuable through his/her experience, education, and importance to the organization going forward. The human capital management component of the overall KM strategy (see Chapter 6) is also an investment in employee selection and development. This contributes to the organization meeting its goals and objectives of not only the merger but also for the new organization on an ongoing basis. In addition, we must keep in mind that executing a KM strategy with a human capital management component can be the catalyst to increased adaptability, enhanced worker performance, and with the current economic climate, having the ability to do more with your existing personnel resources.

M&A: The Basics

The key principle behind buying a company is to create shareholder value over and above that of the sum of the two companies. Two companies together are more valuable than two separate companies—at least, that's the reasoning behind M&A. This rationale is particularly alluring to companies when times are tough. Strong companies will act to buy other companies to create a more competitive, cost-efficient company. The companies will come together hoping to gain a greater market share or to achieve greater efficiency. Because of these potential benefits, target companies will often agree to be purchased when they know they cannot survive alone.

Horizontal merger: Two companies that are in direct competition and share the same product lines and markets.

Vertical merger: A customer and company or a supplier and company. Think of a cone supplier merging with an ice cream maker.

Market-extension merger: Two companies that sell the same products in different markets.

Product-extension merger: Two companies selling different but related products in the same market.

Conglomeration: Two companies that have no common business areas. There are two types of mergers that are distinguished by how the merger is financed. Each has certain implications for the companies involved and for investors:

Purchase merger: As the name suggests, this kind of merger occurs when one company purchases another. The purchase is made with cash or through the issue of some kind of debt instrument; the sale is taxable. Acquiring companies often prefer this type of merger, because it can provide them with a tax benefit. Acquired assets can be written-up to the actual purchase price, and the difference between the book value and the purchase price of the assets can depreciate annually, reducing taxes payable by the acquiring company.

Consolidation mergers: With this merger, a brand new company is formed and both companies are bought and combined under the new entity. The tax terms are the same as those of a purchase merger.

Reverse merger: A reverse merger occurs when a private company that has strong prospects and is eager to raise financing buys a publicly listed shell company, usually one with no business and limited assets. The private company reverse merges into the public company, and together they become an entirely new public corporation with tradable shares. Regardless of their category or structure, all M&A have one common goal: They are all meant to create synergy that makes the value of the combined companies greater than the sum of the two parts. The success of a merger or acquisition depends on whether this synergy is achieved.

Acquisitions

An acquisition may be only slightly different from a merger. In fact, it may be different in name only. Like mergers, acquisitions are actions through which companies seek economies of scale, efficiencies, and enhanced market visibility. Unlike all mergers, all acquisitions involve one firm purchasing another, and there is no exchange of stock or consolidation as a new company. Acquisitions are often amiable, and all parties feel satisfied with the deal. Other times, acquisitions are more hostile. In an acquisition, as in some of the merger deals we discussed above, a company can buy another company with cash, stock, or a combination of the two. Another possibility, which is common in smaller deals, is for one company to acquire all the assets of another company. Company X buys all of Company Y's assets for cash, which means that Company Y will have only cash (and debt, if they had debt before). Of course, Company Y becomes merely a shell and will eventually liquidate or enter another area of business. Another type of acquisition is a reverse merger, a deal that enables a private company to get publicly listed in a relatively short time period.

Distinction between M&A

Although they are often uttered in the same breath and used as though they were synonymous, the terms "merger" and "acquisition" mean slightly different things. When one company takes over another and clearly established itself as the new owner, the purchase is called an "acquisition." From a legal point of view, the target company ceases to exist, the buyer "swallows" the business, and the buyer's stock continues to be traded. In the pure sense of the term, a "merger" happens when two firms, often of about the same size, agree to go forward as a single new company rather than remain separately owned and operated.

This kind of action is more precisely referred to as a "merger of equals." Both companies' stocks are surrendered and new company stock is issued in its place. For example, both Daimler-Benz and Chrysler ceased to exist when the two firms merged, and a new company, DaimlerChrysler, was created. In practice, however, actual mergers of equals don't happen very often. Usually, one company will buy another and, as part of the deal's terms, simply allow the acquired firm to proclaim that the action is a merger of equals, even if it's technically an acquisition. Being bought out often carries negative connotations; therefore, by describing the deal as a merger, deal makers and top managers try to make the takeover more palatable.

A purchase deal will also be called a merger when both CEOs agree that joining together is in the best interest of both of their companies. But when the deal is unfriendly—that is, when the target company does not want to be purchased—it is always regarded as an acquisition. Whether a purchase is considered a merger or an acquisition really depends on whether the purchase is friendly or hostile and how it is announced. In other words, the real difference lies in how the purchase is communicated to and received by the target company's board of directors, employees, and shareholders.

Determining Synergies

Synergies are the magic force that allows for enhanced cost efficiencies of the new business. Synergy takes the form of revenue enhancement and cost savings. By merging, the companies hope to benefit from the following:

Staff reductions: As every employee knows, mergers tend to mean job losses. Consider all the money saved from reducing the number of staff members from accounting, marketing, and other departments. Job cuts will also include the former CEO, who typically leaves with a compensation package.

Economies of scale: Yes, size matters. Whether it's purchasing stationary or a new corporate IT system, a bigger company placing the orders can save more on costs. Mergers also translate into improved purchasing power to buy equipment or office supplies—when placing larger orders, companies have a greater ability to negotiate prices with their suppliers.

Acquiring new technology: To stay competitive, companies need to stay on top of technological developments and their business applications. By buying a smaller company with unique technologies, a large company can maintain or develop a competitive edge.

Improved market reach and industry visibility: Companies buy other companies to reach new markets and grow revenues and earnings. A merger may expand two companies' marketing and distribution, giving them new sales opportunities. A merger can also improve a company's standing in the investment community: bigger firms often have an easier time raising capital than smaller ones.

That said, achieving synergy is easier said than done: It is not automatically realized once two companies merge. Sure, there ought to be economies of scale when two businesses are combined, but sometimes a merger does just the opposite. In many cases, one and one add up to less than two. Sadly, synergy opportunities may exist only in the minds of the corporate leaders and the deal makers. Where there is no value to be created, the CEO and investment bankers—who have much to gain from a successful M&A deal—will try to create an image of enhanced value. The market, however, eventually sees through this and penalizes the company by assigning it a discounted share price.

Synergies can also be uncovered among the knowledge held by the organizations involved. Understanding who are the key knowledge holders, what they know, and the importance of what they know as it pertains to the objectives of the "new" organization is critical to the merger/acquisition being a success or not.

The People Side of the M&A

The people side of M&As as pointed out by Dr. Mark Braverman (2007) in his research entitled "The Human Side of Due Diligence: Protecting the M&A Investment," which is centered around applying KM principles, practices, and policies to produce high-performing, highly effective workforce.

Corporate mergers are about more than numbers and market opportunities, which is why CEOs need to think about the long-term fit of two corporate cultures as well as the financial and market aspects. Here are four bases to touch on the "people side" of M&A due diligence that CEOs should never overlook.

Employees

Employees become naturally fearful when M&A are rumored. Will the employees retain their jobs? Even if they do, will it be the kind of jobs that they are used to? They are all too aware that the executives exiting from their company, once it is acquired, will receive sweetened deals in the forms of settlements, a responsible position in the new organization, or a combination of both. But where are employees left?

In the not-for-profit credit union world, it is standard to retain employees for at least 2 years after a credit union merger. In some cases, these employees are "tried out" in the new organization—and if they do well, they are retained for a long term. The key here for both the acquiring and the acquired organizations is to know what exactly is going to happen to the employees on both sides of the merger—and to be transparent and tell them. At least, one merger was so incredibly "stealth" that it took a major lawsuit and several extra years of employee and management maliciousness before the organization got through it.

Boards

Who is going to sit on the board after a merger or acquisition completes? Often, the acquired organization gets at least one seat on the acquiring company's board. For the CEO, this can be easier said than done. Do you alter your board organization to include more seats? How will the votes be distributed? Will all board positions be voting positions? Are incumbent board members replaced? Because of potential political fallout and a need to retain the highest caliber talent on the board, this should be a major political line item in any merger or acquisition evaluation.

Customers and Other Stakeholders

There are those outside of both companies who have been loyal customers and stakeholders for years. What is going to happen to them once the two companies merge? The CMO and CEO should be integrally involved in this area of strategy—because you could very well lose customers as a consequence of ineffective "advance messaging" to them on what is going to happen to services, products, retail outlets, and so on.

Operations

Most organizations know how important it is to get IT in on early evaluations for potential mergers or acquisitions, because different organizations invariably have different systems, and at some point, these systems must come together. However, it is equally important to pay the same amount of attention to daily operations. How similar are both business and IT governance standards (and work ethics) between the two organizations? Are operations in manufacturing, sales, and the back office sufficiently similar, so that work processes do not have to be redefined and employees retrained?

Communication

Communication can help employee to manage the merger syndrome, because it informs them of the changes in their environment, thus reducing uncertainty and ambiguity. Communication is the most valuable commodity for the successful implementation of a merger or acquisition. The specific communication objectives change for every phase of integration. As the deal moves through its phases, information changes and the circle of knowledge grows. Nothing is a secret for long, and leaders must be prepared, not only for what they know is coming but also for the unexpected. Leaders should follow a phased approach to communication, in which planning is sensitive to continuing information flowing from multiple organizational levels about the progress of integration. Again, if resources or expertise is lacking, leadership can seek out help.

Information flow in a company is one of the most important aspects of a merger that must be understood and consistently adhered to. The trust level in the organization must not deteriorate. An environment must be maintained where people feel they can be straightforward and share information/knowledge with other colleagues. When this environment is compromised, people will often feel that they are afraid to disagree with higher management, let alone new management.

Communication is a requirement for financial success, because low morale, high turnover, direct costs in workers' compensation and healthcare expenditures, and lowered productivity will all have consequences for the level of return on investment. Leaders cannot assume they can and will know everything. But they do have a responsibility to put into place the structures that will maximize their awareness as they go forward. Leaders who confront change effectively are rewarded with superior business performance on the part of their employees. When employees believe their employer is effectively managing change, it is perceived as a gain for shareholders. Conversely, when employees believe their employer is *not* effectively managing change, it is perceived as a loss for shareholders. Avoiding the human issues in M&A is essential for success. Proper planning for the management of people issues in a merger or acquisition should be a top priority.

Productivity

The potential loss in productivity goes beyond mere wasting of time in worry and water cooler talk. After a merger or acquisition, employees who feel uncertain about their job security and mistrustful of leadership regarding the sale may be unmotivated and averse to risk. They will not come forward with new ideas, communicate with leadership, or be creative. The tendency is to try to maintain a low profile and do the minimum, staying "under the radar."

Planning for those employees who will continue on after the merger or acquisition is a key ingredient for success. More often than not, however, this planning is limited to a narrow fixation on payroll and percentages; a shrinking in the employment rolls is often part of the plan, not only in a merger where synergies are expected but also in an acquisition as part of the striving for efficiencies. Formulating a retention plan, leveraging information uncovered as the result in creating a knowledge map will change the typical focus of to a small handful of top people, a few people at the middle and lower levels, creating a climate where valuable staff are vulnerable to poaching by competitors.

An acquisition or merger can create conditions in which a company is at risk for losing those people who may be critical to immediate and longer term business success by virtue of their management skills, knowledge of business systems and processes, and intellectual capital. This can have consequences, not only downstream but also for the transaction itself. Organizations considering mergers or acquisitions should have these "people centric" line items on their M&A checklists—but many do not. The political fallout from a corporate move such as this can be major, which is why organizations that perform their due diligence with attention to people as well as to markets and numbers succeed most often.

Leveraging KM in Company Valuation

Investors in a company who aim to take over another one must determine whether the purchase will be beneficial to them. In order to do so, they must ask themselves how much the company being acquired is really worth.

Naturally, both sides of an M&A deal will have different ideas about the worth of a target company: Its seller will tend to value the company at as high of a price as possible, while the buyer will try to get the lowest price that he or she can. There are, however, many legitimate ways to value companies. The most common method is to look at comparable companies in an industry, but deal makers employ a variety of other methods and tools when assessing a target company. Here are just a few of them:

1. *Comparative ratios*: The following are two examples of the many comparative metrics on which acquiring companies may base their offers:
   a. *Price earnings ratio (P/E ratio)*: With the use of this ratio, an acquiring company makes an offer that is a multiple of the earnings of the target company. Looking at the P/E for all the stocks within the same industry group will give the acquiring company good guidance for what the target's P/E multiple should be.

b. *Enterprise-value-to-sales ratio (EV/sales)*: With this ratio, the acquiring company makes an offer as a multiple of the revenues, again, while being aware of the price-to-sales ratio of other companies in the industry.

2. *Replacement cost*: In a few cases, acquisitions are based on the cost of replacing the target company. For simplicity's sake, suppose the value of a company is simply the sum of all its equipment and staffing costs. The acquiring company can literally order the target to sell at that price, or it will create a competitor for the same cost. Naturally, it takes a long time to assemble good management, acquire property, and get the right equipment. This method of establishing a price certainly wouldn't make much sense in a service industry where the key assets—people and ideas—are hard to value and develop.

3. *Discounted cash flow (DCF)*: A key valuation tool in M&A, DCF analysis determines a company's current value according to its estimated future cash flows. Forecasted free cash flows (operating profit + depreciation + amortization of goodwill – capital expenditures – cash taxes – change in working capital) are discounted to a present value using the company's weighted average costs of capital (WACC). Admittedly, DCF is tricky to get right, but few tools can rival this valuation method.

The need to make the most of organizational knowledge—to get as much value from it as possible—is greater now than in the past. Companies are finding themselves with piles of information within multiple channels, locked away in silos—different systems, different departments, different geographies, and different data types, making it impossible to connect the dots and make sense of critical business information. New computing models such as cloud and social business are exacerbating organizations' ability to collect, analyze, and process data. The data is there, but it isn't being harnessed in the right way to increase our collective knowledge. And it is our collective organizational knowledge that gives us the edge over our competition.

For a potential merger, understanding the value of the organization to be acquired is critical to positioning a price that is both equitable and acceptable to the acquired company. If your organization is positioning itself to be sold, understanding how KM can increase the overall value of the company is essential to obtaining a fair price. So, how do we leverage KM to understand the value of the organization? One such way is to apply the concepts presented in the knowledge value equation (see Figure 8.1) by Mark Clare (2002). This equation aligns with the third method/tool used when assessing a company (stated above), which examines

KM value = F (cost, benefit, and risk)
= Total DCF created over life of KM investment

Figure 8.1 Knowledge value equation.

the use of DCF and presents an equation: KM value = F (cost, benefit, and risk) = Total DCF created over life of KM investment. The equation states that the value created from managing knowledge is a function of the costs, benefits, and risks of the KM investment (project or strategy) in leveraging and protecting the knowledge (Clare, 2002).

An important concept identified in determining the knowledge value equation is to build a knowledge value tree (see Figure 8.2). A knowledge value tree makes the connection between knowledge and value in an organization more visible by understanding the relationship and connection of KM functionality, business impact, and financial impact (Clare, 2002). This viability of the value of knowledge in the organization can be directly tied back to understanding what competitive advantage your organization has in its marketplace, its percentage of that market, and the potential to capture additional market share. An examination of corporate valuation can be found in the book *Valuation: Measuring and Managing the Value of Companies* by McKinsey & Company Inc. This is an important factor when considering buying an organization as well as if you are positioning your organization to be sold.

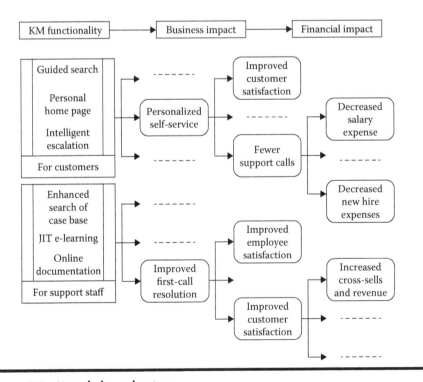

Figure 8.2　Knowledge value tree.

Knowledge and Economic Value

In a 2013 eBook from the Coveo Corporation entitled "Measuring Return on Knowledge in a Big Data World," it is stated that calculating the return on knowledge is not a simple task, and yet it is important that organizational leaders think about increasing return on this critical asset. Better knowledge can lead to measurable efficiencies in product development and production. Employees use it to make more informed decisions about strategy, competitors, customers, distribution channels, and product and service life cycles. However, generally accepted accounting principles do not record these assets.

Accounting research is coming up with ways to calculate the total value of a company's intangible assets, and, fortunately, techniques are improving. The Coveo Corporation eBook outlined a method to calculate intangible value (CIV). This method overcomes the drawbacks of the market-to-book method of valuing intangibles, which simply subtracts a company's book value from its market value and labels the difference. Because it rises and falls with market sentiment, the market-to-book figure cannot give a fixed value of intellectual capital. CIV, on the other hand, examines earnings performance and identifies the assets that produced those earnings.

Through the review of the Coveo Corps research, it can be seen that in the past quarter century, the market value of companies in the S&P 500 has deviated greatly from their book value. This value gap indicates that physical and financial accountable assets reflected on a company's balance sheet comprise less than 20% of the true value of the average organization. Intangible book value, or "goodwill," is calculated by subtracting the tangible book value from the market capitalization of a given company. Companies report tangible book value per share, number of shares outstanding, and market capitalization.

Therefore, intangible book value can also be calculated by subtracting the tangible book value per share multiplied by the number of shares outstanding from the market capitalization. For example, as of February 14, 2013, Apple was worth US$438.2 billion (otherwise known as its market capitalization). Its book value (tangible assets) was valued at US$127.3 billion. Consequently, Apple's intangible assets were worth US$310.9 billion—or 70% of its total value. Using these formulas, once return on knowledge is measured, calculated, and managed, a company is ready to reap the competitive benefits that knowledge brings. Search and relevance technology is an important component of this strategy.

Knowledge and Organizational Culture

An organization's culture evolves from many sources. Culture is manifested in policy and procedures, organizational structure, and everyday behaviors, both formal and informal. These sources are the originators of knowledge within the organization. Knowledge is the differentiator when it comes to increasing competitive intelligence and creating a competitive advantage. Knowledge can be interpreted within and outside of the organization in many ways. Included in this interpretation is how knowledge is exchanged between geographically dispersed employees, suppliers, and partners. The ability to blend (or align) the culture of the companies involved in an M&A transaction is critical to its success. Also critical to the success of an M&A transaction is understanding how the knowledge assets of different organizations culture will fit together. Contextual intelligence becomes an underlying ingredient in combining diverse sources of knowledge during a merger and/or acquisition.

Contextual Intelligence

Contextual Intelligence is, according to Matthew Kutz, "a leadership competency based on empirical research that integrates concepts of diagnosing context and exercising knowledge"; Tarun Khanna (2014) states that "understanding the limits of our knowledge is at the heart of contextual intelligence" and Dr. Charles Brown (2002) states that "Contextual intelligence is the practical application of knowledge and information to real-world situations. This is an external, interactive process that involves both adapting to and modifying an environment to accomplish a desired goal; as well as recognizing when adaptation is not a viable option. This is the ability that is most closely associated with wisdom and practical knowledge."

Although there are several positions on what contextual intelligence is, Dr. Brown's assertion of contextual intelligence is considered to be precise. When it comes to KM and contextual intelligence, context matters! Understanding that contextual intelligence is link to our tacit knowledge, I immediately thought about the connection between KM and contextual intelligence. KM among other aspects is concerned with the ability to understand knowledge and adapt that knowledge across a variety of environments (cultures) different from the origin of that knowledge.

To enable the flow of knowledge to the right person in the right time and in the right context, it is essential to understand the context of that knowledge. Delivering knowledge in the right context to users; organizing, structuring, and associating relevant content in the right context; understanding how content fits together; and connecting questions to answers and people to experts are at the heart of KM.

Understanding the context of knowledge consists of the following:

■ Understanding the intent of the knowledge
■ Understanding the cultural and environmental influences on the knowledge
■ Understanding the role (or who) the knowledge is intended to be used by
■ Understanding the relevancy of the knowledge (the knowledge could only be valid for a specific period of time)
■ Understanding the origin (lineage) of the knowledge

Knowledge Mapping

At a time when organizations need to "know what they know" and use that knowledge effectively, the size and geographic reach of many of them, along with the proliferation of data, make it especially difficult to locate existing knowledge and get it to where it is needed. Knowledge mapping first detailed in Chapter 5 serves as the basis for locating knowledge and knowledge holders anywhere it exist in the organization. Understanding the key knowledge holders within the organizations is essential to knowing who should be terminated and who should continue with the "new" organization. In addition, a knowledge map will serve as a tool to unlock the knowledge in your organization to enable the proper valuation and importance to the organization.

Once you let employees leave, you run the risk of pertinent knowledge leaving with them. The focus of the knowledge mapping effort should center on the employees of the organizations involved. The knowledge mapping deliverable will be an extension of the people side analysis of the M&A transaction.

Before starting to develop the knowledge map (see Figure 8.3), ensure the intentions are clear. This includes understanding the purpose and scope of the knowledge map. The thing to keep in mind is that there is never a single map for every purpose. Knowledge mapping is about relationships (people-to-people and people-to-content), and how these relationships interact within the organization.

To construct the knowledge map, you will go through a process that includes interviewing employees to understand how they work, the processes they use, the content they access, and the people they interact with. This is done because knowledge is found in processes, relationships, policies, people, documents, conversations, and through links to suppliers, competitors, and customers. This information is used

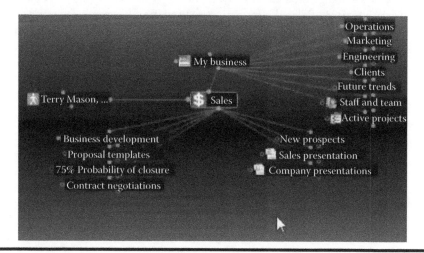

Figure 8.3   Knowledge map example.

to graphically represent these relationships into a map. However, instead of creating a static map, in which several views of the knowledge would need to be created, using of software to create an interactive map is ideal. An interactive knowledge map will provide different perspectives of the relationships and the knowledge each employee has.

Knowledge Profile

A knowledge profile (KP) (see Figure 8.4) records skills, tools, practices, and social networks; it highlights competencies, identifies gaps, helps with learning programs to address deficits, realizes opportunities, and heightens awareness for the owner and colleagues. A KP will provide detailed information about each knowledge holder associated in a knowledge map.

KPs may focus on the individual where they form a key part of your personal KM system or aimed at a "collective" view of a team, group, community, or firm. Profiles may be constructed via manual or automatic means, highly structured, or very informal, maintained by the end user or compiled from test batteries and questionnaires by expert profilers and competency specialists.

A KP goes beyond determining information needs, guiding information seeking behavior, and considers the adoption and use of tools, the condition and functioning of (personal) social networks, and learning desires. Successful KPs focus on the future; they reflect current skills and activities above past positions, awards, and educational achievements, providing some indication of where and how the person can best contribute to organizational and team goals.

KPs are often a key element in knowledge mapping, knowledge audits, and customer relationship management, and play an increasing role in advanced search, expertise location, agent-based work assignments, customer selling strategies, and portal user-interfaces. Related information is found in yellow pages, expertise directories, and academic resumes, but the KP is distinguished by a list and evaluation of relationships (promotes flow), preferences and proficiencies with communication systems/tools, and applicable tacit knowledge strengths.

Figure 8.4   Knowledge profile example.

Why M&A Can Fail?

It's no secret that plenty of mergers don't work. Those who advocate mergers will indicate that the merger will cut costs or boost revenues by more than enough to justify the price being paid. It's not as simple as just combining computer systems, merging a few departments, eliminating redundant suppliers, and the merged company will be more profitable than ever! Historical trends show that roughly two-thirds of large mergers will lose value on the stock market. The motivations that drive mergers can be flawed and efficiencies from economies of scale may prove elusive.

Most research indicates that M&A activity has an overall success rate of about 50%. Chief executives of mid-market companies (generally speaking, businesses with between US$20 and US$300 million in revenue) should keep those odds in mind as deals are offered to them. The consequences of a failed merger or acquisition are far greater for a mid-market company than for large corporations. Large companies usually have enough resources to move on and maintain their business. Most mid-market companies lack the finances or bandwidth to absorb a bad deal.

Most transactions look great on paper, but few organizations pay attention to the details; that is, how the deal will actually work once all the paperwork is signed. This includes thoroughly assessing the culture of your target acquisition, and determining if it is compatible with your company's culture; understanding if the deal in line with your corporate strategy in order to determine what knowledge is necessary for the new company to successfully execute its strategy and identify who the key knowledge holders are that support the strategy moving forward.

Meticulously and diligently screening possible M&A deals may increase your odds of success. However, consider the odds and remember to pay attention to details: Is the deal priced, so that you can afford to put the necessary resources into the integration while still having a return on investment? Is the acquisition, along with all the costs and risks associated with it, a better choice than all other alternatives? How does the organization retain the key knowledge holders? What are the gaps in knowledge the organization needs to fill? How will the gaps in knowledge be mitigated? Mid-market CEOs who can't do the homework will be better off reconsidering the transaction all together.

Key Learnings

The following are some key learnings from this chapter:

■ Planning for those employees who will continue on after the merger or acquisition is a key ingredient for success. Therefore, when planning employee and/or business function consolidation (or elimination), an understanding of what knowledge is needed and the key knowledge holders is essential. Constructing a knowledge map is useful tool in this analysis.

- Before conducting a knowledge mapping initiative, it is important that all employees complete a KP. This will provide the necessary details of the employees in order for the knowledge map to accurately reflect the "key" knowledge holders of the organization.
- Plenty of mergers don't work; it's not as simple as just combining computer systems, merging a few departments, eliminating redundant suppliers, and the merged company will be more profitable than ever! Yes, do your homework!

Tips and Techniques

The following are some of the tips and techniques that are deduced from this chapter:

- Understanding contextual intelligence is an important factor in determining how to integrate knowledge between organizations in an M&A transaction.
- If your organization is positioning itself to be sold, understanding how KM can increase the overall value of the company is essential to obtain a fair price. Leveraging the knowledge value equation will be an essential tool in the valuation process.
- When using the knowledge value equation, build a knowledge value tree. A knowledge value tree makes the connection between knowledge and value in an organization more visible by understanding the relationship and connection of KM functionality, business impact, and financial impact.
- Another point of emphasis is that when calculating the return on knowledge, understand that it is not a simple task, and yet it is important that organizational leaders think about increasing return on this critical asset.

Chapter 9

"Is There a Doctor in the House?": Knowledge Management in Healthcare

Healthcare is a knowledge intensive business. Making the best use of knowledge within any healthcare provider organization (hospital, clinic, pharmacy, physician private practice, etc.) is essential for optimal patient care as well as cutting and/or streamlining costs. Knowledge management (KM) in healthcare is about sharing know-how through collaboration and integration of systems to enable access to knowledge. Applying knowledge sharing and collaboration to healthcare would include sharing medical research, giving visibility to patient decisions, and collaboration between physicians and healthcare provider organizations. Collaborative work environments will bring more effective communication and more physician responsiveness to patients.

Healthcare is also a massive industry, and every healthcare provider organization faces challenges where incorporating KM would be beneficial. The processes and systems that enable the delivery and management of healthcare services to patients are faced with the prospect of failing to prevent (and can indirectly or directly cause) suffering and in some cases death to the various patients. It is for this reason that KM is attracting much attention from the industry as a whole. However, the time has come for the healthcare industry to start implementing KM and to begin realizing the benefits that it can provide.

KM is a particularly complex issue for health organizations. The potential benefits KM implementation could bring are enormous. Some of these benefits include better outcomes for patients, cost reduction, enhanced job flexibility, and improved responsiveness to patients' needs and changing lifestyles and expectations and ensure more effective communication, leading to focused and (hopefully) seamless care interventions and a better patient experience.

In realizing these benefits, it is understood that healthcare delivery is a knowledge-driven process, and KM provides the opportunity to incorporate KM practices to improve the various healthcare processes. Bordoloi and Islam (2012, p. 110) have indicated that "knowledge management is systematically more complex in healthcare and minimal research exist to guide academic and organizational stakeholders."

To leverage KM in the appropriate way to address the complex and process nature of healthcare, healthcare organizations should adopt a broad strategy to capture, communicate, and apply explicit and tacit knowledge throughout the healthcare delivery process (see Figure 9.1). This strategy must include a focus on knowledge sharing and organizational learning. This type of focus will provide

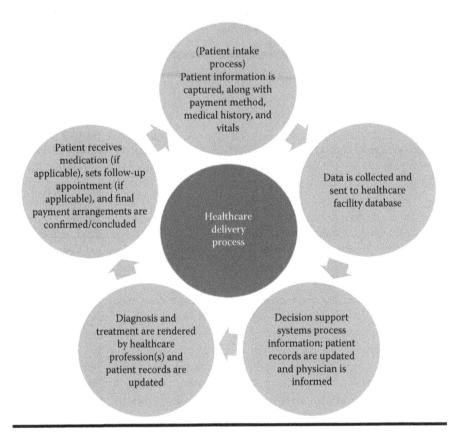

Figure 9.1 Healthcare delivery process.

(codified) evidence-based solutions to the population as a whole, while at the same time providing personalized care for individuals. Tringali and Lusigan (2005) present a KM model for healthcare (see Figure 9.2) that incorporates knowledge and learning as well as a focus on using explicit and tacit knowledge. This model illustrates the elements of KM that should be incorporated into a broader healthcare KM strategy.

With that focus in mind, this chapter will cover the following areas: healthcare delivery process, KM model for healthcare, applying KM to healthcare, constructing healthcare knowledge, KM and healthcare informatics, and knowledge tools and techniques for healthcare.

Healthcare Delivery Process

Delivery of healthcare is a complex endeavor. It includes primary organizations for healthcare delivery such as healthcare providers having interorganizational relationships with other players (i.e., Blue Cross/Blue Shield and its member organizations, physician and hospital affiliations) to provide a foundation. The increasing cost of healthcare is putting pressure on access and quality of healthcare delivery, and this is calling for increased accountability because of high rates of medical errors and globalization, which leads to demands of higher standards of quality.

Furthermore, healthcare delivery is moving away from a physician–patient relationship to a customer–company relationship, and at the same time the traditional single physician–patient relationship is moving toward a situation where healthcare is delivered by a team of healthcare professionals wherein each specialize in a single aspect of healthcare; however, this is all focused on patient-centered care.

The healthcare delivery process depicted in Figure 9.1 presents a simplistic view of each of the major areas (i.e., patient intake, data collection, decision support, diagnosis and treatment, and patient closeout) of healthcare delivery. Each of these areas (depending on medical organization) has more complex processes, procedures, and systems that enable them to integrate and function together. The following provides more details of each of the areas that comprise the healthcare delivery process:

> *Patient intake process*: Because of the increase in patient demand partially caused by health reform initiatives that focus on broadening patient access to insurance, many medical practices are experiencing an increase in new patient enrollment. Whenever new patients use the services of a hospital or physician practice, they must complete forms that list their contact information, medical history, insurance information, and acknowledgment of various Health Insurance Portability and Accountability Act (HIPAA) regulations.
>
> The patient intake process is the first opportunity to capture knowledge about the patient and his/her condition at the time of arrival at the healthcare

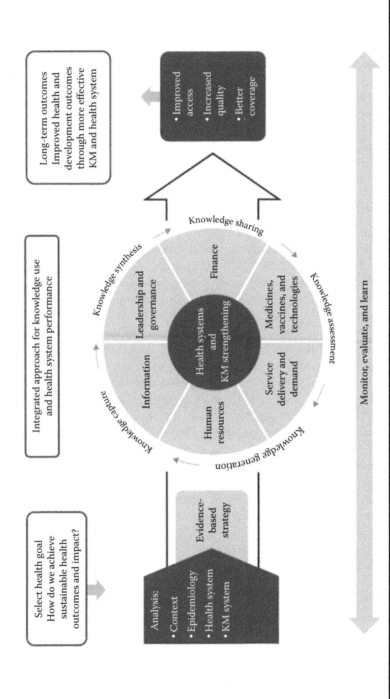

Figure 9.2 Model for KM in healthcare.

facility. At this point, the patient information is captured, along with method of payment, medical history, and current vital condition. All of this data is transitioned to the facilities database. This presents an opportunity for the data to be shared, an opportunity for information to be processed from the data, and knowledge to be acquired from the information.

Data collection: At this point of the process, all the data that was taken during the intake process is collected and sent to the healthcare facilities' database. The collection of healthcare data involves a diverse set of public and private data collection systems, including health surveys, administrative enrollment and billing records, and medical records, used by various entities, including hospitals, clinics, physicians, and health plans. This suggests the potential of each entity to contribute data, information, and knowledge on patients or enrollees. As it stands now, a fragmentation of data flow occurs because of these silos of data collection. One way to increase the flow of data, information, and knowledge is to integrate them with data from other sources. However, it should be noted that a substantial fraction of the U.S. population does not have a regular relationship with a provider who integrates their care (Beal et al., 2007).

Decision support system: This area of the healthcare delivery process involves integrating the clinical decision support systems (CDSSs). The CDSS will enable the standardization and sharing of clinical best practices and protocols with staff, patients, and partners on demand, anywhere, and on any device. Physicians, nurses, and other healthcare professionals use a CDSS to prepare a diagnosis and to review the diagnosis as a means of improving the final result. Data mining (which will be examined later in this chapter) is conducted to examine the patient's medical history in conjunction with relevant clinical research. Such analysis will provide the necessary knowledge to help predict potential events, which can range from drug interactions to disease symptoms. Some physicians may use a combination of a CDSS and their professional experience to determine the best course of care for a patient.

There are two main types of CDSSs. One type of CDSS uses a knowledge base (expert system), which applies rules to patient data using an inference engine and displays the results to the end user. Systems without a knowledge base, on the other hand, rely on machine learning to analyze clinical data. The challenge here is that for a CDSS to be most effective, it must be integrated with the healthcare organizations clinical workflow, which is often very complex. If a CDSS is a standalone system, it will lack the interoperability needed to provide the necessary knowledge for healthcare professionals to determine the best course of care for a patient.

However, the sheer number of clinical research and medical trials being published on an ongoing basis makes it difficult to incorporate the resulting data (Big Data). Additionally, incorporating Big Data into existing systems could cause a significant increase in infrastructure and maintenance.

Diagnosis and treatment: Making a diagnosis is a very complex process, which includes cognitive tasks that involves both logical reasoning and pattern recognition. Although the process happens largely at an unconscious level, there are two essential steps where knowledge can be captured and applied.

In the first step, the healthcare professional will enumerate the diagnostic possibilities and estimate their relative likelihood. Experienced clinicians often group the findings into meaningful clusters and summarize in brief phrases about the symptom, body location, or the organ system involved (Richardson et al., 2002).

In the second step, the healthcare professional would incorporate new data, information, and/or knowledge to change the relative probabilities, rule out some of the possibilities, and ultimately, choose the most likely diagnosis. For each diagnostic possibility, the additional knowledge increases or decreases its likelihood (Richardson et al., 2002). At this point, the diagnosis and treatment is rendered by the healthcare professional and the patient records are updated.

Patient closeout/patient discharge: In the case of a simple patient closeout from a routine/scheduled physician visit or simple visit to the local clinic, the patient receives medication (if applicable), sets follow-up appointments, if necessary, and finalizes payment arrangements and the patient records are updated. However, if you have had a hospital stay, the discharge process can be quite involving. In the case of a discharge, a set series of tasks must occur prior to discharging a patient. These tasks include examination and sign-off by appropriate providers and patient education. For each patient, the time of discharge and the tasks that need to be performed will be provided 1 day ahead of time. This allows for everyone involved in the discharge to self-organize to get the work done within the window necessary to meet the scheduled discharge time (Institute for Health Improvement, 2015). At the conclusion of the discharge, patients receive information and instructions for continued care and follow up; in addition, all patient records should be updated.

KM Model for Healthcare

Before applying the KM model to primary healthcare practices, it is necessary to indicate how the elements of the model will be described or measured. The KM definitional dimensions are matched with commonly employed KM tools. Processes associated with finding information or knowledge include codification, identifying lessons learned and best practices, dissemination/imitation, and loss, and utilizing technical and socially directed tools to connect individuals with existing knowledge sources. "Losing" knowledge arises from gaps or misuse of technical tools, and when people leave. Processes associated with sharing knowledge or information include teaching/training and transfer/diffusion. Social tools, such as apprenticeship interactions, conversations, and cross-functional teams, prevail over more technically oriented ones. Social tools may extend beyond the specific organizational unit.

Processes and tools associated with developing information or knowledge include recombining existing knowledge through categorizing and sorting, as in database utilization (combination); internalizing individual's experiences in the form of shared mental models and technical know-how, as in manuals or oral stories (internalization); acquiring new mental models and technical skills from others, as in interactions with customers and on-the-job training (socialization); and articulating tacit knowledge into more explicit forms of metaphors, analogies, concepts, and hypotheses, as in collective reflection and evaluation (externalization) (Nonaka and Takeuchi, 1995). This process also implies "unlearning" or relinquishing existing knowledge to develop new knowledge.

Patient-Centered Approach

Some of the keys to patient care are the ability to evaluate a large amount of data and information, which includes the use of medical informatics. These are the keys to deliver medical knowledge to the right people, at the right time, in the right context. Electronic health records, data warehouses, laptops, and other mobile devices now provide access to information and knowledge at the point of care. This access facilitates a continuous learning environment in which lessons learned can provide updates to clinical, administrative, and financial processes. Given these advancements, it is imperative that data, information, and knowledge are managed for effective healthcare.

An understanding of how patients fit into the evidence-based medical practice is critical because patients, more than ever, are equipped with a wealth of tacit knowledge about their health needs. Such tacit knowledge can have a dual connotation on healthcare delivery by either promoting or obstructing the acceptance of medical expertise based mainly on explicit knowledge and clinical experience. Incorporating patients' needs, values, and expectations rigorously in medical practice has many benefits. It holds the potential to deal with inappropriate tacit knowledge that patients may have on their health conditions, while at the same time, reinforcing appropriate knowledge that can promote their health. Marginalization of patients' tacit knowledge in the evidence-based equation can easily spell the doom for the healthcare industry. This is because effective healthcare delivery is based not only on rigorous scientific knowledge but also on clinically relevant experience as well as patients' values. Patients' values take into cognizance the unique preferences, concerns, and expectations each patient brings to the clinical encounter. These are values that must be integrated into clinical decisions if they are to serve the patient. In order to ensure optimal clinical outcomes, therefore, there is the need for an effective integration of the three elements espoused by the evidence-based medical paradigm—scientific knowledge of doctors, clinical experience, and patients' values.

Applying principles of KM will/has become the catalyst for quality healthcare delivery and management, and these operational elements will provide the mechanisms to execute a broader healthcare KM strategy. In this chapter, the focus will be to provide a detailed understanding of the practice of KM within the healthcare industry. The content includes critical aspects of healthcare operations, knowledge strategies for healthcare operations, essential knowledge elements for healthcare, knowledge mapping and medical informatics, knowledge creation and discovery in medical informatics, applying KM to healthcare, and knowledge tools and techniques for healthcare.

Applying KM to Healthcare

A critical function in healthcare organizations and more especially for healthcare workers is decision making. In most healthcare organizations, decision making is not structured in a way that follows a consistent healthcare model, as presented in the healthcare delivery process depicted in Figure 9.1. Not only is it important at all times, to ensure that germane knowledge is being extracted during the course of delivering healthcare, but it is also essential that KM does provide a sustained advantage. This necessitates a long-term rather than a single-focus silo approach to capturing, cataloging, using/reusing, and enriching your healthcare knowledge.

Integrated healthcare knowledge that flows between the various areas and systems within the healthcare delivery process is at the confluence of physical, informational, and cognitive domains. The backbone of integrated healthcare operations is the continuous extraction and flow of germane knowledge and pertinent information to all who require it anytime, anywhere throughout the system, so that superior decision making can take place.

It is important that as the knowledge flows within and between the areas of the healthcare delivery process, a proper conceptualization of knowledge occurs. The conceptualization of knowledge within healthcare provides an integrated view of various sources of knowledge that permeate through healthcare organizations. It can also provide access to the latest medical research knowledge as well as locate and identify key areas of knowledge and expertise within the healthcare organization. This can mean the difference between life and death, accurate and inaccurate diagnosis, and between early intervention and prolonged and costly hospital stays, as well as contributing to enabling the delivery and improved patient experience.

Constructing Healthcare Knowledge

Healthcare knowledge is primarily social constructs. For instance, are obesity, binge drinking, and heavy smoking health or social issues? Should people with the problems listed such as obesity, binge drinking, and heavy smoking receive access to treatment as those without these problems? Are the problems listed in question

1 really problems to be solved by healthcare or simply personal choices of lifestyle that individuals must change?

To address this, the healthcare system must influence our institutional logic. Institutional logic refers to organizing principles guiding social actions and refers to a set of belief systems and associated practices. Through healthcare knowledge-sharing campaigns such as forums; awareness campaigns at local, regional, and national events; and by providing pamphlets to patients that detail specific healthcare issues and challenges and their solutions, healthcare organizations will begin to increase patient knowledge and influence the population to improve lifestyle choices and improve overall healthcare.

Knowledge creation, consumption, and management are essentially social processes, which views the construction of knowledge as accomplishing changes that are not only technical but are also cognitive and social. This takes a holistic and realistic approach to the knowledge construction process.

There is a knowledge discourse upon healthcare services. This discourse is the basis on which healthcare services are organized, financed, designed, consumed, and evaluated. Through the use of technology, patients are willing to enter into dialogs with doctors about their healthcare.

Technology also plays a key role in the delivery of healthcare knowledge to the general public. Websites such as WebMD (www.webmd.com), Yahoo Health (https://www.yahoo.com/health), and MedicineNet.com (http://www.medicinenet .com/script/main/hp.asp) are excellent sources for the medical community to share valuable healthcare knowledge to the public.

WebMD

As stated on their website, WebMD provides valuable health information, tools for managing your health, and support to those who seek information. You can trust that our content is timely and credible. In addition, WebMD provides credible information, supportive communities, and in-depth reference material about various health subjects that matter to consumers. WebMD is a source for original and timely health information as well as material from well-known content providers. The website also indicates that the WebMD content staff blends expertise in journalism, content creation, community services, expert commentary, and medical review to give consumers a variety of ways to find what they are looking for. This includes the following: health news for the public; creating and maintaining up-to-date medical reference content databases; medical imagery, graphics, and animation; communities; live web events; and interactive tools. Please note that WebMD does not provide medical advice, diagnosis, or treatment.

Yahoo Health

As stated on their website, Yahoo Health is powered by Healthline.com. This site provides consumers with some of the best and latest health-related content and information available on the Internet. Yahoo Health indicates that it is your ulti-mate source for healthy-living information and inspiration. This site contains a litany of advertisements from various healthcare-related companies to support and promote a healthy lifestyle. Please note that Yahoo Health does not provide medical advice, diagnosis, or treatment.

MedicineNet.com

As stated on their website, MedicineNet.com was founded in 1996 and has had a highly accomplished, uniquely experienced team of qualified executives in the fields of medicine, healthcare, Internet technology, and business to bring to the consumer the most comprehensive, sought-after healthcare information anywhere. In addition, it is indicated that MedicineNet.com brings nationally recognized, doctor-produced (a network of more than 70 U.S. board-certified physicians) trusted sources to their online environment. Please note that MedicineNet.com does not provide medical advice, diagnosis, or treatment.

Patient-Centered Healthcare Knowledge Constructs

Because healthcare knowledge is no longer a doctor-centered process, and is now a patient-centered process, the ideology, cultural, social, institutional, and political circumstances have become major influencers on our healthcare, and as patients, it influences how we view our healthcare services. Social structure refers to the people who are involved in the knowledge construction process as well as the relationship between these people. Understanding social structure is critical to understanding knowledge construction.

Knowledge is created by social interactions based on values, beliefs, experi-ences, expectations, and relationships. These social interactions happen between consumers, providers, agencies, and sponsors. Consumers, which include patients and perspective patients who consume healthcare services; providers, which include doctors, nurses, and other healthcare professionals; agencies, which include govern-ment and other independent bodies that are granted authority and responsibility to evaluate, approve, regulate, and fund healthcare provisions; and sponsors, which include general public, taxpayers, and voters who select government officials to manage healthcare services on their behalf.

KM and Healthcare Informatics

Healthcare informatics combines the fields of information technology and health to develop the systems required to administer the expansion of information, advance-ment in clinical work flow, and improvement in the security of the healthcare system. It involves the integration of information science, computer technology, and medicines to collect, organize, and secure information systems and health-related data.

The design and implementation of an electronic medical record system also pose significant epistemological and practical complexities. As we move to integrate electronic capture of medical records into the contribution to the quality of care, we know that their implementation and deployment into various clinical settings has been a challenge. As a result, the extraordinary explosion of medical knowledge, technologies, as well as ground-breaking drugs may vastly improve healthcare delivery to consumers, and keeping the information related to these advancements organized and accessible is the key.

Health informatics can also yield computational insight in assimilating knowledge from large clinical datasets for both research and policy discussion. The adoption of computerized patient records by healthcare organizations promises to expand the sources potential research data to include clinical patient data. Applications of health informatics can enhance health services and clinical research, as well as improve healthcare quality.

A primary goal of health informatics is to gain expertise in the understanding of clinical knowledge and the mapping of this knowledge to alternative taxonomies and meta-languages. A computational approach to this clinical knowledge will enable the creation of methodologies for aggregating clinical data from disparate data storage systems for large analysis.

Knowledge Tools and Techniques for Healthcare

There are key tools and techniques closely related to contemporary KM. Some of these techniques use information technology but all rely on an effective human component to both enliven and enable them. These include taxonomies and ontologies (see Chapter 4 section on Information Architecture), expert systems, data mining, text mining, business intelligence and analytics, communities of practices (CoPs), and social networks (with the growth social networking sites being of contemporary relevance).

KM is centered on people, process, and technology. It leverages processes to gather, analyze, organize, and discover knowledge. The following tools are prevalent in the delivery of healthcare knowledge and assist in the decision making process for improved patient care.

Expert Systems

Expert systems offer benefits in many areas of healthcare. They provide an environment for experts to develop and test disease models, and this research can provide valuable answers to complex health problems. To this end, expert systems for healthcare services are widely used where accuracy of diagnosis and efficiency for various services are needed. The cooperation of all parties in the healthcare delivery process is crucial in analyzing and managing the data of patients to detect abnormal patterns in order to provide an advance treatment; expert systems are an essential tool in providing this analysis. Expert systems often take the form of CDSSs. A CDSS is an application that analyzes data to help healthcare providers make clinical decisions. It is an adaptation of a decision support system commonly used to support business management.

Data Mining

Data mining is used during the knowledge discovery process and aims to analyze a set of given data or information in order to identify patterns (i.e., decision trees, artificial neural networks, and algorithms). Traditional data mining tools help companies establish data patterns and trends by using a number of complex algorithms and techniques. Some of these tools are installed on the desktop to monitor the data and highlight trends, whereas others capture information residing outside a database. Most data mining tools are able to handle any data using online analytical processing or a similar technology.

Data Mining Tools and Techniques—Dashboards

Dashboards are used to monitor information in a database; dashboards reflect data changes and updates onscreen often in the form of a chart or table, enabling the user to see how the business is performing. Historical data can also be referenced, enabling the user to see where things have changed (e.g., increase in sales from the same period last year). This functionality makes dashboards easy to use and particularly appealing to healthcare providers who wish to have an overview of the patients' history and changes over time.

The following are the typical steps taken in data mining:

1. Develop an understanding of the application
   a. Relevant prior knowledge
   b. Determine end user's goals
2. Create target dataset to be used for discovery
3. Clean and preprocess the data
4. Reduce the number of variables
5. Choose the data mining tasks (classification, regression, clustering, etc.)
6. Choose the data mining algorithm
7. Search for patterns of interest
8. Interpret the patterns mined
9. Consolidate the knowledge discovered, prepare reports, use/reuse the newly created knowledge

a. *Text gathering*: Locating and identifying relevant documents in all forms (word, PDF, etc.).
b. *Text preprocessing*: Text preprocessing classically means division of text into words or terms and then part-of-speech tagging.
c. *Data analysis*: Many text mining and data mining techniques are applicable here, as this is where the actual information extraction happens. The data analysis is very dependent on the preprocessing and the data representation model that was chosen in preprocessing.
d. *Visualization*: The simplest is just to make a table for the user to look up the information he needs.
e. *Evaluation*: Use one or multiple text mining evaluation techniques.

Text Mining

Data mining and text mining techniques have been applied to different areas of biomedicine, ranging from patient record management to clinical diagnosis. Text mining aims to extract useful knowledge from textual data or documents. It is called text mining because of its ability to mine data from different kinds of text. This includes from Microsoft Word and Acrobat PDF documents to simple text files. These text mining tools scan content and convert the selected data into a format that is compatible with the tool's database, thus providing users with an easy and convenient way of accessing data without the need to open different applications. Scanned content can be unstructured (i.e., information is scattered almost randomly across the document, including e-mails, Internet pages, audio, and video data) or structured (i.e., the data's form and purpose is known, such as content found in a database). Capturing these inputs can provide healthcare organizations with a wealth of information that can be mined to discover trends, patterns, and anomalies in the patient's health history.

Business Intelligence and Analytics

Healthcare business intelligence can provide organizations the ability to use their data to improve quality of care, increase financial efficiency and operational effectiveness, conduct innovative research, and satisfy regulatory requirements. Healthcare organizational data have a wide range of uses. From surgical analytics, service line profitability, and quality analysis to claims management, revenue cycle management, and utilization, analytics can provide the critical insights in meeting the organizations goals and gain competitive advantage.

Business intelligence and analytics combined with decision support systems can provide a holistic examination of all of the patients' data from the combined areas of the healthcare delivery process. As hospitals and other healthcare organizations move toward a data-driven healthcare environment, business intelligence and decision support systems will provide the catalyst hospitals are looking for to improve healthcare delivery and make improvements on cost reductions.

Communities of Practice

CoPs support collaborative networks of individuals and organizations working together to improve their own operations and provide improved patient care. By sharing knowledge, concerns, and passions, healthcare providers can use CoPs as tools to facilitate the sharing of knowledge throughout the healthcare delivery process. The knowledge base of a healthcare organization is the result of many interactions with colleagues and mentors.

Some examples of CoPs in healthcare organizations include clubs, committees, associations, academies, study groups, coalitions, social network discussion threads, medical staffs of local hospitals, and community-oriented primary care groups. CoPs can exist in many different forms and professions, but all CoPs share three key dimensions: a domain of knowledge, a community, and a shared interest or practice.

- *Domain of knowledge*: In a CoP specific to family medicine, the common domain of knowledge among all of its members may be the specialty of family medicine, a focus on specific populations, and performance of specific procedures or a particular need or interest, such as becoming more competitive with other specialties or physicians.
- *Community*: People in a CoP share a voluntary commitment to relationship building.
- *Shared practice*: In a shared practice, members develop and share knowledge and build expertise by compiling resources, tools, and strategies that support future learning for all involved.

Social Networks

Social networks are playing an increasingly prominent role in healthcare. More and more physicians are becoming members of social networking sites such as Sermo (http://www.sermo.com/). Sermo has been rated the number one social networking site for doctors in the United States and globally. Because consumers and clinicians are using social networks, healthcare organizations have an opportunity to leverage their influence across multiple audiences.

Many social media tools are available for healthcare professionals, including social networking platforms, blogs, microblogs, wikis, and media sharing sites. They use these tools to improve or enhance professional networking and education, organizational promotion, patient care, patient education, and public health programs (Chauhan et al., 2012). However, these tools also present potential risks to patients and healthcare professionals regarding the distribution of poor quality information, damage to professional image, breaches of patient privacy, violation of personal–professional boundaries, and licensing or legal issues (Lambert et al., 2012). This has caused many healthcare institutions and professional organizations have issued guidelines to prevent these risks.

As more consumers are going online for health information and knowledge rather than going to see a physician, healthcare professionals have an obligation to create educational content to be shared across social media that will help accurately inform consumers about health-related issues. This is extremely important because the opinions of others on social media are often trusted but aren't always accurate sources of insights, especially when it comes to a subject as sensitive as health.

Top Five Trends in KM for Healthcare 2016 and Beyond

There will be a focus on empowering consumers, e-health adaptability, and a shift to focus on prevention, not just cure! Here are the top five trends for KM as it pertains to healthcare for 2016 and beyond!

1. Technological advancements

   The proliferation of new technology is transforming the entire healthcare industry. The two areas of opportunity and concern are wearable technology (specifically wearable tracking devices) and data security.

   • *Wearable tracking devices*: It is estimated that nearly 70 million people in the United States are using wearable tracking devices to monitor their physical activity, sleep patterns, calorie consumption, and much more. This new frontier presents a great deal of potential to improve patient care. Only time will tell the impact this trend has on improved patient care.

   • *Data security*: Patient privacy issues (including concerns about data breaches) will continue to be top-of-mind for providers, payers, and consumers, especially with ongoing data breaches in the news. Providers and payers will need to step up data security to avoid the type of HIPAA violations that can negatively impact an organization.

2. Collaboration between healthcare providers

   Owing to the changes in healthcare laws and the strain on healthcare organizations due to difficult financial climate, it has put a premium on the importance of partnerships and collaboration when it comes to providing value-based healthcare. This will not be changing anytime soon. This is evident by the following recent examples of healthcare partnerships:

- Trinity Health System joined forces with Heritage Provider Network to deliver population health management in select markets throughout the country.
- Anthem Blue Cross Blue Shield of Wisconsin joined forces with Aurora Healthcare and its Aurora Accountable Care Network. They agreed upon a shared-risk program to support value-based reimbursement payment models.
- Allina Health formed a dozen Citizen Health Action Teams (called CHATs) to bring community members together to discuss neighborhood health issues and come up with solutions.
- Henry Ford Health System is seeking ways to "hardwire the safety net." It is pursuing more seamless integration between itself and the various navigators and volunteers it deploys to address community engagement. The safety net program alone required the participation of more than 30 community partners, including competing health systems in the Detroit region.

3. Patient-centered care

A significant change in the healthcare industry's approach to providing care is underway—putting the patient at the center of care. The goal is to improve patient satisfaction scores and engagement. The healthcare industry as a whole is starting to look into ways to engage with patients outside of a traditional office visit. This includes tapping into social media to build relationships with their customers. This will continue to be essential in gaining new customers, as patients begin to shop for healthcare online, including through social media interactions; this includes searching for patient reviews and comparing prices.

4. Need for Big Data

Researchers, clinicians, and administrative leaders are leveraging for data to develop new drugs, improve patient diagnosis, make decisions, and guide their planning. Access to Big Data resources is becoming essential to create this competitive advantage. Access to Big Data resources is key to overcoming the current data challenges. As demands for access to high-quality, accurate Big Data sources continue to grow, healthcare organizations will want better analytics tools, so they can improve care and reduce costs.

5. Population health management

Population health management is a proactive application of strategies and interventions to defined cohorts of individuals across the continuum of healthcare delivery in an effort to maintain and/or improve the health of the individuals within the cohort at the lowest necessary cost. As the risk for a population of patients shift based on demographics (age, due to people living longer, and the baby boomer population increasing the elderly population) health systems need to know more about the patients they serve and how to continue to provide improved healthcare services.

Key Learnings

The following are some key learnings from this chapter:

- The patient intake process is the first opportunity to capture knowledge about the patient and his/her condition at the time of arrival at the healthcare facility.
- The collection of healthcare data involves a diverse set of public and private data collection systems, including health surveys, administrative enrollment and billing records, and medical records, used by various entities, including hospitals, clinics, physicians, and health plans. This suggests the potential of each entity to contribute data, information, and knowledge on patients or enrollees.
- It is important at all times to ensure that germane knowledge is being extracted during the course of delivering healthcare. This necessitates a long-term rather than a single-focus silo approach to capturing, cataloging, using/reusing, and enriching your healthcare knowledge.
- It is important that as the knowledge flows within and between the areas of the healthcare delivery process that a proper conceptualization of knowledge occurs. The conceptualization of knowledge within healthcare provides an integrated view of various sources of knowledge that permeate through healthcare organizations.

Tips and Techniques

The following are some of the tips and techniques deduced after reading this chapter:

- In order for a CDSS to be most effective, it must be integrated with the healthcare organization's clinical workflow, which is often very complex.
- To avoid your CDSS missing the necessary interoperability, it must be integrated into the other systems that support your healthcare delivery process. Otherwise, it will lack the delivery of knowledge necessary for healthcare professionals to determine the best course of care for a patient.
- Be aware that incorporating Big Data into existing CDSS could cause a significant increase in infrastructure and maintenance costs.

Chapter 10

"Show Me the Money!": Knowledge Management for Financial Services

Financial service enterprises operate in a highly challenged market where consolidation, increasing regulation, and economic realities are negatively impacting their ability to achieve key objectives. This has created a culture where there is a constant need to find more predictable revenue streams and cost-efficiency gains.

Regulatory bodies such as the Financial Industry Regulatory Authority (FINRA), Securities and Exchange Commission (SEC), Commodity Futures Trading Commission (CFTC), and the various international bodies' present challenges to financial service organizations to deliver fair and open products and services while providing answers and direction to the various customers interacting with their organizations. In order to address these challenges, KM is needed to streamline processes and deliver content at the right time, in the right way, and in the right context to meet the demand of customers.

In meeting the demand for customers, it is increasingly important for financial service organizations to address customer needs. KM through the implementation of processes and technology (including information architecture—see Chapter 4) will ensure that customer information is shared with the right people at the right time across the organization. By utilizing a customer-focused, integrated knowledge management system (KMS), all employees interacting with a customer will have up-to-date knowledge of that customer's breadth of relationship and experience with the organization. This will assist the organization with cross-selling, up-selling, and reporting on the effectiveness of any new customer initiatives.

In addition, the staff must start (if they are not already doing so) working together using knowledge as a focal point to service the customer. With this emphasis, as more financial products and services become available through mobile devices, the ability for those financial companies to respond rapidly to customer demands with the right answers, at the right time, and in the right context will be met.

Empowering Employees to Satisfy Customers

The objective of KM is to capture knowledge of different stakeholders of the organization and make it explicitly available to all employees. Sharing of knowledge will enable improved and quicker decision making. Employees empowered with improved decision making will increase the ability to address customer needs and create more satisfied customers. Empowering your employees through KM will assist your organization in addressing competition driven by reduced barriers to switch companies, the proliferation of products and product commoditization, mergers and acquisitions and the ever-changing product portfolios, and shifts in customer behaviors.

Financial service organizations (including banks) value KM as a business practice. From managing intellectual capital, to the vast array of customer data, one of the goals of KM is to enhance customer satisfaction and increase revenue.

Whether the organization is regional or global, a key aspect of your business and specifically your KM strategy must be to treat each client as an individual with individual needs. By implementing a comprehensive KM program and associated processes and systems, a determination as to which customers are most likely to buy which products, who is at the risk of leaving, which unprofitable clients are most likely to be profitable again, and who is most likely to respond to which marketing campaigns based on their demographics, can start to be addressed and the organization will have a sustainable model for success!

Firms within this industry are predominantly knowledge based, as are most of the industry's products, processes, and services. The application of KM represents a clear opportunity for financial services firms to confront challenges. A KM model for financial services (brokerage and banking being the focus here) should contain a multilevel approach integrating a resource-based knowledge view of the firm should be implemented. This model offers renewed opportunities for financial firms to become more efficient and effective in their use of KM.

This chapter focuses on the use of KM within the financial industry. Specifically this chapter will present how KM is being leveraged by brokerage companies, which include commodity (futures and options) organizations and online trading financial companies, as well as banking institutions.

KM Leveraged by Brokerage Companies

Brokerage organizations are constantly evolving, offering new products and services. At the same time, product specifications are becoming more stringent and legislation is tightening around safer operational limits. Additionally, new capabilities of information technology (IT) are enabling effective collaboration, even across large global organizations. It is now realistic to gather real-time knowledge from operating sites and provide meaningful analytics that help users collaborate to make the best possible decisions.

In order to keep pace with the new commodity-trading environment, businesses need to unlock their business information and intelligence. That means breaking up existing data silos and deploying the tools necessary to capture, access, and share data, information, and knowledge accurately, efficiently, and in real-time, across the organization. A common set of information must be accessible to everyone right from the execution of each trade to the shipping, receipt, and delivery of commodities if applicable, including those responsible for managing credit, market risk, and controlling the finances.

Achieving this involves real-time processing and delivery of data, information, and knowledge, all the way from the front to back office. That means using highly integrated and scalable systems that are capable of seamlessly managing physical operations, scheduling, financial trading, and corporate compliance issues for multiple commodities that have the analytical, business modeling, and reporting tools necessary to support delivering the necessary knowledge to achieve intelligent decision making at every step of a trade's life cycle. To fulfill the promise of delivering knowledge throughout the trading cycle and to achieve intelligent decision making, a holistic KM framework must be developed. An example of this framework is illustrated in Figure 10.1.

The brokerage organization KM framework offers a platform that can facilitate the integration of operations, scheduling, and financial trading. This framework integrates trading platforms with search capabilities to quickly access trading knowledge and make it available on the KM platform. In addition, this framework enables the managing and maintaining of data, information and knowledge, access to corporate content and a brokerage operation, and retail trading and institutional trading view through an integrated business taxonomy structure.

Brokerage Institution KM Model

The brokerage KM model (see Figure 10.2) integrates various business units; policies; products; trading content; client; and systems to gather, catalog, store, and disseminate knowledge across the enterprise. Brokerage companies, which include commodity (futures and options) organizations and online trading firms, will leverage KM to capture knowledge to contribute to the products and features offered by brokerage companies to its customers.

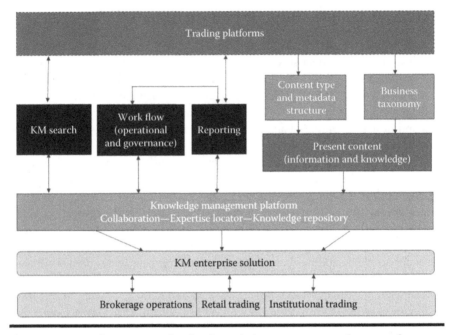

Figure 10.1 Brokerage organization knowledge management framework.

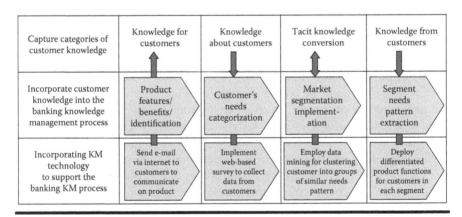

Figure 10.2 Brokerage knowledge management model.

This model supports collaboration, communication, improved employee skills, better decision making, and increased innovation. In order to respond quickly and effectively within the marketplace, brokerage institutions need to create and capture corporate knowledge, rapidly disseminate it, and integrate it with new products and services.

The following are the core principles that the brokerage institution KM model must support:

- The ability to analyze and synthesize knowledge in order to generate an additional value.
- The ability to connect, collect, catalog, store, use/reuse, learn, and create, which contributes to growing intelligently reusable knowledge that supports product and service innovation.
- The ability to incorporate KM technology to support the brokerage KM processes.
- The ability to acquire desired knowledge, by induction of the desired quality of talent through all business units (brokerage operations, retail trading, and institutional trading).
- The ability to develop, knowledge pool, knowledge repository within the organization and manage/maintain the knowledge through governance processes.
- The ability to make available the appropriate updated knowledge to employees (the users) anytime and anywhere.

KM Leveraged by Banking Institutions

Globalization of financial markets has forced bankers to be knowledge based and be more efficient in managing knowledge in their banking operations. Through the practices of KM, an organization focuses on the systematic exploitation and reuse of knowledge. The firm should identify the organization's competitive knowledge position in order to define the strategic gaps in its organization's knowledge.

In accounting and finance, knowledge can be categorized as an intangible asset, but organizations downplay the importance of their intangible assets. Highly competitive business organizations have found out that many types of sources (tangible and intangible) are needed to gain a competitive edge in order to maintain competition and superiority in the marketplace. This is shown by an increasing number of firms that give more emphasis to their intangible assets. Managing this type of asset (knowledge) through organizing, creating, sharing, and acquisition between employees, such an organization will enhance its existence in the marketplace and probably maintain progress in its banking operations.

The ongoing knowledge sharing and continuous discussions among employees, management, and customers will enhance the convergence of a perspective that is required for effective partnering. This will enhance such mutual benefits working in the direction of creating value for all partners.

The practices of KM in the banking industry will enable these institutions to implement appropriate strategies within their financial systems. Expertise in the first level of management will leverage the available optimum capacity of their organization, and enhance and reshape their policy in the long term. In service industries like banking, the application of KM concepts is not an easy task. Although the application of KM does not differ from other industries, the complexity of the banking environment makes KM implementation difficult.

There are eight factors contributing to KM success: technology infrastructure; organizational infrastructure; balance of flexibility; ease-of-accessibility to knowledge; shared knowledge; knowledge-friendly culture; motivated workers who develop, share, and use knowledge (means of knowledge transfer using various IT infrastructure); and senior management support and commitment.

For many years, banks have been actively automating their manual processes. This has resulted in the creation of many information systems. Although these information systems were able to help banks to better manage their processes and resources, they also have created a number of challenges.

One challenge is to take advantage of the proliferation of data, information, and knowledge that has been created as a result of automating the various manual processes. In today's modern banking, data, information, and especially knowledge are treasured assets. Banks have realized the crucial role of KM in gaining an edge in this competitive field, but they have been slow adopters of KM, usually due to wait-and-see attitude of what will be the true benefits and pitfalls from the early adopters. With a greater awareness of the importance and success of KM, industry experts from International Data Corporation (IDC)s expect KM will become a priority for the banking sector. Apart from large volumes of knowledge, the use of IT in managing knowledge has given KM a new dimension. Employing the appropriate KM strategies, IT as an enabler and facilitator will be able to carry out and maximize the benefits of KM.

Banking Institution KM Model

The banking KM model (see Figure 10.3) integrates customer relationship management (CRM) with KM to capture customer-related knowledge to contribute to the products and features offered by banks to its customers. This model supports the notion that in order to ensure business excellence, a products feature must meet the needs of specific customer groups in the market. This is accomplished by a target market-oriented customer KM model supported by implementing KM technology.

The following are the core principles (similar to brokerage institutions) that the banking institution KM model must support:

- Improve the organization's performance through increased efficiency, productivity, quality, and innovation.
- Connect, collect, catalog, store, use/reuse, learn, and create, which contributes to growing intelligently reusable knowledge that supports product and service innovation.

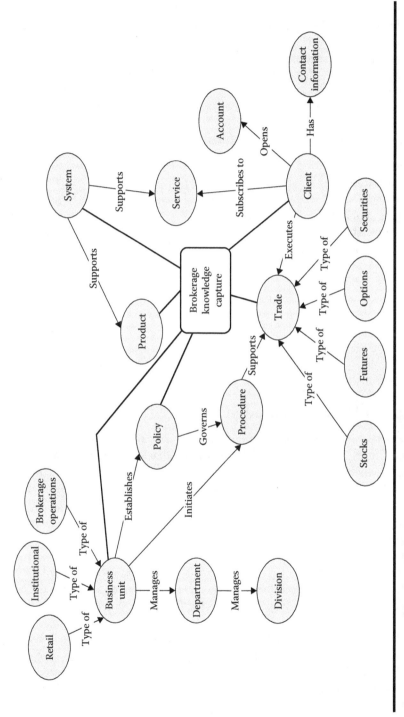

Figure 10.3   Banking knowledge management model.

- Incorporate customer knowledge into the banking KM process.
- Incorporate KM technology to support the banking KM processes.
- Develop knowledge pool, knowledge repository within the organization and manage/maintain the knowledge through governance processes.
- Make available the appropriate updated knowledge to employees (the users) anytime and anywhere.

Increased Sales through Customer Satisfaction

Customer satisfaction is a prime target to make improvements through the implementation of KM. Improved customer satisfaction will lead to increases in revenue. This is accomplished through the process of knowledge creation, cataloging, and dispersion. The most common areas of banking that the application of KM will affect include risk management, marketing management, and CRM and performance measurements. Investments in KMSs such as a decision support systems and data mining are making the most impact.

KM in financial services covers the organizations' intellectual capital to the wealth of knowledge collected as a result of customer transactions. Banking personnel are often required to have knowledge of not only their immediate job but the jobs around them. This heightens the need for effective implementation of KM (knowledge sharing, knowledge transfer).

Arguments for Knowledge Management

A recent study by the Institute of Financial Services and by JD Powers Financial Services Industry Market Research has shown that companies in the financial industry are failing to fully realize the benefits of KM. This survey, conducted among the top 200 banks and insurance companies, showed that only one-third of the companies questioned have KM initiatives in place; in 37% of the cases, no individual is responsible for KM; and that only 36% of the companies with KM programs have realized and implemented that program within a 2-year timeframe.

However, 90% of employees in the financial industry endorse the need for KM, and organizations are beginning to focus more and more on the management of knowledge. This realization and interest is motivated by the following:

- Processes in the financial industry have become more knowledge intensive.
- Professionals are scarce and lifetime employment does not exist anymore.
- Economic trends necessitate that organizations cut costs dramatically.
- Nontraditional financial industry companies have started to offer financial products as well.

Technology

The increasing interest in KM was initially fostered by the IT industry. Technically, it is now possible to extract information and knowledge from employees in order to share it with others through the use, for example, of knowledge bases/repositories, collaboration environments, business intelligence tools, and decision support systems; tool vendors have positioned themselves as KM solutions providers, offering a broad range of KM-supporting tools.

Banking KM Framework

A KM framework positioned to support banks and their various knowledge needs must include the following: the ability to support knowledge intensive processes across bank functions and departments; bank employee needs for knowledge; the consumer needs for knowledge in order to execute self/help capabilities; and business needs for bank knowledge as well as suppliers. Figure 10.4 depicts this framework on a broad level.

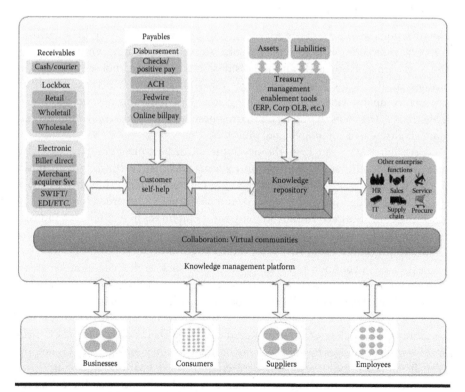

Figure 10.4 Banking knowledge management framework.

Knowledge-Intensive Processes

Processes have also become more knowledge intensive. Technology vendors such as Microsoft, Oracle, and IBM have introduced a new technology to automate/facilitate financial process management. In the financial industry, the focus is now on attracting clients with new products and concepts. These products need to be introduced faster than the competition can manage, and as such time to market has decreased substantially.

Scarce Talent

Only 10 years ago, people had to apply at dozens of potential employers in the hope that they would be invited for a job interview. Presently, when an employer does not satisfy an employee's career demands, the employee has more options to move to another organization. It is vital that an employer keeps the knowledge worker engaged, by providing an environment in which he or she can evolve and is rewarded for the knowledge he or she provides in the organization. People want to be rewarded for their added value, which stems from the contribution they can make in sharing their knowledge with others.

Cost-Cutting Environments

Organizations in the financial sector have to deal with increasing pressure from the outside environment. Financial results are very important; witness the malaise in the financial markets and the disillusion affecting technology and telecom businesses. This leads toward a stronger focus on short-term benefits and often to large, company-wide cost-cutting programs. KM programs have to respond to these trends. The focus should be on sharing best or better practices in order to gain more efficiency in a company's core processes.

Although KM is not new, the development of best practices is needed. The success of KM ultimately depends on its users and their enthusiasm and initiative. In practice, user indifference is the most common pitfall. Thus, users need to experience an added value in their work and be (formally) rewarded for knowledge usage and contributions. At the moment, most employees in the financial industry are rewarded for attaining their (financial) targets, and not for sharing valuable knowledge. In many cases, KM is viewed to be extra work.

Fear is also a common problem. Some people stick to the paradigm *knowledge is power* and refuse to participate actively and share experiences, ideas, and insights. But knowledge kept to oneself quickly becomes useless. Also, many managers fear that by sharing their knowledge and encouraging their employees to do so, they lose control of the flow of information and thereby their power. Perhaps the rise of this type of manager depends heavily on their role in KM activities (as laid out in their job description), reward structures, and strong boardroom support. Only when you exchange knowledge with others can you be of influence. There is a need to accept the fact that sharing of knowledge is power.

Virtual Communities

Virtual communities can be thought of as a digital environment in which people gather to exchange knowledge, experiences, and ideas relating to a common interest. Virtual communities have radically changed the nature of traditional ideas of communication within groups of people. They overcome time and place barriers and synthesize the benefits of the codification (knowledge is made explicit in documents, databases, etc.) and personalization (knowledge is shared through a person-to-person interaction) approaches to managing knowledge.

Virtual communities are organic by nature; they are born, grown, and eventually die. These processes are highly intertwined with and reflect the development of the social networks that use the virtual communities. These networks don't necessarily have to follow organizational structures. In fact, they tend to encompass people from different (functional) departments at different echelons, and change in composition over time. A key characteristic of virtual communities is that they *mold* themselves to the dynamics of these social networks. Thus, unlike traditional meetings, they don't impose a rigid structure on the interaction in terms of subject (which topics are most important?), participants (who may/can participate?), location (which place is convenient for most people?), and time (what time is convenient for most people?).

Benefits of Virtual Communities

The fact that virtual communities tear down organizational time and place barriers doesn't mean that they will be immediately successful. It is equally possible to lose money and work in an inefficient manner when these barriers have been removed. When starting an initiative, it is important to consider the achievements and goals the community needs to fulfill.

Exchanging best or better practices will make employees more aware of processes performed in other parts of the organization. Large financial conglomerates in particular can benefit from this. Internationally dispersed managers in the same line of business are able to learn from each other, while constant reinvention of the wheel is prevented. Incorporating this form of knowledge exchange in their way of doing business will lead to more efficient and effective processes and synergy.

An interesting aspect of communities is their ability to combine knowledge in organizations across borders, or even with suppliers or customers. Through this combination of knowledge, areas of the company can gain new insights into the development of products and markets, and in securing new customers. Depending on the strategy and position a company is in, it can choose to implement virtual communities to cut costs or to develop a new business (or, even better, both).

The benefit of virtual communities lies in their ability to ease the transition associated with mergers and acquisitions (see Chapter 8). In the financial industry, integration programs do not always result in a stronger organization, and the effects of former mergers can still be felt a long way down the line. Old cultures remain and people are often afraid to socialize and break down the barriers between them. By bringing these people together, based on their field of expertise and interest, these barriers can be overcome. At the same time, knowledge gaps in the new organization will be quickly revealed, and the necessary knowledge developed to plug these holes.

Although virtual communities are based on a technological platform, because of their organic and social nature, critical success factors are also found in broader organizational and cultural dimensions. These dimensions are intimately related to each other, resulting in a complex web of interdependent issues. A multidisciplinary team is therefore needed, with technical, managerial, and social skills, to make successful implementation possible. Special attention should be applied to the following sections.

Tool Selection

Implementing the right tool to do the job involves a deep analysis of the expected size, usage, and growth of the community to prevent a mismatch between the needed and actual tool properties. Also, the tool chosen should be easy to implement on the existing IT platform of the organization (dedicated servers, available bandwidth, integration with knowledge bases or CRM tools, etc). Heavy involvement from the IT department is therefore necessary. In addition, the selection of the desired functionalities of the community, such as e-mail notification of new entries, anonymous access, and chat options are also important. A clear understanding of management and user expectations and needs is always necessary.

Cultural Dimension

The residing culture (the attitude and atmosphere) should support the transition of social to virtual, informal networks. To respect the latent and sometimes fragile structure of informal networks, there has to be an environment in which KM initiatives are valued and encouraged. Clear management support and a strong managerial vision are therefore keys. If these conditions are satisfied, and the value of KM is clear, bottom-up community initiatives with a sufficient social basis will emerge, or can be initiated in co-operation with enthusiastic employees.

Key Learnings

The following are key learnings gained from this chapter:

- To realize the full potential of KM at financial institutions, break up existing data silos and deploy the tools necessary to capture; access; and share data, information, and knowledge accurately, efficiently, and in real-time, across the organization. Leveraging a KM framework as depicted in the brokerage organization and banking KM frameworks (Figures 10.1 and 10.4) will provide the basis for implementing the necessary systems.

■ In this era of knowledge intensification and global competition, we believe virtual communities are excellent enablers of knowledge sharing and creation, within and between organizations, to the point that they can become a key source of competitive advantage in the financial industry. However, organizations often fail in successfully implementing KM programs, usually due to a failure to integrate them fully with business activities, and the fact that KM is seen as an additional *chore* rather than a core process. A cultural change is often necessary to facilitate the implementation of KM and the use of virtual communities.

Tips and Techniques

The following are some tips and techniques that can be applied from this chapter:

■ A key to successful implementation of KM is to incorporate the principle supported by both the brokerage institution and banking KM models.

■ A key ingredient of delivering knowledge effectively is to establish the core principle of connect, collect, catalog, store, use/reuse, learn, and create, which contributes to growing intelligently reusable knowledge that supports product and service innovation.

■ It is important to consider what a community will bring to its users and the business as a whole before jumping right in. Try to facilitate bottom-up thinking and create a knowledge-sharing atmosphere instead of forcing KM solutions upon the organization.

■ In your KM offerings, provide self-service options by establishing the ability for consumers to access information, get answers, and complete basic tasks without your assistance.

Chapter 11

"Are You in Good Hands?": Knowledge Management in Insurance

Conveying a consistent message to the customer base, which is supported by consistent and up-to-date knowledge, is essential to servicing the needs of both customer and customer service representatives (CSRs) (which is an extension of your insurance organization). Knowledge management (KM) will play a key role in servicing customers and CSRs in a consistent manner. Developing and executing processes and communication aimed at capturing, cataloging, and delivering content (information and knowledge) are keys to producing positive results. However, we must understand that it is the human element of KM, and the positive impact that KM has on the efficacy and attitudes of customers, CSRs, and business executives that will deliver quantifiable business benefits to insurance companies today.

Specifically, investments in facilitating a knowledge culture can directly enhance an insurer's business performance by improving the experiences of four core constituencies: customers, agents, and executives. The primary goal of sustaining business through attracting and retaining more customers has three categories: focusing on customers, managing the business effectively, and developing your knowledge workers. The following depicts how KM will align with the insurance company's corporate goals and objectives.

Insurance Business Challenges

Knowledge drain: One of the primary challenges being faced by insurance companies today is the high turnover of employees, CSRs, brokers, and other third-party assessors. When they leave, they take with them the wealth of knowledge acquired as a result of their association with the organization. This results in lower productivity as the onboarding time for new hires is high.

Lack of structured information: Most insurance companies collect a huge amount of content (information and knowledge). Usually this content is collected in silos as part of employees' ongoing activities. This unstructured information leads to loss of knowledge, as it is not shared with people who need it.

Diverse markets: The Asian market is very complex, in the sense that each of the markets has their own set of business processes. Some are mature whereas some are emerging; some are well regulated whereas some are open. A global insurance company will have to leverage their knowledge framework to streamline processes across the market to achieve operational efficiency.

Lack of a sound knowledge platform: Currently, the industry does not have a robust knowledge platform, which can be used to promote a knowledge culture within the organization. With the outburst of emerging technology platforms, there is a huge opportunity for insurance organizations to apply these and build an innovative knowledge framework.

This chapter centers on how insurance companies should be leveraging KM to address the needs of customer, call center, underwriting claims, and the knowledge workers employed by the insurance company (talent management).

Focusing on Customers

KM through its knowledge processes/architecture, governance, and technical guidance will be the catalyst in delivering a consistent customer experience by delivering knowledge and responding to the customer in a consistent voice and message no matter where the insurance company engages with the customer (contact centers, CSRs, mobile or Web) or with what media (online chat, e-mail, postal service, help center, and/or frequently asked questions [FAQs]).

Managing the Business Effectively

KM will enable all key decisions and governance regarding knowledge. This includes the capturing, cataloging, storing, availability, and maintenance of all knowledge assets. In support of managing the business effectively, KM will manage the knowledge assets of the insurance company to:

- Provide full visibility to knowledge in all areas.
- Capture and disseminate key decisions.
- Synchronize knowledge enterprise-wide.
- Enable collaboration between all knowledge and key knowledge holders.
- Enable common, enterprise-wide knowledge processes.
- Establish holistic governance and taxonomy.
- Form solid foundation to build continuing KM maturity.

Managing knowledge and achieving competitive advantages are the ingredients of success for today's insurance companies. Knowledge has been perceived to be a key corporate asset in terms of increasing a firm's competitiveness, corresponding to the organization's ability to act intelligently to sustain its long-term competitive advantages via developing, building, and organizing its knowledge assets. This is relevant within insurance companies because the key business consideration of managing risk in this industry is through client relationships. Insurance companies could achieve competitive advantage if they manage knowledge pertaining to service quality and performance.

An organization's employees are relatively proficient at interpreting knowledge within a broader context, which includes combining knowledge with other types of information and synthesizing various unstructured forms of knowledge (Davenport and Prusak, 2002). The employees in the insurance industry play an important role in the business performance, and their cooperation, attitude, and empowerment could be important in determining whether their companies are ready for KM initiatives or not.

Insurance Call Center

In a call center, customers are assigned to CSRs by routing policies that seek to balance several objectives. Usually, these policies follow myopic rules in order to minimize the waiting time or maximize the quality experienced by each customer. However, there is a secondary effect of the routing assignment: by learning-on-the-job, the development of the CSRs' expertise depends on the calls they take.

A major influence on a customer's satisfaction at a call center is the knowledge level of the CSR who takes their call. KM, in particular maintaining or increasing the cumulative knowledge of the CSRs, is therefore a key issue for ensuring service quality. This is especially true when the call center operates within dynamic markets, and CSRs are required to keep pace with trends and advances.

KM has a number of practical tools and strategies for meeting this challenge, and call center managers have much to gain by implementing KM principles.

As indicated in Dimension Data's 2015 Global Contact Centre Benchmarking Report, a call center is confronted with a number of considerable challenges.

A call center is confronted with a number of considerable challenges:

- Potentially wide range of customer enquiries
- Legal accountability for information provided to customers
- Customers expect "instant" answers to questions
- High-stress work environment for call center operators
- High staff turnover
- Large and complex body of knowledge to be learned by new staff
- Constant pressure to reduce call handling times
- Continuous tracking and assessment of efficiency measures

Inbound centers have an average annual turnover of 26% for full-time representatives and 33% for part-timers.

Benefits of KM to Call Centers

In meeting these challenges, KM has the potential to deliver some (or all) of these benefits:

- Reduced training time and costs for new staff
- Improved call handling and response times
- Increased staff satisfaction and morale
- Greater consistency and accuracy of information provided to customers
- Greater flexibility in handling changing business processes, products, and information
- Fewer calls to second-level support or the help desk

Applying KM to Call Centers

There are two aspects to KM that must be covered in a call center:

- Efficient processes must be put in place to ensure that the right knowledge is captured, managed, and kept up-to-date.
- KM systems must be established to support these processes. These IT systems are the core of a KM-based call center.

Meeting both these areas will ensure that you have the resources in place to support frontline staff, and the processes to maximize their value. However, more important than any IT system you may implement is the knowledge itself. Identify the knowledge your tier 1 staff and customers require, and accumulate it. Once you have the raw information, shape this into a structured and usable knowledge repository. Only then will you be in a position to deliver a complete KM solution.

Spend the necessary time to identify the actual data, information, and knowledge requirements of your customers and staff. This will ensure that you get the maximum benefit out of building your center's knowledge resources.

There are a number of practical ways of identifying information needs:

- Talk to both experienced and novice staff, to find out their requirements first-hand.
- Conduct an information review of the resources currently available (both online and on paper).
- Survey both call center staff and customers (if possible).
- Talk to business and product representatives, to identify the areas they would like highlighted to customers.
- Examine the daily activities of frontline staff to identify key information needs.
- Analyze call logs and other statistics to find out areas of customer interest or confusion.
- Identify the typical questions and problems addressed by the help desk or second-level support.
- Evaluate whether sufficient documentation exists for frontline IT systems.

The end product of these efforts should be a long list of comprehensive call center KM requirements. This list must be prioritized and implemented as part of delivering the KM system.

Structure Your Knowledge

It is surprising how often businesses spend considerable time and money building online knowledge bases, only to discover that staff can't work out how to use them.

Effective structure and navigation leveraging sound information architecture (IA) principles (see section "Information Architecture" in Chapter 4) is critical to the success of a knowledge base. Without this, staff will not be able to find required knowledge during the limited duration of a customer's call.

Take these practical steps:

- Involve staff throughout the design process, to ensure that their needs are identified.
- Develop prototypes for new KM systems, and test these with real users.
- Apply IA principles and methods to all information repositories. This will determine appropriate groupings, menu items, and navigation.
- Use card sorting to determine structure, to identify any missed categories (see section "Card Sorting" in Chapter 4).

Up to a third of any KM project should be spend designing and testing. Without this, the risks of developing a solution that does not meet your center's needs are much higher.

Ensure Knowledge Is Accurate and Up-to-Date

Customer queries often relate to recent changes or product releases. The call center must therefore be supported by up-to-date knowledge on these areas. This is typically done by following a comprehensive knowledge governance process.

Call center operators must also be able to access the knowledge repositories and be confident that the knowledge provided is both accurate and current. With a customer on the line, there is no time for double-checking against other information sources.

If your staff does not trust the KM systems, they will rapidly find other sources, such as hand-written notes, or photocopied "cheat sheets." There are a number of practical steps you can take to ensure information accuracy:

- Put in place a permanent team to create and update content.
- Establish communication channels with the sources of new information (policy groups, business units, etc.).
- Ensure that updating the call center knowledge base is part of the "sign off" requirements for business development.
- Provide a simple mechanism for frontline staff to report errors and omissions

Ensure that your staff is fully trained to use KM systems and processes. Make sure they are aware of the full range of information that is available to them.

Knowledge Repository

One such KM system focused on call centers is a knowledge repository. The knowledge repositories in a call center are the primary (or sole) source of information provided to your customers. As such, they warrant a substantial amount of effort to ensure that they are both useful, and used.

Although this may be considered a large system effort, the payoff justifies the benefits that can be realized. A knowledge repository will help to reduce call handling times, and increase the consistency of knowledge provided to customers. Call center staffs typically have only a minute to find the information requested by their customer. Under this pressure, it is critical that staffs have effective and efficient ways of locating answers.

A well-designed search engine is a necessary first step toward meeting this goal. Spend time designing and configuring the search engine: It must be simple to use, but still return a useful set of results. A search engine does not deliver the complete solution. It is also important to provide staff with structured and meaningful browsing and navigation methods. This ranges from ensuring the correct items are on the main menu, to creating related links between pages. All of this must be supported with comprehensive metadata, such as title, description, and keywords. These combine to increase the effectiveness of both searching and browsing.

Integrate Customer Relationship Management and KM systems

Customer relationship management (CRM) systems are all about knowing your customers, and their needs.

This ties in closely with the operation of your KM systems:

- Demographic information about your customers will allow you to ensure that the right information is in your knowledge repository.
- Tracking customer queries is an excellent way of identifying FAQs.
- These FAQs should be easily available from within the CRM, to facilitate rapid responses.
- Information in KM systems should be broken down according to customer groupings in the CRM software.
- Escalation from the CRM system should be closely tied in with KM processes.
- Usage statistics gathered from the knowledge repository provide an indication of the "hot topics" for customers. This is a valuable source of information for CRM activities.

Integrate Help Desk and KM Systems

Most help desks and second-level support teams are equipped with "call logging" systems, which track the status of the reported problems and issues. In conjunction with this, a repository of common problems and resolutions should be developed. (This may already be provided as part of the call logging software.)

This reduces the amount of knowledge the help desk staffs have to "keep in their heads" (tacit knowledge). It also helps to ensure that consistent responses are provided to frontline staff. This repository is also an excellent source of frontline information. Distil the most common problems, write these up as procedures or workarounds, and provide them to frontline staff. Such information will reduce the number of "simple" calls to the help desk, which eases the workload, and allows help desk staff to concentrate on the more difficult cases.

Integrate Interactive Voice Response and KM Systems

Most phone queues are now fronted with an interactive voice response (IVR) system. These may simply direct incoming callers to an appropriate phone queue, or provide sophisticated phone transaction systems.

Integrate the IVR with your center's KM systems:

- Ensure that information provided via the IVR is consistent with the details in your information repository.
- Gather detailed breakdowns on the usage of the IVR. This will tell you the areas your customers are interested in.
- Document the exact script of the IVR for call center staff. This will assist them to manage a clean handover when they answer calls.

IVR systems are normally only the first step in the customers' interaction with a call center, and they must be managed as such. There must be consistency across all methods of information delivery.

Customer-Facing Resources

Many call centers now respond to online and e-mail queries, in addition to phone calls. With this broadened responsibility, call centers must manage the additional workload.

The call center knowledge repository can be used in a number of practical ways:

- Publish a selection of customer questions (FAQs) to the website.
- Ensure online sales and product information are accurate and comprehensive. This will reduce the number of calls in these areas.
- Develop "standard responses" to a range of common e-mail or website queries. Products even exist that will analyze incoming e-mails, and automatically select appropriate responses.

It is important that the information provided to customers is drawn out of the same repository used by call center staff (also known as "single sourcing"). In this way, duplication is reduced and errors are avoided. Maintenance efforts are similarly reduced.

Insurance KM Model

The insurance KM Model (see Figure 11.1) depicts the various stages of knowledge and the areas within an insurance organization that must leverage knowledge in order to effectively and efficiently execute their tasks. The following describes each element of the insurance KM model:

Connect: This part of the model focuses on determining what knowledge exists, where the knowledge is located, and who are the holders or authoritative voice(s) for your organization's knowledge. Executing a content/knowledge audit is a method for determining this. This audit focuses on those activities that are concerned with understanding what knowledge is needed to support all business areas within the insurance organization.

Collect: Once the knowledge has been identified, it must be gathered in one central location. If any gaps exist in the knowledge, new knowledge must be captured or created. This will be accomplished through leveraging consistent guidelines and templates for the specific knowledge being created.

Catalog: This part of the model focuses on categorization and organization of knowledge. Designing and constructing a taxonomy to determine the structure in which the knowledge will be categorized and stored is the major activity in this part of the model. Once this categorization is designed, it will be implemented within the specified knowledge repository.

Use/reuse: This part of the model will focus on the ability to find and leverage knowledge across the organization. Accessing the knowledge via the identification, design, and implementation of filters based on keywords and synonyms will be incorporated here.

Enrich: This part of the model focuses on maintainability and sustainability of knowledge within the designated repository. The governance plan will be a key input into the maintainability and sustainability of all knowledge through the continuous review, update, and archiving of outdated knowledge.

Share: This part of the model focuses on incorporating those mechanisms necessary to exchange knowledge between all employees and business areas within the insurance organization. This is accomplished by creating environments and opportunities to exchange (transfer) knowledge. Once new knowledge is gathered, it must then become part of the "corporate knowledge base" and follow the continuous flow of the knowledge life cycle as identified in the insurance KM model.

Underwriting

Emerging technologies such as discussion databases, document management, Internet search capabilities, case-based reasoning, rule-based systems, data mining, and neural networks are powerful tools that can improve organizational communications and decision-making performance. To be effective however, technology must be aligned with and support the human and selected management practices of the organization.

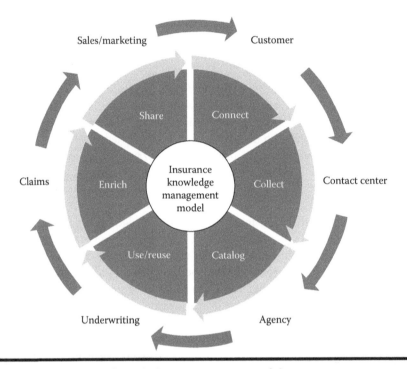

Figure 11.1 Insurance knowledge management model.

KM utilizes these management practices and emerging technologies to support the human art and management science of underwriting. Underwriters are expected to analyze and price risks to meet customers' needs for risk management, while containing loss within acceptable levels to assure adequate cash flow and return on premium.

Underwriters ask questions, gather information, analyze data, and leverage the knowledge and experience of the organization to make decisions. The higher the probability or potential size of loss, the more questions, information, data, knowledge and experience involved in the underwriting decision-making process.

Technology is used in varying degrees to support the risk assessment and pricing processes within each segment of the insurance industry. The more simple or straightforward the decision-making process, the more automated it has become.

The initial underwriting of individual term life insurance, personal auto insurance and other standardized commodity products has been largely automated through the use of rule-based or risk-scoring technologies. In these situations, underwriting is becoming increasingly more of a science that automates the explicit knowledge of the frontline professional.

As the probability or size of loss increases, so does the complexity of the decision-making process. The underwriting of group life and health, long-term disability, and commercial property and casualty risks require more complex and situational-based analysis best left to the judgment of the underwriter. KM focuses on providing underwriters with the information, data, and tools they need to accurately assess risk and make better and faster decisions. Frontline professionals rely on two primary methods for making complex decisions.

First, they try to relate the current case to similar situations they have dealt with in the past. For example, a commercial property underwriter evaluating the submission of a hotel will rely on his or her previous experience with this class of business to begin and conduct the underwriting process. The more experience the underwriter has, the more sensitive he or she will be to the cues that help evaluate the probability of risk.

With the second method, if the submission, in whole or in part, is unfamiliar to anything the underwriter has previously handled, he or she begins to look for components of the risk that present problems or issues that can be solved. These components act as recognition footholds to support a deeper analysis of the account.

In either case, experts tend to ask more questions, use more information, and conduct more implicit and explicit analysis than their less experienced counterparts—and they do it in less time as well. KM can help organizations evaluate complex risks through the review of the decision-making processes used by expert professionals.

What questions do experts ask? What information and data do they use? What analyses do they conduct? What outcomes do they consider? When and how do they access and use knowledge and expertise—both within and outside the organization? These cognitive tasks determine context and timing for content delivery to support the frontline professional.

Once completed, the analysis provides the key business requirements for the design, development, and integration of information system capabilities to support the frontline underwriter. Finally, KM system solutions need to be easy to use. They must integrate relevant mainframe, client-server, and Web technologies, and their disparate data types, through a common user interface that supports the capture and use of the knowledge and experience of the organization as a normal part of the decision-making process.

KM can deliver significant short-term cycle-time and productivity improvements through "just-in-time" access and delivery of information, data, analytical tools, and knowledge to frontline underwriters.

Claims

Insurance companies often have to validate claim information and enter it manually before even starting the adjudication process. Delays are constant. Multiple priorities must be balanced, including regulatory compliance, fraudulent claim detection, invalid claim identification, and customer service. In order to best serve all of these goals at once, processes must be optimized and paired with technology designed to support a streamlined claims experience.

We can provide our wealth of domain expertise in insurance, process management, and technology to provide your company with the following benefits:

- Reduced claims delays through streamlined processes
- Fewer claims errors
- Improved communication and access to information about claim status for higher customer satisfaction
- Reduced operational costs through process improvements and automated decision making
- Enhanced compliance with regulations such as Sarbanes–Oxley Act, Health Insurance Portability and Accountability Act, and the PATRIOT Act
- Better fraud detection through advanced identification and analysis of abnormal patterns
- Decreased erroneous claims payments
- Reduced paper processes (and associated duplication and inefficient use of labor)

Big Data. Big Data. Big Data. Yeah … so what? What does Big Data have to do with insurers? Just think about it. You sift and search and sort an incredible amount of data—adjusters' hand-written notes, data from fraud lists and the information from claims management systems, and the National Insurance Crime Bureau (NICB) claims database. Are you getting the most from that data?

With so many claims to handle, your adjusters don't have time to sift through all of that data to evaluate each claim. But they may not make the best decision if they miss a valuable piece of information. That means many of their decisions are based on experience, gut feeling and the limited information that is readily at hand.

For this reason—and many others—Big Data analytics is playing an increasingly important role in the insurance business. Working alongside adjusters, analytics can flag claims for closer inspection, priority handling, and more. Here are six areas where analytics can make a big difference:

Fraud: One out of 10 insurance claims is fraudulent. How do you spot those before a hefty payout is made? Most fraud solutions on the market today are rules-based. Unfortunately, it is too easy for fraudsters to manipulate and get around the rules. Predictive analysis, on the other hand, uses a combination of rules, modeling, text mining, database searches, and exception reporting to identify fraud sooner and more effectively at each stage of the claims cycle.

Subrogation: Opportunities for subrogation often get lost in the sheer volume of data—most of it in the form of police records, adjuster notes, and medical records. Text analytics searches through this unstructured data to find phrases that typically indicate a subrogation case. By pinpointing subrogation opportunities earlier, you can maximize loss recovery while reducing loss expenses.

Settlement: To lower costs and ensure fairness, insurers often implement fast-track processes that settle claims instantly. But settling a claim on-the-fly can be costly if you overpay. Any insurer who has seen a rash of home payments in an area hit by natural disaster knows how that works. By analyzing claims and claim histories, you can optimize the limits for instant payouts. Analytics can also shorten claims cycle times for higher customer satisfaction and reduced labor costs. It also ensures significant savings on things such as rental cars for auto repair claims.

Loss reserve: When a claim is first reported, it is nearly impossible to predict its size and duration. But accurate loss reserving and claims forecasting is essential, especially in long-tail claims such as liability and workers' compensation. Analytics can more accurately calculate loss reserve by comparing a loss with similar claims. Then, whenever the claims data is updated, analytics can reassess the loss reserve, so you understand exactly how much money you need on hand to meet future claims.

Activity: It makes sense to put your more experienced adjusters on the most complex claims. But claims are usually assigned based on limited data—resulting in high reassignment rates that effect claim duration, settlement amounts, and ultimately, the customer experience. Data mining techniques cluster and group loss characteristics to score, prioritize, and assign claims to the most appropriate adjuster based on experience and loss type. In some cases, claims can even be automatically adjudicated and settled.

Litigation: A significant portion of a company's loss adjustment expense ratio goes to defending disputed claims. Insurers can use analytics to calculate a litigation propensity score to determine which claims are more likely to result in litigation. You can then assign those claims to more senior adjusters who are more likely to be able to settle the claims sooner and for a lower amount.

Why make analytics a part of your claims processing? As insurance becomes a commodity, it becomes more important for carriers to differentiate themselves. Adding analytics to the claims life cycle can deliver a measurable ROI with cost savings. Just a 1% improvement in the loss ratio for a $1 billion insurer is worth more than $7 million on the bottom line.

Developing Your Knowledge Workers

Both public and private sector organizations are struggling with knowledge loss resulting from employee turnover. Moreover, costs of recruiting, of lost productivity, and training to replace employees can reach huge values. Capturing knowledge inside an organization seems to be one of the main purposes of a KM professional. In the insurance industry, trade secrets, confidential information, and valuable ideas are part of the workforce knowledge. Recruiting, selecting, training, and managing insurance CSRs constitute a real challenge for insurance companies all over the world, and a sensitive ethics-related issue is the case of insurance CSRs leaving their employer, in order to transfer to a competitor insurance company, while trying to take along as many clients as possible from the old employer.

KM will provide the mechanisms, policies, procedures, and governance to facilitate associate collaboration, knowledge sharing (lunch-n-learn, knowledge café, and communities of practice), knowledge transfer, associate enrichment through focus training and learning (instructor lead, workshops, web or computer based). KM will provide the strategy and processes to capture and disseminate tacit and explicit knowledge from employees to be shared across the organization, which will support organizational learning and evolve the company and its associates into a lifelong learning community and organization.

Talent Management

The focus here is about addressing the specific needs of the insurance company employee. In Chapter 6, a broader perspective on talent management was detailed. Talent management must address the business costs and the impact of employee turnover. Employee turnover can be grouped in four main categories:

■ Costs due to a person leaving (other employees must fill in for the person leaving; the lost productivity of the employee; the cost of training the company has provided; the cost of lost knowledge, skills, and contacts; and the cost of lost customers the departing employee is taking with him).

■ Hiring costs (costs associated with identifying, recruiting, selecting, and hiring a replacement, such as advertising, Internet posting, costs in terms of time spent arranging the interviews, or calling references). These costs also translate into lost productivity.

■ Training costs (the replacement person's orientation, product knowledge, industry knowledge, and on the job training).

■ Lost productivity costs (the new employee will go through a few stages before becoming fully productive; his supervisor will spend time guiding him or her and correcting his or her potential mistakes).

■ Given that companies are increasingly gaining competitive advantages from intellectual assets rather than physical assets, organizations that do not implement effective knowledge capturing strategies will face difficulties.

Role of Technology

The role of technology as it pertains to KM is that of a facilitator and enabler. Technology enables the capture, catalog, and dissemination of knowledge to occur. Technology facilitates the use/reuse of knowledge assets across the organization.

This is true for all organizations, including insurance companies, when leveraging KM. The following provides awareness into a few technology platforms that help insurance organizations achieve knowledge creation, storage distribution and most importantly, knowledge application.

> *Content management and IA*: Enterprise Content Management (ECM) and tools are used to capture, categorize, save, and supply relevant content related to organizational processes. ECM/IA tools are also needed to automate processes involving workflows, document management, along with taxonomy and meta-data management. The content and collaboration strategies would remain ineffective in the absence of a good content management system. Thus, ECM/IA should be seen as a foundation to KM rather than an enabler. ECM/IA solutions will lead to higher process efficiency in areas such as new business, underwriting, and claims.
>
> *Collaboration*: Essentially, KM is a collaborative effort. An assortment of collaboration technologies such as cloud and SharePoint can be used to support KM practices in insurance organizations. They allow people to send secure emails, share artifacts, participate in discussions, blog, web conference, and perform secure instant messaging, thereby supporting collective learning. A typical example would be a CSR collaboration platform, which would allow CSRs to collaborate more easily with all the stakeholders. Mobile technologies and social media have also seen unprecedented reach, adoption, and impact. Social media can help insurers promote collaboration among CSRs, brokers, and customers, while mobility could empower CSRs with information anytime, anywhere, and on any device.
>
> *E-learning*: In national, global, and/or multicultural insurance organizations, there is a huge amount of information present across multiple locations and languages. There is a need for on-the-job training to enhance knowledge and skill bases, thereby avoiding re-inventing the wheel. E-learning platforms are proving to be a reliable solution to this. These platforms could be used by insurance brokers to enhance their knowledge and skills. Through such courses, insurance organizations can develop a cost-effective way to onboard qualified/certified CSRs in their field force. E-learning platforms are also being extensively used to render "application—knowledge transfer applications" to business users using the IT application.

Insurance Knowledge Management Systems Framework

The insurance knowledge management systems (IKMS) framework (see Figure 11.2 depicts the majority of the areas in which knowledge has to be enabled and/or facilitated within an insurance organization. The following describes each element of the IKMS framework:

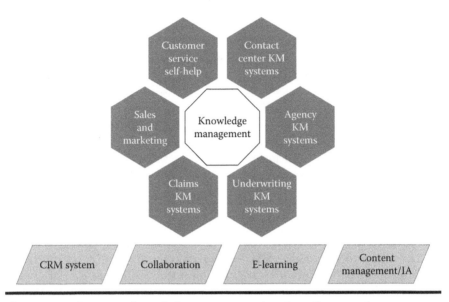

Figure 11.2   Insurance knowledge management systems framework.

Customer service self-help: Establish FAQs, knowledge articles, and other self-help content in order for customers to solve issues without needing customer service assistance. Providing answers to questions efficiently, effectively, and in a consistent manner is the main purpose here. This is accomplished by providing standardized internal processes and knowledge results for faster resolution.

Contact center KM systems: Establish a contact center-centric KM system that delivers consumable knowledge that can be communicated to customers succinctly over the phone, chat, and/or e-mail. The type of knowledge will consist of primarily knowledge articles, procedures, and job-aids. Specific escalation from first-level support through third-level support should also be established.

Agency KM systems: Provides CSRs and CSR office staffs with the necessary knowledge to enable the ability to educate and consult with customers in order to facilitate the transaction of purchasing insurance products. This environment will also provide the ability to point out appropriate coverage and gaps therein as well.

Underwriting KM Systems

The underwriting KM functionality will provide the underwriter with the following:

■ *Risk selection*: Enable the underwriter to decide whether to accept a particular risk or not. It involves securing factual information from the applicant, evaluating that information, and deciding on a course of action.

- *Classification and rating*: Enable the underwriter to classify and rate the policy. Several tentative classifications are usually assigned before a final decision on classifying the risk is reached. Insurers may have their own classification and rating system, or they may obtain a system from a rating bureau.
- *Policy forms*: The underwriter will leverage the necessary knowledge to determine the acceptability of an applicant and assigning the proper classification and rating; the underwriter is ready to issue an insurance policy. The underwriter functionality of the KM system will assist in identifying the different types of policies available as well as recommending modifications to fit the needs of the applicant.
- *Retention and reinsurance*: The underwriting function of the KM system will enable the underwriter to protect the company from undue financial strain by retaining only a certain portion of the risk and securing reinsurance for the remainder of the risk.

Claims KM Systems

The claims KM functionality will provide the following:

Settling claims: Settling insurance claims is just one aspect of the claims management process. The claims KM functionality will provide the necessary knowledge to the claims processors to timely process a claim by

- *Detecting fraud*: Claims KM functionality will provide underwriting guidelines, examine payment history, and evaluate trends in claim payoffs to help insurance companies detect fraud.
- *Lowering costs*: Claims KM functionality will provide improved efficiency by decreasing the number of claim errors, detecting fraud early, and reducing the time it takes to process and settle a claim.
- *Avoiding litigation*: Claims KM functionality will provide knowledge to quickly settle a claim and avoid the chances for litigation and provide accurate liability assessment.

Sales and Marketing

KM for sales and marketing will provide improved operational efficiency by reducing time to market for new product launching; more effectively enhance insurance products by modifying and/or adding new features; target specific customers/ markets with campaigns that are effective and more likely to increase revenue; make specific sales and marketing data, information and knowledge available that includes historical data and processes to make accurate forecasts.

CRM System

Integration of your KM system with your organizations CRM system will enable knowledge about customers to be directly tied to specific customer data. This integration will improve services for customers; prioritize customers using their purchase history, which allows a company to delineate which customers are most important and target most of their efforts toward; and see and know the customer's complete history, which will enable employees to review customer history and allow them to analyze customer activity that will aid in selling more product or service to that customer.

Collaboration

Collaboration is a key benefit of any KM system. Integration with your organization's collaboration tools/environment with social media will empower your organization to tap into the voice of the customer. This integration will enable your organization to establish a better relationship with your customer by responding quickly to issues, and to launch products and services that tie directly to customer needs and being proactive about sharing pertinent news about your organization.

E-Learning

Integration of your KM system with your organization's e-learning platform will address specific knowledge gaps your employees are experiencing and tie them directly to training and learning opportunities that will fill those gaps. The e-learning platform integrated with KM will improve training event management (i.e., scheduling and tracking), skills and competencies management, skill gap analysis, and delivering of an individual development plan.

Content Management/IA

Integration of your KM system with your organization's content management system powered by IA will provide all content (information and knowledge) with a consistent organization structure, labeling, descriptive elements (metadata), and consistent (improved) search experience.

Key Learnings

The following are key learnings from this chapter:

■ Experience has shown that the use of a KM system is maximized by incorporating it into the initial training provided to the new staff. In this way, it becomes the "default" way of resolving problems, and finding answers. (For further information on KM adoption, refer to Chapter 17.)

Take these practical steps to ensure information accuracy:

■ Establish a permanent team to create and update content.
■ Establish communication channels with the sources of new information (policy groups, business units, etc.).
■ Ensure that updating the call center knowledgebase is part of the "sign off" requirements for business development.
■ Provide a simple mechanism for frontline staff to report errors and omissions.
■ IVR systems are normally only the first step in the customers' interaction with a call center, and they must be managed as such. All call center interaction with the customer must be consistent across all methods of information delivery.

Tips and Techniques

The following are some of the tips and techniques that are deduced from this chapter:

■ Up to a third of any KM project should be spent designing and testing. Without this, the risks of developing a solution that does not meet your call center's needs are much higher.
■ Once you have the raw information, shape this into a structured and usable knowledge repository. But remember that your organization is legally accountable for every piece of information provided to customers.
■ It is important that the information provided to customers is drawn out of the same repository used by call center staff (also known as "single sourcing"). In this way, duplication is reduced, and errors avoided. Maintenance efforts are similarly reduced.

Chapter 12

"Sign Right Here!": Knowledge Management in the Legal Profession

Knowledge management (KM) is becoming more prevalent within law firms as well as legal departments, as the practice of KM has become more mature. KM policies, procedures, techniques, and technologies have been proven in other industries to the point where legal entities are taking notice. As with all applications of KM in other industries, KM in law firms will vary from firm to firm and from lawyer to lawyer. This chapter will focus on KM in the management of law firms and legal practitioners, specifically in the following areas: training lawyers (talent management), legal project management (LPM), legal research, precedent/case law, client support, competitive intelligence (CI), and governance of law firm knowledge assets.

In March 2012, I discussed in a blog post that KM in law firms centers on client relationships and understanding the clients' legal needs. These needs can range from but are not limited to litigation, intellectual property, criminal, divorce, and bankruptcy (Rhem, 2012). In understanding what a client needs, the law firm partner has to determine who would be the best (lawyer/lawyers) to address specific needs of the client and how they can effectively and efficiently handle these needs. Therefore, knowledge around servicing the client would be a good start for a legal KM strategy to focus. The legal KM strategy should address the knowledge needs, processes, initiatives, and tools that will increase the performance of the staff and provide outstanding services and increase revenue of the firm (Rhem, 2012). The legal KM strategy should incorporate specific KM drivers to insure that KM is adopted and sustained within the firm.

KM Drivers for Legal Professionals and Firms

In order for KM to take hold and be adopted across the firm, there are several drivers that will lead to law firms incorporating KM into the organization. The KM drivers for legal professionals and firms include the following:

- *Cost pressures*: KM can be used to work more efficiently to meet client demands and become more cost-effective with the various services being provided.
- *Efficiency and consistency*: KM (through explicit knowledge capture) will produce standard and consistent forms, templates, processes, and procedures to become more efficient in delivering services to clients.
- *Flexibility and responsiveness*: KM (through incorporating expertise locators as an example) will facilitate flexibility and responsiveness to client needs by assigning the "right resources (lawyers) at the right time in the right way to address the particular need(s) of clients."
- *Training and learning*: KM (in particular, by implementing knowledge transfer, sharing, collaboration processes, policies, and tools) will create an atmosphere where lawyers can learn from each other, share best practices, and provide practical training for inexperienced associates.
- *Retention (people and knowledge)*: Successful KM practices, policies, and tools will create an environment where all staff will experience enrichment through collaboration and sharing. In addition, expertise management will foster lawyers being assigned to cases where their expertise can be best leveraged, and this will foster an environment where the retention of staff is high. Establishing a knowledge portal will enable individual knowledge to be captured and included as part of the corporate knowledge base, where it can be accessed across the firm, and this will facilitate the retention of the firm's knowledge.
- *Workplace satisfaction*: Establishing KM to address retention of people and the accessibility of knowledge contributes greatly toward workplace satisfaction. Fostering an environment where you are rewarding employees for sharing knowledge and open communication for collaboration will continue to enrich the workplace.

Some of the benefits KM has for legal professionals and firms are as follows:

- The ability through expertise locators to quickly build teams to address cases and client situations
- The ability through search engine optimization techniques (taxonomies, ontology, and associated information architectures for legal information and knowledge objects) to improve retrieval of case history, enable associations of related cases and rulings, as well as locate knowledge resources (subject matter experts) based on knowledge objects that are retrieved

- The ability to share, collaborate, and store communication around intellectual capital
- The ability to mentor and cross-train new, associate, and experienced lawyers
- The ability to manage and expand the talent and experiences of lawyers in the firm
- The ability to infuse KM in managing law firms
- The ability to reuse internally developed knowledge assets such as precedents, letters, research findings, and case history information

Knowledge capture and transfer to prepare the law firm for when partners and/ or associates leave the firm, infusing knowledge sharing to continue building the expertise of the firm, and improving learning through lessons learned, assessments, and continual process improvement for better client service are all valuable assets that KM will impart to the firm.

This chapter focuses on how law firms manage their vast array of explicit and tacit knowledge. It also examines how law firms are leveraging precedent development, legal research, talent management, expertise locator, LPM, and client support, all in relation to instituting KM within their legal institutions to provide the law firm with a distinct advantage over its competitors.

Talent Management in Law Firms

As stated in Chapter 6, infusing a human capital/talent management strategy with KM that includes knowledge capture, knowledge cataloging and reuse, knowledge sharing, and connecting expertise throughout your organization will improve the talents of your people and increase the organizational competency. This section will explore lawyer training and expertise locators to improve performance and align the right knowledge to the right task(s).

Lawyer/Legal Staff Training

KM will provide law firms with the mechanisms to manage the development of and access to core practice content. In this capacity, KM will supplement lawyer training by providing access to knowledge relating to internal memoranda on practice legal issues and practice process checklists; identifying work product precedents (exemplar documents); providing knowledge about internal and external firm publications, presentations, and training; detailing results from legal knowledge projects and systems in the assigned practice area(s); as well as providing access to legal knowledge bases and repositories.

It is important that lawyers new to the firm are trained and mentored to use the firm's relevant knowledge tools (if they exist) and information resources. An effort to coordinate with peers in other practice areas to exchange best practices regarding knowledge resources, including monitoring and sharing practitioner's recent, relevant legal developments and current market practice developments and trends, is another essential aspect of KM, providing a holistic approach to speed up new lawyers and thereby taking less time to become productive.

Not only is the training for lawyers important, but the training for all legal staff on the management of the law firm is also important. Essential to that training is access to mentors and knowledge in order to become productive quickly by supporting the needs of the lawyers. The following are details concerning the evolution of the legal support staff due to technology and access to knowledge tools and information resources.

Legal Secretaries/Legal Assistants/Paralegals

The increase in use of laptops, smartphones, and tablets in law firms allows attorneys to work independently anywhere, anytime. These devices are just a few of the technological advancements that have vastly affected legal secretaries' duties. Younger tech-savvy attorneys type their own correspondence and use smart devices to carry out their day-to-day duties. This decrease in traditional clerical duties is causing a major change in the role and the necessary knowledge needed to be a legal secretary.

Legal secretaries, who once supported one or two attorneys, are now often supporting many more as well as performing many more duties, such that they are now being retitled as "legal assistants." These legal assistant positions represent a new transitional opportunity that can be leveraged to entice a new generation of entry-level college-degree workers into the legal profession.

The role of the paralegal is also evolving into that of the legal assistant due to the mobility and access that technology has created. Technology has enabled the ability to achieve more than normal, access legal knowledge repositories whenever and wherever required, share knowledge, and support multiple lawyers. Legal assistants in many firms are now performing legal research. This requires that a legal assistant know precisely where to go for any necessary information. Because of this, today most firms have discarded their books in favor of online services such as Westlaw and Lexis for legal research as well as utilizing other Internet resources. This allows a legal assistant to perform the research in less than half the time, and with this faster technology, the answer is often expected within minutes.

Another major change in the role of legal assistants involves the handling of discovery. Paralegals play a critical role in assisting attorneys with discovery. They help manage the discovery process, especially when large volumes of documents are involved. These are no longer paper documents; instead, through the use of document, content, and KM software, discovery documents and associated knowledge are stored, providing easy access.

Therefore, the traditional role of a legal assistant has transformed into a more tech-savvy one, and paralegals are now training and working with IT personnel to assist in managing the discovery process. The knowledge necessary to perform in this role requires familiarity with document, content, and KM software and state and federal e-discovery rules, and they must be able to coordinate with outside litigation support vendors. As a result, the evolution of technology has created a new legal support staff member who merges the skills of a paralegal and a computer specialist into a legal technology specialist.

Legal Technology Specialist

A legal technology specialist provides technical support for large e-discovery projects, document production, and document reviews. He or she requires not only advanced knowledge of document, content, and KM software but also a thorough understanding of federal and state rules of civil procedure.

It is because of technology and the access provided to legal information through document, content, and KM software that law firms need to begin to reclassify and create new job descriptions, duties, and titles to better reflect the support staff's actual responsibilities. This will trickle down to providing not only the necessary training but also the necessary reorganization to deliver the best client services.

Law firm business model must produce increased profits through greater efficiency from decreased revenues. This model demands a strong team of knowledgeable, resourceful, and talented professionals. Having access to the firm's corporate knowledge will enable that to happen.

Expertise Locators

An expertise locator is a system that is intended to be used to connect people to others whose expertise (capabilities) are needed. This system includes tools and techniques that allow for identification of who has the expertise on a certain topic(s). The seeker of an expert can expect to accrue the benefits of accessing one or more experts from a pool of talent within the organization.

It is often said that "we don't know what we know," and at an organizational level, this can be extended to mean "we don't know who knows what." If you were to ask someone if they know who has expertise about a certain topic, they will probably be able to name a few people. But ask them to name more than five people in the organization who have this expertise and they will likely struggle to list the names of these individuals. The expertise locator will look up the available expertise within the organization, when solving a problem, rather than rediscovering what someone has done already.

The expertise locator (see Figure 12.1) can be used not only for fields of expertise but for any way of classifying and tagging (see section on "Metadata" in Chapter 4) user profiles that are useful to your organization. Each different type of expertise or

Figure 12.1 Expertise locator example.

attribute that you wish to use can be added as a custom field to users' profile pages. The unique type of custom field used for this purpose is called a "tag custom field." The benefit of these tag custom fields is that the tags associated with them are used to identify only the people, not content. This challenge of finding experts is an issue across all industries. Most companies have systems that identify and classify experts using some sort of searchable directory or database that includes a description of the person's role and the team he or she belongs to, but these systems have limited functionality.

These kinds of tools are needed when we are considering assembling a team with certain expertise that is needed to address a problem. This capability is essential in putting a team of lawyers together in order to address a client's legal issue. Locating experts is often a time-consuming and tedious process. An expertise locator will reduce the time needed to put the right team together and contribute in facilitating reducing costs and gaining efficiencies for clients.

However, there are some disparagements around expertise locators. One is that the method identifies the knowledge at the individual level and does not capture the knowledge of groups or teams. Another is criticism about the notion of "the expert" itself, as the level of "expert" is really limited to a very few people. One solution to this issue is to identify in the expertise locator a person's capabilities and fields of experience and associate the person to actual content within your knowledge base such as briefings authored or other project documentation, as opposed to just identifying capabilities.

The benefit of these tag custom fields is that the tags associated with them are used to identify only the people, not content. For example, a regular tag called "Criminal Law" can be applied to pages, profiles, groups, or any other type of content. So selecting this as a search facet would return results of all kinds. But if "Criminal Law" is added to a tag custom field on users' profiles, selecting it as a search facet will narrow your search down to only the people with the expertise that you are looking for!

Legal Project Management

LPM focuses on leveraging the application and concepts of project management in order to control and manage the business of providing legal services. Law firms working under fee arrangements such as fixed or flat fees, cost limits, and success bonuses are commonly utilizing project management. Project management (see section on "Software Methodologies" in Chapter 2) will provide management of schedule, risk, and cost in a more rigorous and structured manner. LPM is becoming standard practice for law departments and firms using hourly billing as they are faced with the need to be more efficient in the delivery of legal services.

LPM can be an effective tool for improving efficiency in the delivery of legal services. LPM techniques can help identify best practices for scoping a matter, effectively communicating across the team, managing a budget, and monitoring progress. However, to realize these benefits, the lawyers will have to buy-in and realize benefits from this right away. A best practice would be to start with a pilot with a few lawyers in order to demonstrate the value of LPM and to achieve a quick win. Once some level of buy-in has been accomplished, continue implementing the LPM practice, capturing and applying lessons learned along the way.

Palomaki and Wagner (2011; [emphasis added]) have indicated 10 aspects of what they found instrumental in getting lawyers to buy into LPM inside a law firm and they are listed below:

1. *Embrace it, lawyers know everything*: Many lawyers will rightfully rebel against the notion that PM training is teaching them something new. PM includes skills and techniques that most lawyers currently know and use. Acknowledging that the attorneys already possess the basic skills and that PM techniques merely provide more structure around what they are already doing, is key to gaining attorneys' buy-in. And, if you talk to the lawyers about a time they have exceeded budget and had to explain it to a client that can be a good starting point for helping them identify what they can do better to avoid that conversation in the future.

2. *Consider a bottom-up approach*: Many of the firms who are on the path to PM have taken a top-down approach. It is no surprise that the "Do it because I said so" method is ineffective. Rather than dictating a one-size-fits-all tactic, consider starting with individual client or project teams. In order to help improve efficiencies, first identify what the inefficiencies are. All lawyers are not inefficient in the same way, and neither is the solution to help them. Training on a team level and helping individual teams analyze the way they work will be more effective and more successful—one team at a time.

3. *KISS (Keep it simple, stupid)*: Lawyers hate non-legal training, and if you make them attend training that is longer than 90 minutes, they get **really** cranky. Instead of trying to cram all that could be taught into 90 minutes or forcing our lawyers to submit to daylong sessions, we found it more effective to develop training programs that are unique and specific to the individual teams on just those areas in which that team wants help. By approaching the training this way, our lawyers really hone in on the areas where they want to focus. They don't learn everything, but they learn what they want to know, they use it and they get results. Then, they come back for more.

4. *Encourage debate*: We hired an outside consultant to jump-start Sutherland's PM initiative. Throughout the training course, the consultant both anticipated and enjoyed the debates that occurred during the session and was able to use those discussions to emphasize key points on many concepts. We learned that our lawyers got the most out of PM training when we opened up the discussion and encouraged them to debate the concepts and best practices. Our lawyers fiercely debated the appropriate time to talk to clients about a change in scope, how much to involve associates in the overall project plan, what the best practices are for team meetings and communication, and how to share a post-project review with the team. And, as is usually the case in the law, there is no right answer. The "right" answer is team, practice and client specific. What works for one team may not work for the other. The most critical piece is that the team and the client are on the same page. Listen to the debate, and you will be better positioned to help your lawyers where they need it most.

5. *Do ONE thing better*: Every lawyer, every practice, every client, and every team has different strengths and weaknesses. Still, there is always *one* thing the team can do better. Encourage everyone to be involved in identifying inefficiencies, our team members have ownership in the solution, and everyone works together to improve the process.

6. *Talk about task codes*: Task codes can be a sticking point for project management efforts in law firms. The codes are intended to systematically categorize legal work by grouping relevant tasks for a matter. Executed correctly, the codes can provide a platform for tracking the scope and budget of a matter based on task (e.g., case assessment, pre-trial pleadings, discovery, trial preparation). Task codes can also provide historical data that allows for better budget forecasting. There can be a few challenges with using task codes, however. Using codes requires the lawyers to know and

understand how to segment their time without overlap and all team members must use the codes consistently. Without consistent standards and definitions, the data that results is "garbage in, garbage out." Our approach is to let the client's objectives dictate how task codes will be used and then to implement them for the specific team.

7. *Follow up and reward success*: Once a team has identified an inefficiency, how will you know if they have improved? Following up with them at regular intervals—a couple of weeks, 30 days, and so on—will ensure everyone stays motivated. Ask them how they are progressing. Did the solution work the way they thought it would? Has improving one area created a more inefficient process somewhere else? Have they developed a best practice that can be shared with another team doing similar work? In addition to following up, recognizing success is essential. Make sure firm management is aware of the progress the team is making. Helping the lawyers along the way and promoting them internally when they succeed helps everyone achieve their client goals.

8. *Be resourceful*: An area for improvement we identified was better sharing of resources. In conjunction with our KM initiative, we are working with teams and individual lawyers to pool the resources they use repeatedly, making them easily accessible to anyone who may need them. We are identifying various templates and tools considered to be "best practices" and making them available in our KM system. Sharing across the firm helps everyone do a better job for their clients.

9. *Use technology*: When we began the PM initiative, none of the available software products had been fully tested. Since we had the capabilities internally to create our own tool, we took the "build it yourself" approach. We knew we wanted a platform that would help our lawyers better track the progress on matter scope and budgets, ensuring there were no surprises for the client at the end of the month. We also knew we wanted the flexibility to customize the platform for each client or individual matter.

10. *Include your clients!* By conducting client feedback interviews proved by far the most effective tool we have to hear what clients really think about our firm and its services. Clients want the best service possible, and they want to help their favorite outside counsel be the best they can be.

The practice of LPM varies from law-firm-specific practices to corporate law entities when it comes to the approach to legal work. In recent years, clients have begun demanding more alternative fee arrangements, greater predictability, improved accountability, and, above all, cost containment from their law firms (Palomaki and Wagner, 2011). Project management (specifically LPM) is a disciplined, systematic, task-based approach to work process that can provide law firms with some key tools to respond to client demands. The knowledge that is gained and reused in the LPM paradigm is essential to gaining efficiencies and the cost containment that law firms and legal entities are looking for.

KM in LPM

Knowledge is generated throughout the execution of a project. KM within projects is intended to make relevant knowledge available to the project team throughout the execution of the project. Project management methodologies usually define standard project phases, processes, templates, or actions that are repeated in the course of different projects.

The LPM execution addresses why the project idea exists, the problem(s) it is addressing, the products or the deliverables of the project, who will take part in the project, and how will people working on the project be organized, as well as the project location and deadlines. KM as a part of the LPM process will document and share decisions and assumptions regarding resources, timelines, quality requirements, and costs. KM will also document and share domain knowledge: knowledge about the industry, technology, processes, current situation, business products, and services (i.e., the software development life cycle); institutional knowledge: knowledge that a project team or member has about the organization (i.e., organization structure and reporting structure); and process knowledge: knowledge about the project tasks, methodologies, timelines, structure, deliverables, and processes (i.e., project plan), as well as sharing and transferring knowledge through mentoring and lessons learned (which are documented after every phase and at the end of the project).

According to Lisa Kellar Gianakos, director of KM at Pillsbury Winthrop Shaw Pittman and the author of *The Intersection of Knowledge and Legal Project Management* (2013, p. 1), "KM professionals understand the process of law practice, project management, finance, and technology. They also tend to be analytical and logical thinkers. Furthermore, in many firms the KM professionals have already built bridges to both lawyers and multiple staff departments. Since LPM is a collaborative effort, those bridges turn out to be very important in the difficult LPM change management process" (Gianakos, 2013).

Gianakos also quotes Toby Brown. Brown is a well-known LPM evangelist with a strong history in KM. "In his keynote on the Economics of Law and the Future of KM, he discussed why, for KM to remain a vital function for firms, it needs to be focused on solving the core challenges facing firms" (Gianakos, 2013, p. 1). KM applied to LPM is one of the vehicles for KM to remain in front of law firms in the foreseeable future. The project development life cycle enables many traditional KM goals to become closely aligned with those of LPM (cultivating efficiencies, delivering better predictability, and improving communications and processes). It is with this understanding that KM enables project team members to reduce rework and squeezes the time that it takes to plan project execution. Sharing lessons learned and advanced practices is key to helping others excel in the LPM process and execution.

Legal Research

This section is not intended to provide an examination of legal research tools that are available to legal professionals and law firms. It is intended, however, to examine the role that legal research and the access to its resources plays in the overall KM within law firms and for legal professionals.

In order to understand where to find the right content that is buried deep within your firm's thousands of research repositories and outside sources (such as WestLawNext®, LexisNexis®, and VersusLaw®) and understand who in the firm has a deep knowledge of specific content, in addition to wondering if what you have in your repositories are up-to-date and relevant, you quickly realize that KM is a challenge! Multiply that by the number of trial and appellate briefs, memoranda, pleadings, depositions, e-mails, letters, and spreadsheets prepared by inside and outside counsel alike and the challenge becomes even more daunting. Without incorporating KM, your firm runs the risk of paying for research over and over again.

During the early years of a lawyer's career, research and document drafting are the predominant professional activities that are being performed. Legal research tools and sources are key resources to assist the early stage lawyers in performing their tasks. The tools of legal research are considered KM tools that help legal professionals locate the knowledge and analysis previously written by judges, expert scholars, and lawyers for adaptation and use in the context presented by a current client. LexisNexis research tools that include citation tools, treatises by authors and competitive publishers, as well as integrated search functionality are all delivered to the legal researchers via laptops, tablets, and other mobile devices (Staudt, 2003).

Legal research tools benefit users by helping them improve their research speed and accuracy and enable a precision of collaboration, which the combination of research resources and tools makes possible. Realizing the benefits that the various legal research tools bring to the law firm will depend in large measure on the current structure of the firm's internal data and on the past and future ability of the firm's data infrastructure to insure that the firm data is of very high quality. A brief synopsis of three popular legal research platforms, namely WestLawNext, LexisNexis, and VersusLaw, are presented subsequently.

WestLawNext

WestLawNext (see Figure 12.2) provides an authoritative content (primary law and exclusive secondary law titles), attorney-editor expertise, with access to primary law, analytical materials, practice area insights, litigation resources, public records, and

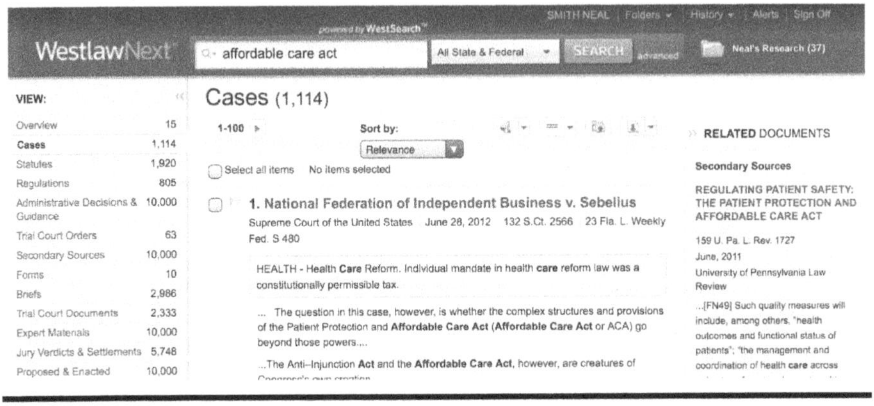

Figure 12.2   WestLawNext Legal Research Platform.

more. This platform enables users to build a legal research page that's ideal for the way you work, through organizing your favorite content and legal research tools. It also provides access to legal encyclopedias, treatises, legal periodicals, and law reviews that provide well-reasoned statements of the law.

LexisNexis

LexisNexis (see Figure 12.3) is a global provider of content-enabled workflow solutions, and is designed specifically for professionals in the legal, risk management, corporate, government, law enforcement, accounting, and academic markets. This platform originally pioneered online information with its Lexis® and Nexis®

Figure 12.3   LexisNexis® Legal Research Platform.

services. It is part of RELX Group (London, UK) and serves customers in more than 100 countries, with more than 15,000 employees worldwide.

LexisNexis provides an integration of information and technology. It unites proprietary brands, advanced web technologies, and premium information sources. Across the globe, LexisNexis provides customers with access to billions of searchable documents and records from more than 45,000 legal, news, and business sources. LexisNexis encompasses authoritative legal-publishing brands, dating back to the nineteenth century, including Butterworths® in the United Kingdom, Canada, and the Asia-Pacific region; Les Editions du Juris Classeur in France; and Matthew Bender® worldwide.

VersusLaw

VersusLaw (see Figure 12.4) was founded in 1985 as Timeline Publishing Company (Minneapolis, MN). The company's focus was originally to provide the legal community with accurate, current, and in-depth information, exclusively on one topic: professional liability. The company created a monthly journal on legal ethics titled *Lawyers Liability Review (LLR)* and published the first issue in February 1986.

In the early 1990s, Timeline began the electronic collection and distribution of court opinions and other primary research materials. Timeline was an early adopter of the Internet, and in August 1995, it was among the first web-based legal content providers, carrying opinions from the US Supreme Court, the Federal Circuit Courts of Appeals, and State appellate courts. Reflecting a new direction and the company's commitment to electronic distribution of legal research materials, in 1996, Timeline Publishing changed its name to VersusLaw, Inc. and launched a new website devoted exclusively to the distribution of primary materials to the legal profession.

Today, VersusLaw continues to broaden its focus and mission: to provide all legal practitioners access to current, in-depth, easy-to-use legal research, regardless of the size of their firms, by using the power of technology.

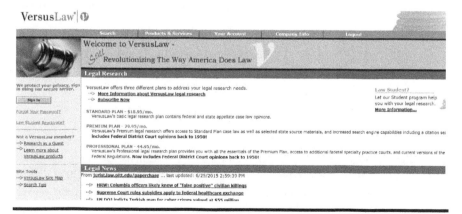

Figure 12.4   VersusLaw® Legal Research Platform.

Precedent/Case Law Knowledge

An essential part of any law firm's legal research knowledge base is having access to precedent case law information. Having access to judicial precedent/case law information and incorporating that knowledge within the overall KM infrastructure are essential for law firm performance.

Enabling access to previous judicial decisions or proceedings must be relied upon for future similar cases. This is an important part of any law firm's knowledge base because all courts are bound to follow decisions made by courts higher than themselves in the hierarchy, and all appellate courts are usually bound by their own previous decisions. This supports the idea of fairness and certainty throughout the courts. However, precedent can only stand if the reason for the decision is known, so at the end of a case a judgment is given. This is what creates the precedent for judges to follow in future cases.

The value of a case law knowledge base is that the law can be adapted to situations that were not contemplated by the legislature. With hundreds of cases being decided every day, having a knowledge base with access to this knowledge will enable the law firm to keep up with relevant decisions. It is not unusual for several courts to be deciding cases on the same subject at the same time, with no good way to coordinate their opinions. Frequently, the courts will reach different conclusions about the law.

A companion knowledge base to include is the civil law system. In civil law, the legislatures pass very specific statutes, and these are applied by the courts. Each judge who decides a case looks to the statute, rather than the previous cases, for guidance. The judges' decisions (or interpretations, where they are free to reinterpret the statute as necessary to fit the facts of the specific case) are an excellent source of knowledge for any law firm involved in civil cases. Another important note is that civil law judges do try to ensure some consistency in the application of the law by taking into consideration previous court decisions, further strengthening the reason for having both case law and civil law knowledge sources.

In some instances, law firms can positively increase their visibility through publishing their own case decisions that contribute to setting a precedence (legal questions of first impression).

Legal KM and Client Support

The differentiators between law firms and legal practitioners are the intangibles, and one such intangible is true client care and service. In a Forbes 2014 article, Micah Solomon indicates that creating true client loyalty is one of the most powerful and reliable ways to build a strategic, sustainable advantage for your (law) practice and that truly loyal clients are less price sensitive, more willing to forgive your small foibles, and largely immune to competitive entreaties from the firm across the street or across the continent (Solomon, 2014).

Client support specifically focuses on dramatically improving the client experience. It is the expectation of all clients that legal professionals and law firms will provide high-quality legal services, and it's the promise and demonstration of high-quality legal services that are the intangibles that will set the firm apart.

KM plays a key role in ensuring a high level of client support. KM staffs operate smoothly between lawyers and a range of operational functions—ideally situated to increase intra-firm collaboration, communication, and understanding. Some KM programs have worked on operations for some time, but business conditions are now ripe for more extensive applications of KM to firm operations—arguably critical to keeping operational teams relevant and law firms profitable.

KM in law firms provides the ability to identify and provide business process and technology solutions to improve the business and increase profitability. Establishing KM groups in firm operations to facilitate collaboration and knowledge transfer within the operation functions of the firm is another area where KM can be applied. LPM (detailed earlier in this chapter) focuses on what the client needs and structures a cohesive plan to deliver client-specific services in the most expeditious and cost-effective manner. In addition, KM can be leverage to standardize the onboarding process across the firm delivering consistent role-based knowledge (see section on "Role-Based Knowledge" in Chapter 6) to legal professionals based on their role and job functions at the firm. KM will also provide process mapping, help understanding workflow and critical touch points, and enhance the handling of the flow of knowledge throughout the firm.

Competitive Intelligence

As law firms mature in their use of knowledge and KM, incorporating the use of CI to gain an advantage when serving clients is a logical next or synergistic next step. KM and CI are about the process of gathering actionable knowledge on the law firms' competitive landscape. CI essentially means understanding and learning what's happening in the world outside your business, so you can be as competitive as possible. It means learning as much as possible—as soon as possible—about your industry in general and your competitors.

CI is the process of collecting and analyzing information about competitors' strengths and weaknesses in a legal and ethical manner to enhance business decision making. CI activities can be basically grouped into two main types: (1) tactical, which is shorter term and seeks to provide input into issues such as capturing market share or increasing revenues, and (2) strategic, which focuses on longer term issues such as key risks and opportunities facing the enterprise. CI is different from corporate or industrial espionage, which uses illegal and unethical methods to gain an unfair competitive advantage.

KM infuses CI strategy through centering on a firm's ability to expand relationships with clients and make faster and more informed decisions that help enhance the firm's thought leadership position. CI initiatives leveraging KM will aid in the intelligence-gathering process, empowering practice group initiatives, while elevating the firm to the role of a trusted advisor providing knowledge of industry trends, legislation, litigation, and other legal precedents.

Ann Lee Gibson states that although CI is indeed based on information, it is created only when that information is analyzed, refined, and distilled into something that has very clear implications for decision making. It offers the most benefits to firms where important decisions and actions are being considered, particularly the kinds with big upsides and downsides. In these settings, CI can significantly reduce risk.

KM Architecture in Law Firms

To realize the potential that KM offers to law firms, a holistic KM architecture should be implemented. A KM architecture that includes the aspects of legal KM, presented in this chapter, provides the roadmap and consistent structure for implementing KM in law firms (see Figure 12.5). The development of communities of practice, blogs, and wikis' knowledge repositories of work products (i.e., forms, letters, and factums) needs a holistic KM system approach. Just incorporating a document management and/or enterprise content management system does not incorporate necessary key KM capabilities (i.e., collaboration and expertise locator). In addition, implementing workflow is important for managing the flow of knowledge and to execute the governance of digital assets to insure they are kept relevant, accessible, and up to date.

Information Architecture

Information architecture through the implementation of an understanding of content relationships, taxonomies, and metadata (see Chapter 4) will improve retrieval of case history and enable associations of related cases and rulings, including locating knowledge resources (SMEs) needed for specific cases.

Creating/Modifying Taxonomy

The core benefit of KM is the ability to classify, retain, and find critical knowledge. Navigation, taxonomy, and search are important for long-term adoption and success of KM, because they are the framework by which users find the information they are looking for when they do not know where it is located. If

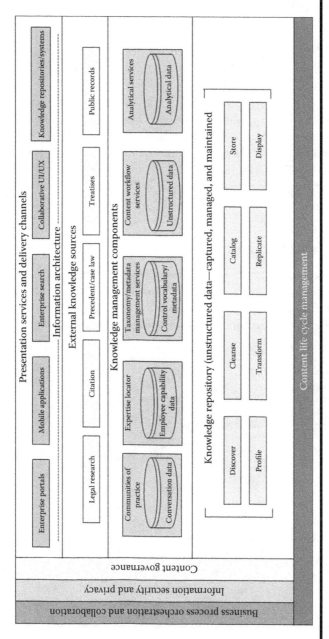

Figure 12.5   Law firm knowledge management architecture—(Sample).

users are unable to find the content they need, the value to the user is almost entirely lost. The KM taxonomy can be changed based on recommendation of the knowledge architect.

Creating/Modifying/Managing Metadata

Requests for Metadata Changes

Any user may suggest metadata changes. The knowledge architect administrator is solely authorized to raise a request for metadata changes. This request needs to be vetted and approved before moving ahead. Metadata reuse is highly recommended. This means that metadata values should be enforced during the artifact creation/check-in processes within the KM. It also means that determining metadata values should not be a "one system/silo" view of values. Critical metadata values will reflect the overall information architecture.

Governance of Law Firm Knowledge

KM governance ensures policy adherence and successful capture, cataloging, reuse, monitoring, managing, and maintaining of explicit knowledge of the firm (see Figure 12.6). The KM governance plan describes the policies, procedures, roles, and responsibilities as it pertains to explicit knowledge. Effective governance planning

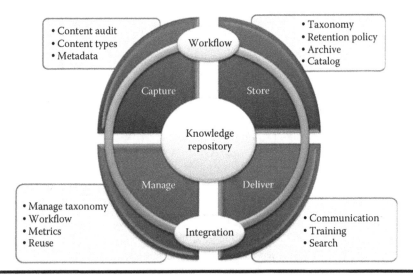

Figure 12.6 **Information architecture view of areas for knowledge management governance.**

and the application of the governance plan are critical for the ongoing success of the managing and maintaining of explicit knowledge.

The KM governance plan will establish the processes and policies to

- Avoid explicit knowledge proliferation.
- Ensure explicit knowledge is maintained by implementing quality management policies.
- Establish clear decision-making authority and escalation procedures, so that policy deviations are managed and conflicts are resolved quickly.
- Ensure the solution strategy is aligned with business objectives so it continuously delivers business value.
- Ensure explicit knowledge is retained in compliance with KM guidelines.

Benefits of Governance

The following are some of the benefits of governance:

- It provides an enterprise-wide common infrastructure for all explicit knowledge.
- It provides more reliable and relevant search.
- It ensures that the explicit knowledge, taxonomy, and metadata schema remain relevant to its users.
- It employs best practices to improve usability.
- It lowers total cost of information/content development and management through increased efficiencies throughout the KM life cycle.

Policies and Standards

Policies define rules for use; standards describe best practices. From a governance perspective, policies are usually driven by statutory, regulatory, or organizational requirements. Users are expected to meet policies without deviation. These standards are established to encourage consistent practices.

Governing Information Architecture

Information architecture must be governed in order to ensure that

- It is implemented and maintained.
- It meets the regulatory requirements, privacy needs, and security goals of the enterprise.
- It meets an organization's business goals. A well-designed and governed information architecture can multiply that organization's effectiveness.

Enforcing Metadata Quality

Metadata quality in the repository is a direct reflection on the effectiveness of knowledge that is attainable now and in the future. The governance plan will indicate what should be measured to determine the effectiveness of metadata by evaluating number of artifacts without metadata, metadata reuse, watching search relevancy, seeking inputs from users, and proactive monitoring.

Archiving—Record Retention Governance

The various content (information and knowledge) repositories are locations for valued artifacts. Often, the various sites used to contain the content must not only contain the current content but also the content that has expired. A policy should be put in place to remove the archived content from search results and to retain based on the company retention policy. The KM governance policy should align with the current record retention policy of the firm.

Governing Content

The governing of knowledge content must leverage the following best practices:

- Use workflows and approval for content centers and site pages wherever official content is stored.
- Use version history and version control to maintain a history and the authoritative source of the content.
- Audit, manage, and maintain content repositories according to the content life-cycle management.
- Use site usage confirmation and deletion to manage site collection life cycles.
- Identify important corporate assets and sites that contain personally identifiable information to be sure that they are properly secured and audited.
- Integrate the information architecture with the environment's search strategy. Take advantage of enterprise search features such as people search, content sources, and connectors for external content.

Governing KM Effectiveness

Assessing Value with Metrics

Measuring effectiveness is a key component of governance and thus included here. Metrics are a component to measuring overall adequacy and effectiveness of the KM tool. Initial rollout of KM will take some time across the first business area(s). Experience shows even then that adoption takes time. Measurements at the beginning, middle (during adoption), and end (fully matured) can be different.

Search—Tuning and Optimization

Site owners/administrators should constantly observe and evaluate effectiveness of search results. Site administrators/owners oftentimes can get the "Search Query and Search Result" reports from the search tools administrator periodically (every two weeks). From these reports, they can analyze the type of keywords users are searching for and the sites from which most of the search queries are coming. Based on this, site administrators/owners can "tune" the search for their sites. If any newly added metadata column needs to be available in advanced search filters, then the search administrator will ensure this metadata is configured.

Key Learnings

The following are some key learnings from this chapter:

- A support structure to adopt when considering restructuring the law firm management office is to leverage collaborative teams consisting of partners, associates, paralegals, legal assistants, and legal technology specialists, all dedicated to performing the necessary tasks to provide quality services to clients and to ensure that the firm is running in a highly efficient and cost-effective manner.
- Training programs must be established to assist all law firm management team members to retool and shift their thinking and approach to work in a more technologically advanced and collaborative law firm.
- A best practice for instituting LPM is to start with a pilot with a few lawyers in order to demonstrate the value of LPM and to achieve a quick win.
- When considering implementing governance, institute a comprehensive KM governance process to ensure the monitoring, managing, and maintenance of your legal/law firm knowledge. This will contribute greatly to keeping this knowledge relevant and up to date.
- For LPM to be successful, understanding your law firm's culture as well as applying Palomaki and Wagner's 10 aspects in getting lawyers to buy into LPM will be a key ingredient to the success of implementing LPM.

Tips and Techniques

The following are some tips and techniques deduced after reading this chapter:

- When considering incorporating KM with the law firm/law practice, begin with the benefits that KM can bring.
- Identify the key benefits and align them to the KM drivers to facilitate the adoption of KM at the law firm.

■ The use of technology is changing the way law firms operate and the way legal professionals work. Acquiring the right technical personnel to assist in transitioning technology into the firm as well as providing the necessary training to all legal staff will facilitate adoption and proper use of technology (see section "TTF Model" in Chapter 16 for details on facilitating technology adoption).

■ Expertise locators are a great tool for streamlining the process of assigning the right legal resource to the right problem. Consider implementing an expertise locator; this will contribute to retaining clients and attracting new ones enabling the firm to resolve client issues and address client needs more succinctly.

Chapter 13

"A Mind Is a Terrible Thing to Waste!": Knowledge Management Education

As knowledge management (KM) challenges top the agenda of many CEOs (Yunginger, 2013), an emphasis on getting more value from corporate knowledge assets has heightened the interest in KM as a professional area of practice. Providing education in KM, which can include specialized courses, seminars, certifications, and formal undergraduate, graduate, and doctoral programs, is leading the way in preparing future KM practitioners to meet this challenge. On the other hand, it has also raised questions about the educational foundation needed to support the profession.

Despite the wealth of published and informal literature, although derived from practice, and dialog on the foundational learning needs of KM practitioners, there is no consensus on what comprises professional education and training in KM. In 2011, the Knowledge Management Education Forum (KMEF)—a collaboration between Kent State University and George Washington University—was formed.

> The mission of KMEF in part is to provide an ongoing, annual dialog to identify and grow consensus on the knowledge management body of knowledge, competencies, roles and curriculum. The goal of the KMEF is to create an environment in which a consensus can evolve. It brings together the current and past thought leaders in the field of

knowledge management to discuss their work and to open the dialog where others can contribute. (KMEF, 2011: http://kmatkent.cim3.net/wiki/Welcome)

Besides the educational options mentioned in section "KM education programs", KM education opportunities are occurring in KM-focused departments, which are delivering subject-specific education and strategic learning programs. All of these KM educational products must operate under one cohesive and holistic set of standards and policies in order to provide the KM practitioners with consistent industry-recognized education. According to the KMEF, a special effort will be needed to connect the various educational entities to the business community and vice versa, while providing "the core and elective elements of a knowledge management curriculum for the 21st century." (KMEF, 2011: http://kmatkent.cim3.net/wiki/Welcome)

While participating in the KMEF, it is generally recognized that

there is general agreement that KM, knowledge services, and knowledge strategy require, an understanding of shared concepts, a basic lexicon, and some level of mutual understanding about the elements and framework of KM, there continues to be concern that too much "standardization" might work against the success of KM in the workplace. (KMEF, 2011: http://kmatkent.cim3.net/wiki/Welcome)

As a KM practitioner who has worked (and continues to work) across various sectors and industries of the twenty-first-century "knowledge economy," I recognize that every organization is different and, therefore, the success of KM, knowledge services, and knowledge strategy in each is going to depend on how well the elements of KM align with the corporate objectives, unique management methodologies, and leadership structures of the various organizations implementing KM programs.

As KM education evolves for the twenty-first century and beyond, especially as the delivery of education and the workforce becomes more mobile, there is a need to establish a philosophy of teach-and-learn anywhere and anytime. This will facilitate the need to incorporate the following:

■ Standards for KM course design
■ Need to provide students (class participants) a practical way to apply KM
■ The delivery of technology that will facilitate the ability to teach and learn anywhere and anytime
■ Provide learning outcomes and assess them
■ An understanding of the various KM roles and responsibilities

This chapter will cover topics that include roles and responsibilities of knowledge professionals, educational needs of these professionals, core KM competencies, KM curriculum development and delivery, and KM education programs and teaching methodologies.

Roles and Responsibilities of Knowledge Professionals

The roles of knowledge professionals cover areas from strategic, tactical, program-related to executing specific projects and system development. The KM roles and responsibilities vary according to the category in which the knowledge professional works. The roles and responsibilities depicted here (see Table 13.1) consist of but are not limited to chief knowledge officer (CKO), KM program manager, KM project manager, KM director, operations KM director, KM author, KM lead, KM liaison, KM specialist, KM system administrator, knowledge engineer, knowledge architect, KM writer, knowledge manager, and KM analyst.

Core KM Competencies

In determining core KM competencies (see Table 13.1), we must first understand what it takes to perform in the various KM roles and execute their responsibilities. The KM core competencies include connecting education and strategic learning competencies with skill and ability in knowledge strategy development and operationalization, collaboration, leadership and management skills, in addition to technical competencies.

KM has both soft and hard competencies. The soft competencies include ensuring that knowledge processing is aligned with the organization's business goals and objectives and is integrated into the organization's everyday business and work. It also includes software development, business and systems architecture, and workflow management. The hard competencies include elicitation and representation of knowledge (both tacit and explicit) and structural knowledge in the form of business rules and business processes.

The KM Competency Model

KM focuses on people, process, and technology that enable and support knowledge sharing, transfer, access, and identification. KM competencies represent what KM practitioners must understand to facilitate KM methods established by the organization. A KM competency model (see Figure 13.1) reflects the strategies, goals, and objectives of an organization. Competency alone is not sufficient; it must be accompanied by a cultural shift in the organization toward knowledge sharing.

Table 13.1 KM Roles, Responsibilities, and Core Competencies

KM Role	Role Description	Responsibilities	Core Competencies
Chief knowledge officer (CKO)	The CKO is the executive leader of the KM discipline at the organization and key figure for all KM activities initiated from the KM program.	The CKO manages the knowledge sharing process at the organizational level; leads efforts to move the organization to knowledge centricity; requires dedication to KM principles, the ability to discuss the benefits of knowledge sharing, and the vision to ensure that KM initiatives are adopted by the organization; ensures that the best, relevant knowledge for the area of practice is accessible to all personnel and implements the knowledge sharing strategy in alignment with corporate guidelines; champions cross-organizational CoP; forms relationship with HR, IT/systems, organizational learning; establishes incentive programs for knowledge sharing and re-use; fosters cultural change; defines roles, skill sets, and opportunities for knowledge workers; and facilitates training and education of knowledge workers.	CKOs must have skills across a wide variety of areas. They must be good at developing/ understanding the big picture, advocacy (articulation, promotion, and justification of the knowledge agenda, sometimes against cynicism or even open hostility), project and people management (oversight of a variety of activities, attention to detail, ability to motivate), communications (communicating clearly the knowledge agenda, having good listening skills, and being sensitive to organizational opportunities and obstacles), leadership, team working, influencing, and interpersonal skills. The CKO who successfully combines these skills is well equipped as an excellent agent of change for his or her organization.

(Continued)

Table 13.1 (*Continued*) KM Roles, Responsibilities, and Core Competencies

KM Role	Role Description	Responsibilities	Core Competencies
KM program manager	The KM program manager orchestrates the activities of the KM program and approves the projects to be initiated.	The KM program manager is responsible for running KM programs and specific initiatives: • Ensures that all the KM projects follow the established KM Governance procedures • Undertakes strategy creation for contingency planning and risk mitigation • Responsible for planning and scheduling project goals, milestones, and deliverables • Defines requirements and plans the project life-cycle deployment • Defines resources for project and program implementation • Identifies and solves program issues effectively • Exhibits leadership qualities to define requirements and identify risks • Possesses organization, presentation, and customer service skills	The KM program manager must have capabilities in program management, strategy and planning, leading people and building teams, collaboration and partnerships, analysis and decision making, applying program knowledge, contract management and budgeting, and personal management. Also, KM, risk management, and project and process management competencies are needed.

(Continued)

Table 13.1 (*Continued*) KM Roles, Responsibilities, and Core Competencies

KM Role	Role Description	Responsibilities	Core Competencies
		• Reports the progress as well as the problems to assigned KM director, CKO, and/or other designated stakeholders	
KM director	The KM director oversees the KM efforts that pertain to their specific area of the organization. This includes efforts that are driven by the CKO as well as the KM program manager.	The KM director manages the KM strategy, governance, and processes at their specific area of the organization and leads efforts to move the organization to knowledge centricity by aligning efforts of KM to the overall enterprise KM strategy.	*Communication:* Ability to get consensus and collaboration across many business units; ability to explain complex concepts in layman's language; ability to generate enthusiasm; ability to communicate with all levels of management and staff. Establishing straightforward, productive relationships; treating all individuals with fairness and respect; demonstrating sensitivity for cultural and gender differences; showing great drive and commitment to the organization's mission; inspiring others; maintaining high standards of personal integrity

(*Continued*)

Table 13.1 (*Continued*) KM Roles, Responsibilities, and Core Competencies

KM Role	Role Description	Responsibilities	Core Competencies
			Client orientation: Understands clients' needs and concerns; responds promptly and effectively to client needs; customizes services and products as appropriate *Teamwork:* Collaborates with others in own unit and across boundaries; acknowledges others' contributions; works effectively with individuals of different culture and gender; willing to seek help as needed. Influencing and resolving differences across organizational boundaries; gaining support and commitment from others even without formal authority; resolving differences by determining needs and forging solutions that benefit all parties; promoting collaboration and facilitating teamwork across organizational boundaries

(Continued)

Table 13.1 (Continued) KM Roles, Responsibilities, and Core Competencies

KM Role	Role Description	Responsibilities	Core Competencies
			Learning and knowledge sharing: Open to new ideas; shares own knowledge; applies knowledge in daily work; builds partnerships for learning and knowledge sharing. *Analytical thinking and decisive judgment:* Analyzing issues and problems systematically; gathering broad and balanced inputs; drawing sound conclusions; and translating conclusions into timely decisions and actions
Operations KM director	The operations KM director oversees the efforts that pertain to operational KM area. This will include efforts that are driven by the KM program manager as it pertains to operations.	The operations KM director manages the KM strategy, governance, and processes at the operations KM program level and leads efforts to move the organization to knowledge centricity by aligning efforts of operations KM to the overall KM enterprise KM strategy.	Business experience in KM and IT and experience working with the following: • Budget management; leadership (experience in building, leading, managing, and setting the strategic direction of a team) • Strong understanding of client needs and client service

(Continued)

Table 13.1 (*Continued*) KM Roles, Responsibilities, and Core Competencies

KM Role	Role Description	Responsibilities	Core Competencies
			• Must be a responsible, self-motivated individual with strong communication/relationship management skills • Demonstrated track record of successful interactions with all levels within an organization, especially senior leaders • Demonstrated ability to work autonomously and in a team environment • Ability to build successful relationships • Team leadership and motivational skills • Organization and project management skills • Ability to multitask, manage competing priorities and conflicting agendas • Understanding of and experience with intranet and KM technologies

(Continued)

Table 13.1 (*Continued*) KM Roles, Responsibilities, and Core Competencies

KM Role	Role Description	Responsibilities	Core Competencies
			• Ability to use and adapt to new technologies and applications, as well as guide the team and our users in doing so as well • Generally understand IT development methodologies
KM project manager	The KM project manager oversees the overall direction, coordination, implementation, execution, control, and completion of specific KM and KM director-initiated projects ensuring consistency with KM program strategy, commitments, and goals.	The KM project manager is assigned to a designated KM director and is responsible for running KM projects: • Leads the planning and implementation of KM project • Facilitates the definition of project scope, goals, and deliverables • Defines project tasks and resource requirements • Develops full-scale project plans • Assembles and coordinates with project staff • Plans and schedules project timelines • Tracks project deliverables using appropriate tools • Provides direction and support to project team	The core competencies include KM, risk management, project and process management, financial management, planning and organization, communications. In addition, knowledge of utilizing professional, online communities for knowledge sharing and/or collaboration purposes is required. A proven record of excellent management, leadership, decision-making, and interpersonal skills is required along with strong analytical, written, and oral communication skills.

(Continued)

Table 13.1 (*Continued*) KM Roles, Responsibilities, and Core Competencies

KM Role	Role Description	Responsibilities	Core Competencies
		• Constantly monitors and reports on the progress of the project to KM director and all stakeholders • Presents reports defining project progress, problems, and solutions • Implements and manages project changes and interventions to achieve project outputs • Facilitates project evaluations and assessment of results	
Knowledge manager	Knowledge manager works with the KM program and/or project manager to implement KM initiatives.	The knowledge manager has the following responsibilities: • Manages KM efforts (often serves as a KM project manager or product owner) • Looks across KM processes to capture tacit and explicit knowledge • Balances technology, information, processes, and individual and organizational learning within a culture of shared values • Creates ways to maintain a sustainable competitive advantage	Knowledge managers should also have a general understanding of knowledge architecture, but do not need an in-depth knowledge Extensive experience and senior technical expertise in the field of KM or capacity development are required, preferably in an international development organization, with a proven track record of successfully delivering KM strategies. The knowledge manager should have worked in a developing

(Continued)

Table 13.1 (*Continued*) KM Roles, Responsibilities, and Core Competencies

KM Role	Role Description	Responsibilities	Core Competencies
			country and have a good knowledge of international development issues, trends, and approaches. Proven experience in the design and delivery of capacity development, coaching and mentoring activities, particularly adult learning techniques, and replication of best practices is required. Strong knowledge and practice of results-based management (RBM), and experience in performance measurement and program evaluation are needed. Strong communication skills, both written and verbal, and excellent report writing and organizational skills are needed. The core competencies also include the following: • Leadership • Excellent communication • Time management/ability to prioritize

(Continued)

Table 13.1 (Continued) KM Roles, Responsibilities, and Core Competencies

KM Role	Role Description	Responsibilities	Core Competencies
			• Development or management of information systems to support complex business processes • Project management of IT projects • Significant knowledge and use of relational database systems • Survey design • Finding, assembling, and analyzing verbal and numerical data from Internet, databases, and paper-based sources • Dissemination of information in a way that is accessible, manageable, and which supports the work of individuals in an organization • Experience of working effectively in a diverse team, maintaining good working relationships • Experience of working effectively in a diverse team, maintaining good working relationships

(Continued)

Table 13.1 (*Continued*) KM Roles, Responsibilities, and Core Competencies

KM Role	Role Description	Responsibilities	Core Competencies
			• Excellent information technology skills, including relationship database programming and/or reporting skills
KM (systems) administrator	The KM administrator promotes, facilitates, and supports the KM system within the organization, with optimized outputs and process management. The KM system administrator is the person(s) with administration rights and privileges within the specific knowledge repository.	Responsibilities: • Maintains the knowledge repository • Can serve as a KM author • Subject matter expert (SME) for all knowledge repository upgrades, capability issues, and approved configuration updates The KM administrator coordinates and executes governance of knowledge within the knowledge repository.	The core competencies include understanding of KM governance best practices, initial configuration, system administration, content administration, and product-specific knowledge of implementing KM security policies.
Knowledge engineer	A knowledge engineer researches, designs, and implements computer software programs that can accomplish a wide variety of problem-	It is essential for a knowledge engineer to be highly detail-oriented and organized. When writing a new program, he or she must be sure that no mistakes are made. Even a tiny error in a code can disrupt an entire program and mangle data output.	Knowledge engineers need in-depth competency as it pertains to knowledge architectures as well as knowledge sharing, collaboration, and transfer techniques and methods.

(*Continued*)

Table 13.1 (*Continued*)   KM Roles, Responsibilities, and Core Competencies

KM Role	Role Description	Responsibilities	Core Competencies
	solving tasks. Professionals work with knowledge-based systems (KBSs) that incorporate artificial intelligence into data mining, data entry, calculation tasks, and decision-making applications. They try to formulate codes and programs that operate in a similar fashion to a human expert on a given task, such as solving complicated physics equations. Most knowledge engineers are employed by software development companies, though some work for private corporations and consulting groups.	In addition, a knowledge engineer must have the foresight to include special instructions for the program that may be overlooked by a less experienced programmer. For example, he or she might be able to prevent common data entry errors in a spreadsheet application by programming the computer to recognize when one piece of data is very different from previous entries. If the application detects that a 100 was entered instead of a 10, for example, it could ask the user if he or she is sure that the entry is correct.	A person who is interested in becoming a knowledge engineer can look into bachelor's degree programs at accredited colleges and universities. Relatively few schools offer degrees specifically in knowledge engineering, but a program in computer science or software engineering can provide the appropriate training. Many future engineers decide to pursue master's degrees or higher before looking for jobs in the specialty. A new knowledge engineer usually has the chance to work alongside experienced professionals for several weeks or months to master his or her skills.

(Continued)

Table 13.1 (*Continued*)   KM Roles, Responsibilities, and Core Competencies

KM Role	Role Description	Responsibilities	Core Competencies
KM liaison	The KM liaison is the KM resource assigned to various teams across the organization that executes KM-specific duties for their teams on behalf of the KM director.	*Responsibilities:* • Executes KM initiatives on behalf of the specific KM director • Serves as a champion for the KM and specific KM director • Serves as the primary SME for the specific KM director area	KM liaison must have a general understanding of KM, including knowledge sharing, collaboration, and transfer techniques and methods.
KM specialist	The KM specialist is engaged in the support of the KM policy, planning research, and metrics for KM.	KM specialist's responsibilities include the following: • Leads/contributes to the development of a KM strategy and associated implementation plan • Leads/contributes to the development and execution of the KM governance plan • Develops a comprehensive mapping of KM information sources and knowledge, including processes • Contributes to the development and ongoing maintenance of the KM system(s)	KM specialist need in depth competency as it pertains to knowledge architectures as well as knowledge sharing, collaboration and transfer techniques and methods.

(Continued)

Table 13.1 (*Continued*) KM Roles, Responsibilities, and Core Competencies

KM Role	Role Description	Responsibilities	Core Competencies
		• Creates an approach for guiding ongoing analyses needed to address observed KM gaps and for identifying opportunities for innovation, process, procedure, and policy making/adjustments • Oversees capacity building and support for internal knowledge acquisition, management, and sharing; ensures relevant CoPs are developed and strengthened; supports development of staff, consultants, and key partners and of all aspects of KM	
Knowledge architect	The knowledge architect is a cross-organizational and interdisciplinary role. This role has knowledge of taxonomies and ontology analysis/design/creation, and understanding and creating knowledge flows to capture tacit and explicit knowledge. The individual who oversees	This person is charged with the design of dynamic systems of knowledge creation and transfer, and the design of semantic structures that range from taxonomies to models of knowledge flows (explicit and tacit) within an organization. This person also deals with the development of those semantic structures and designs them for their use and application. A critical part of creating these designs is research into an	Knowledge architects provide the tools and skills to help them design knowledge into the organization's business processes. Their core competencies include understanding of knowledge structures (tacit and explicit) and understanding of data modeling (structured data) and content modeling (unstructured data focus).

(*Continued*)

Table 13.1 (*Continued*) KM Roles, Responsibilities, and Core Competencies

KM Role	Role Description	Responsibilities	Core Competencies
	implementation of the enterprise's knowledge architecture, who leads the "knowledge architecture team" in identifying, organizing, and providing access to scattered, heterogeneous information in digital and paper form, and who leads the knowledge audit to determine and continually reevaluate the specific knowledge needs of users and their business processes. The knowledge architect defines knowledge processes and identifies the technology requirements for creating, capturing, organizing, accessing, and using knowledge assets.	organization's knowledge, the knowledge contained in the people of the organization, and, the information/knowledge component of the activities of the organization.	

(*Continued*)

Table 13.1 (*Continued*) KM Roles, Responsibilities, and Core Competencies

KM Role	Role Description	Responsibilities	Core Competencies
KM author/ writer	KM author/writer is the primary person(s) involved in creating knowledge within the knowledge repository. The KM author is a member of the KM staff who applies plain language and information design (PLAID) to the construction of knowledge articles, FAQs, and other content being leveraged for KM.	Responsibilities include the following: • PLAID • Collaboration with key SMEs • Establish/maintain adherence and governance of style guide	KM author/writer must have experience in PLAID as well as linguistics. Also, the KM author must have a general understanding of KM, including knowledge sharing, collaboration, and transfer techniques and methods.
KM analyst	The KM analyst analyses and proposes improvements to the overall effectiveness and efficiency of the KM program at all levels by applying advanced KM methods and practices for all users of KM at the organization.	KM analyst's responsibilities include the following: • Implementing a range of methods and tools to capture and document knowledge • Contributing to the analysis and configuration of knowledge maintenance approaches and practices	KM analyst's core competencies include deep analysis competency as it pertains to leveraging various KM methods. KM analysts provide means to communicate the business needs in a way that engineers and architects can understand. While this competency focuses on

(*Continued*)

Table 13.1 (*Continued*) KM Roles, Responsibilities, and Core Competencies

KM Role	Role Description	Responsibilities	Core Competencies
		• Contributing to the analysis and configuration of knowledge sharing approaches and practices • Working closely with other staff members of the specific KM director and/or KM to ensure that new elements of KM using innovative technology and media are retained and developed, and advising on the mechanisms for their implementation	operations in knowledge organizations, it is also of value to business professionals.

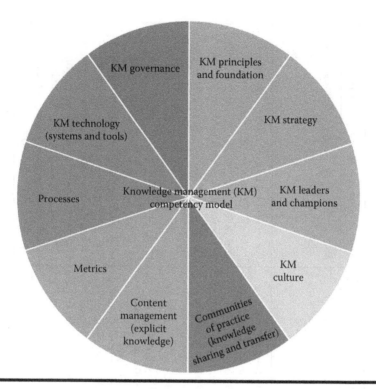

Figure 13.1 KM competency model.

To determine the KM competency model, a rigorous process was initiated to provide consensus on core competency areas (see Table 13.2). This methodology will apply to any modern organization, regardless of the establishment of a CKO role. It can be used by any department or individual who has the vision, leadership, and determination to infuse KM principles in the enterprise. A KM competency model serves as the foundation for functions such as training, education, development, and performance management, because it specifies what essential knowledge, skills, and abilities are required.

The KM competency model will serve as the foundation for enterprise-wide KM adoption and use, and it will create a culture of collaboration and knowledge sharing in the army, where personalized and contextual information and knowledge are "pushed and pulled" from across the enterprise to meet mission objectives, where good ideas are valued regardless of the source, where knowledge sharing is recognized and rewarded, and where the knowledge base is accessible without technological or structural barriers.

Table 13.2 KM Competency Model Details

Competency Area	Goal(s)	Action to Achieve Goal(s)	Suggested Learning Methods
KM principles and foundation	Understand KM principles, methods, and their applications.	Formal training is either developed or accessed by an accredited (creditable) institution.	Standardized KM courses are taught via instructor lead and/or online.
KM strategy	Develop and socialize the vision and mission of KM by developing and operationalizing a detailed KM strategy.	Develop an effective KM strategy to support your KM program through the establishment of a short-term (1–3 years) and a long-term (3–5 years) roadmap that includes the identification of initiatives to support the vision, mission, and objectives of your organization.	Focus on building a holistic, enterprise-wide KM program. Your organization may want to pilot certain KM methods, KM practices, and/or tools in targeted areas of the business, but do this as part of a larger plan.
KM leaders and champions	Understand what KM professionals do, their roles and responsibilities, and how they influence the use of KM practices within an organization.	Seek out KM champions throughout the organization to support KM activities. Develop specific KM expertise within the organization.	KM champions act as liaisons between the KM professionals and practitioners. Explore the need to create leadership and lead technical positions such as CKO, knowledge architect, and CoP leaders and facilitators.

(Continued)

Table 13.2 (Continued) KM Competency Model Details

Competency Area	Goal(s)	Action to Achieve Goal(s)	Suggested Learning Methods
KM culture	Identify and understand the cultural issues that impact the adoption and use of KM practices, procedures, and methods.	Establish a "lifelong learning culture" to ensure the capture and use of lessons learned throughout activities and initiatives at the organization. Reward and recognize knowledge sharing and collaboration to ensure staff remains motivated to contribute.	Develop KM executive councils, along with the development and execution of KM policies, procedures, and standards.
CoPs	Understand the KM approaches to knowledge sharing, transfer, and collaboration.	Encourage the establishment of CoP around professional activities and communities of interest (CoI) around nonprofessional activities. Establish policies and practices to best use your SME resources.	Provide the resources to allow CoP and CoI activities to emerge and grow throughout the organization and encourage participation. CoPs provide a forum to share expertise and build a body of knowledge. As people interact and network, they build trust and relationships that cross departmental boundaries. SME activities include CoP facilitation, mentoring and coaching, internal consulting, and expertise transfer techniques.

(Continued)

Table 13.2 (Continued)   KM Competency Model Details

Competency Area	Goal(s)	Action to Achieve Goal(s)	Suggested Learning Methods
Content management (explicit knowledge)	Understand content-life-cycle management, content library structures, content labeling and tagging, and search as it pertains to KM practices (IA).	Review current content management procedures to ensure compliance with formal policies and guidance; ensure all content is credible (has authoritative source, has contextual consistency, is actively managed); develop a consistent organizational approach to metadata along with the structure and guidelines to enforce metadata tagging by utilizing IA.	Assess how documents are created, stored, accessed, and archived; audit records to ensure compliance with formal record-keeping requirements; develop an IA plan/strategy for addressing discrepancies and poor practices. Create metadata elements that will enhance the retrieval of content across the organization; look at both manual and automated methods of metadata creation; explore methods to provide social tagging to content to supplement controlled terms (details should be included in the IA plan/strategy).
Metrics	Understand the reasons for monitoring and evaluating performance, considerations of what to measure, and using metrics to refine KM strategies.	Use metrics to assess the accomplishment of organizational strategic goals and objectives.	Measurement against strategic goals and objectives provides insight on how KM efforts are closing the knowledge gap between what your organization knows and what it needs to know to be successful.

(Continued)

Table 13.2 (Continued) KM Competency Model Details

Competency Area	Goal(s)	Action to Achieve Goal(s)	Suggested Learning Methods
		Use metrics to measure efficiency (output—activity based) and effectiveness (outcome—results based). Standardize measures across the organization to ensure they are focused on strategic outcomes. Measure only what is necessary to drive the intended results.	Use a combination of both output and outcome metrics to track both hard (factual) and soft (perceptual) measures. Focus organizational metrics on strategic goals and accomplish the mission; ensure alignment across all departments. When measuring for outcomes, it is best to manage no more than five to seven measurements; the results should drive decisions that refine KM strategy.
Processes	Understand the use of KM techniques in order to find opportunities for simplifying current processes or making them more efficient or effective.	Use KM techniques to simplify or increase the efficiency or effectiveness of current business processes. Create process maps and conduct knowledge audits to identify where critical information and knowledge inputs and outputs are.	Assess current processes that may be streamlined or eliminated; understand why the process steps must be performed as is to achieve the desired result. Process maps used in conjunction with knowledge maps can drive process redesign projects that help define the most appropriate roles and responsibilities for information and knowledge management, tightly integrated into the operational workflow.

(Continued)

Table 13.2 (Continued) KM Competency Model Details

Competency Area	Goal(s)	Action to Achieve Goal(s)	Suggested Learning Methods
KM technology (systems/tools)	Understand how technology impacts KM and the tools that are available to facilitate knowledge sharing and collaboration.	Ensure the organization IA fits the needs of its primary user groups, whether it's for a single platform such as an intranet or knowledge portal, or across several platforms. Assess how the organization currently uses technology to accomplish tasks such as content creation, capturing, reviewing, sharing, collaborating, and archiving. Stay abreast of current and emerging technologies and how they can be (or are being unofficially) used within your organization.	An IA will make sense of how the different platforms relate to each other, how users will navigate between them, and how expectations for content discovery (search) can be met. Develop a list of tools that are used by the organization to connect people to explicit knowledge and tacit knowledge—these include everything from e-mail, phone books, and meetings to technologies such as blogs, wikis, and podcasts; map how these technologies work within the IA and how they help the organization meet its strategic goals and objectives—use this information to guide KM strategy.

(Continued)

Table 13.2 (*Continued*) KM Competency Model Details

Competency Area	Goal(s)	Action to Achieve Goal(s)	Suggested Learning Methods
KM governance	Understand balancing the need to know with the need to share and how KM coexists with information management policy.	Accept that KM and content assurance must coexist and that secure KM takes into account the aspects of confidentiality, trust, and privacy management. Balance the need to know with the need to share. Develop security strategies, policies, plans, and procedures (comprehensive content governance plan) that not only address content management but also consider KM strategies and are tightly integrated with business strategies.	Understand that secure KM is much more than protecting classified information; security strategies, secure operation processes, and security metrics need to be incorporated into KM strategy and plans. Organizational assets such as intellectual property, trade secrets, and privacy information need to be protected from malicious or unintentional access and use; ensure technology incorporates access controls, credential mechanisms, and encryption systems to secure KM practices. Review existing content management policies; consider supplemental policies that incorporate security controls into the KM life cycle while maintaining appropriate access to knowledge. This should be part of the content governance plan and the subsequent development of the Content Governance Board.

KM Curriculum Development and Delivery

KM curriculum development and delivery must support the twenty-first century model of being able to learn anywhere, anytime, and on a varied number of platforms, applications, and mobile devices.

To embark on the challenge of providing KM curriculum for the twenty-first century, the four pillars of KM were leveraged as a foundation by the KMEF (Green, 2011). These four pillars of KM are as follows:

1. *Leadership*: This deals with the environmental, strategic, and enterprise-level decision-making processes.
2. *Organization*: This deals with the operational aspects of knowledge assets.
3. *Learning*: This deals with behavioral aspects and social engineering of the organization.
4. *Technology*: This deals with the various information technologies that support and/or enable KM strategies and operations.

The curriculum must not only focus on concepts and theories but also on practical aspects (based on real-world implementation of KM), and how it is implemented and used. The curriculum must also include the various methods, tools, applications, and systems that are developed and utilized to enable KM to be an actionable event. Another essential ingredient of KM curriculum development and delivery for the twenty-first century would be to incorporate the use of case studies, storytelling, affinity diagrams, knowledge cafés, and similar experience-sharing mechanisms.

This is the type of education that will lead to KM career enhancement, enrichment, and planning. Other curriculum "basics" as pointed out by the KMEF to be included in KM are courses in measures and metrics, collaboration techniques, networking, and organizational development and effectiveness.

Teaching Philosophy/Methodology

The KM professional must be able to learn knowledge concepts and apply them in a variety of ways. KM education comes in a variety of forms to enable the KM professional to speed up on a particular concept and apply it to meet a specific need. Knowledge transfer, communities of practice (CoPs), capturing tacit and explicit knowledge, and KM governance are only a few of the concepts that today's KM education must focus on to assist the KM professional in execution of their jobs.

My goal of instruction delivery has always been to improve student comprehension, application, and performance. It's further based on the premise that learning should not occur in a haphazard way but should be developed in accordance with orderly processes, be specifically tailored to the target audience, and have measurable outcomes. To accomplish the goals set forth in the delivery of KM education, I have incorporated the use of Bloom's Taxonomy of Learning. As a KM professor, I recommend Bloom's Taxonomy to be part of any curriculum that teaches KM.

Objectives of Bloom's Taxonomy of Learning

The revised version of Bloom's Taxonomy represents a taxonomy for learning, teaching, and assessing. This version describes six revised categories that include the following:

1. *Remembering*: Recall data or information. (for further details refer Table 13.3)
2. *Understanding*: Understand the meaning, translation, interpolation, and interpretation of instructions and problems. State a problem in one's own words.
3. *Applying*: Use a concept in a new situation or unprompted use of an abstraction. Apply what was learned in the classroom into novel situations in the work place.
4. *Analyzing*: Separate material or concepts into component parts, so that their organizational structure may be understood. Distinguish between facts and inferences
5. *Evaluating*: Make judgments about the value of ideas or materials.
6. *Creating*: Build a structure or pattern from diverse elements. Put parts together to form a whole, with emphasis on creating a new meaning or structure.

This version of Bloom's Taxonomy from Iowa State University Center of Excellence in Learning and Teaching (2012) includes an alignment of knowledge (see Figure 13.2). This alignment of knowledge, called "knowledge dimension," identifies four types of knowledge that learners are expected to acquire and/or construct. This knowledge includes (1) metacognitive—knowledge about when and how to use particular strategies for learning or for problem solving; (2) procedural—knowledge exercised in the performance of some task; (3) conceptual—knowledge rich in relationships and understanding; it is a connected web of knowledge, a network in which the linking relationships are as prominent as the discrete bits of information; and (4) factual—the basic elements students must know to be acquainted with a discipline or solve problems in it.

Bloom's Six Cognitive Taxonomy Categories

Table 13.3 outlines each of the categories to include an example of the category and how it is demonstrated. In applying Bloom's six cognitive taxonomy categories, we must consider the following sections.

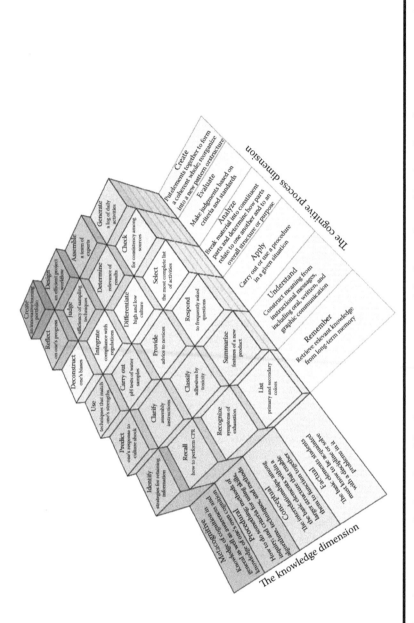

Figure 13.2 Bloom's taxonomy for learning objectives. (R. Heer, A Model of Learning Objectives based on A Taxonomy for Learning, Teaching, and Assessing: A Revision of Bloom's Taxonomy of Educational Objectives. Center for Excellence in Learning and Teaching, Iowa State University, Ames, Iowa.)

Table 13.3 Bloom's Six Cognitive Taxonomy Categories

Category	Examples	Demonstration
Remembering: Recall data or information.	Conduct lecture presentations on specific course topics; solicit feedback during the lecture.	Knowledge is demonstrated through students responding to questions during the lecture.
Understanding: Understand the meaning, translation, interpolation, and interpretation of instructions and problems. State a problem in one's own words.	Work with students to understand concepts; put the interpretation of concepts in their own words; ask students to interpolate and extrapolate the given concepts to specific circumstances.	Comprehension is demonstrated through assignment, quiz, and midterm and final exams.
Applying: Use a concept in a new situation or unprompted use of an abstraction. Apply what was learned in the classroom into novel situations in the work place.	Guidance is given to students on approaches to analyze case studies that reflect real-world problems.	Through the use of case studies, each student leverages the knowledge gained through understanding of and the interpolation and extrapolation of concepts and apply them to solve real-world problems.
Analyzing: Separate material or concepts into component parts so that its organizational structure may be understood. Distinguish between facts and inferences.	Students are instructed to use logical deduction as well as interpolation and extrapolation of concepts during their analysis of problems and situations presented during the course.	Demonstration of analysis takes place during assignments, exams, and case studies. Students are instructed to analyze, break down, compare, contrast, diagram, deconstruct, and often differentiate situations that are presented.

(Continued)

Table 13.3 (Continued) Bloom's Six Cognitive Taxonomy Categories

Category	Examples	Demonstration
Evaluating: Make judgments about the value of ideas or materials.	Students as well as course materials are evaluated. Students are evaluated and feedback is given during every class session, and course materials are evaluated by students and professors and any necessary adjustments are made.	Students are worked with to sharpen values and ideas. Course materials are constantly supplemented with videos and other pertinent research materials.
Creating: Build a structure or pattern from diverse elements. Put parts together to form a whole, with emphasis on creating a new meaning or structure.	Students are instructed on how to design artifacts to address solutions and perform tasks, as well as integrate course instruction from several sources to solve problems.	Students demonstrate synthesis during the execution of case studies and often during exams and assignments. Students are often instructed to categorize; combine; compile; compose; create; devise; design; and explain their solutions, approaches, and measurements.

KM Education Programs

Sometime ago, I had participated in a discussion and the associated comments on KM education, which included university courses (master's programs), certification programs, and certificate programs. This discussion was hosted by Art Schlussel in the CKO Forum at LinkedIn. This discussion inspired me to elaborate on my thoughts concerning KM education. As I stated in my comments to Art, for any education to be effective, it must be supported by practical application, including having experienced mentors work with participants who have recently completed any number of various KM training programs.

In this discussion, Art mentioned that a partnership between the US military and a well-known accredited university to build a comprehensive KM training program is in its preliminary stages. However, the major issue is what does or will this training consist of and the fact that the US military wants it to follow their KM competency model (see earlier).

I believe that the KM training should have a holistic approach, which will cover the following:

- The basics of and differences between data, information, and knowledge
- Establishing "your" definition of KM
- Developing/executing KM strategy (including knowledge audits, knowledge mapping, and KM process)
- Identifying and addressing knowledge gaps (result from knowledge audit)
- Collaboration and knowledge sharing (CoPs)
- Knowledge transfer planning (mentor–protégé relationship and knowledge codification)
- Collecting/applying KM metrics
- Identifying, planning, and executing KM projects/initiatives
- KM tools (wikis, blogs, search, and KM systems)

Although this is not an exhaustive list, the approach must include planning, strategies, and processes applied for KM as well as the software that will enable and suport the execution of the KM program initiatives. The US army's KM competency model serves as a foundation to how the army will approach KM and forms the basis of what KM will address from the army's perspective. The army's enterprise KM competency model represents a holistic approach to institutionalizing KM. I believe that a holistic approach to KM is where we must begin in our training as well as our execution of KM at our organizations.

KM at Institutions of Higher Education

You may not know that KM continues to be a growing discipline in which organizations are seeking qualified individuals. A master of science (MS) concentration in KM offers students an opportunity to enter the knowledge economy and become an important asset to organizations working to get the right knowledge to the right people at the right time. When considering a master's in KM, each student should consider a university program that presents a holistic approach to the principles, practices, policies, and technologies that are being deployed today at organizations in the field of KM.

An MS concentration in KM will provide the successful student with the ability to assist organizations in making better decisions, understand where knowledge exists, and uncover knowledge gaps that will lead to better performance and communication between workers.

Here are some universities' certification programs that offer master's and certifications in KM. This is not meant to be an exhaustive list of schools or programs. However, these institutions offer educational experiences that support gaining the necessary knowledge to fill various KM roles, responsibilities, and core competencies previously indicated.

Knowledge Systems Institute

KM at Knowledge Systems Institute (KSI)'s (http://www.ksi.edu/) Master of Science Graduate School is an area of concentration most suitable for people who already have a career in a field other than information technology, but now find the need to acquire new IT skills in order to remain technologically competent. Because knowledge industry is the wave of the future, acquiring the necessary data management and KM skills enables an individual to compete successfully in a demanding job market. KSI offers coursework and research in the field of KM. The program is designed as concentration for individuals who need to acquire actionable insights into KM methodologies and strategies to enhance knowledge transfer and collaboration as a driving principle of organizational success. Business processes naturally involve generating knowledge and sharing of knowledge to ensure that an organization maximizes the value it achieves through its knowledge base. Contact KSI for specific up-to-date information regarding this program.

George Mason University

At George Mason University, KM is taught within the School of Policy, Government, and International Affairs (http://spgia.gmu.edu/programs/graduate-degrees/organization-development-knowledge-management-odkm/). The curriculum combines organizational development and KM. In the George Mason University Organization Development & Knowledge Management Development (ODKM) cohort master's program, you will explore organizational leadership theory and practice, the shift from hierarchical structures to group-based learning, and best practices to promote the creation of adaptive, collaborative work environments. You will graduate with the capacity to manage, evaluate, and affect rapid change in government, corporate, and nonprofit organizations.

The ODKM program is designed to meet the needs of contemporary society and of organizations undergoing rapid changes and shifting from hierarchical structures to more group-based learning environments. While focusing on the human and social aspects of organizing, the program also emphasizes the use of collaborative groupware technologies to support interactive learning, knowledge sharing, and knowledge creation.

This unique cohort program is offered in a part-time executive format with classes offered primarily on Friday evenings and Saturdays on alternating weekends. Contact George Mason University for specific up-to-date information regarding this program.

The George Washington University

The Department of Engineering Management and Systems Engineering (EMSE), The George Washington University (http://www.emse.seas.gwu.edu/knowledge-and-information-management-research), offers research areas in knowledge and information management. The Department of EMSE faculty, as stated on their website, is an active research faculty whose members balance both research and teaching responsibilities. A large research component is the joint research between faculty members and their doctoral students. Prior to completion of their program, doctoral students are required to submit a journal article describing their research contribution. Faculty and students conduct research in eight subfields of the EMSE disciplines. The specific research topics include knowledge-based economy, knowledge-intensive enterprises, knowledge security/assurance, and strategic assets management. Contact The George Washington University for specific up-to-date information regarding this program.

Kent State University

Kent State University offers an MS in KM within the School of Library and Information Science (SLIS; http://www.kent.edu/slis). The SLIS at Kent State University offers several learning opportunities to students, scholars, and professionals interested in KM careers. The MS concentration in KM prepares you to take a leadership role in this engaging profession. Dual degree options—Kent State University allows students to work on two degrees concurrently and to double-count up to 12 credit hours between any two programs. This dual degree designation requires admission to each program (separately) and approval from each program to share the credits.

In addition, Kent State University offers a master's degree in information architecture and knowledge management (IAKM). Within the IAKM degree program, Kent State University offers concentrations in health informatics, KM, and user experience design; these programs are dynamic and continually respond to changes in marketplace helping information and knowledge professionals and their evolving skill sets. Contact Kent State University for specific up-to-date information regarding these programs.

Here are some additional universities that offer an MS in KM programs

Notre Dame of Maryland University

Notre Dame of Maryland (NDM) offers an MS in analytics in knowledge management (AKM; http://www.ndm.edu/academics/school-of-arts-and-sciences/ programs/ms-in-knowledge-management/). NDM states that this program will "Transform Big Data into powerful knowledge for your company or clients." NDM indicates that AKM is the systematic process of developing, organizing, retaining, and using knowledge resources that contribute to an organization's sustained success. To adapt to the fast-changing and competitive economy, public and private organizations have hired KM professionals to enhance their ability to serve clients and realize strategic priorities. Contact NDM for specific up-to-date information regarding this program.

Columbia University

Columbia University's MS in information and knowledge strategy (IKNS) program (http://ce.columbia.edu/information-and-knowledge-strategy) prepares individuals who are invested in the strategic potential of business-knowledge strategy alignment, collaboration, and business analytics to expand or branch out from their current roles, or become entrepreneurs of ventures in the knowledge domain. Contact Columbia University for specific up-to-date information regarding this program.

Drexel University

Drexel University's online accredited master of science in library and information science (MSLIS) program (http://online.drexel.edu/online-degrees/information-sciences-degrees/ms-di/index.aspx) is an industry leader in digital information management and is ranked top 10 among library science programs nationally. Drexel's College of Computing and Informatics, with the MSLIS program in 2014, was named one of "America's Best Graduate Schools" by *U.S. News & World Report*. The College of Computing and Informatics offers a concentration in competitive intelligence and knowledge management. In this program, students will learn to apply commonly used techniques to identify and evaluate an organization's knowledge-based assets, design knowledge sharing opportunities within organizations, design information services to meet organizational information needs, relate business resources to real-world situations and needs of individuals and institutions, and utilize competitive intelligence activities to support strategic decision making in the organization. Contact Drexel University for specific up-to-date information regarding this program.

The Hong Kong Polytechnic University

The Hong Kong Polytechnic University promotes a flexible program that allows students to develop their own learning plan with a combination of on-site and online classes (http://www.ise.polyu.edu.hk/app/webroot/html/academic_program/km//). The curriculum is codeveloped by an international team of leading experts and scholars in KM. Delivery of the program is via a balanced mix of in-person seminars and workshops, online tutorials, and web-based study with enhanced pedagogy. The in-person workshops are conducted in weekday evenings or during weekends. Some subjects have open book examination; some operate with continuous assessments. Contact the Hong Kong Polytechnic University for specific up-to-date information regarding this program.

KM Certification Programs

KM certification programs are often designed for working professionals. These programs are leveraged to provide the tools and methods for understanding and implementing KM relatively quickly. More often than not, the participants have specific issues in KM that they need to address and/or they are moved into a KM role not fully understanding what KM is really about, or how to be effective in their KM position. A good KM certification should be based on standards disseminated by the industry and professional KM organizations. Once the participant completes an in-class project and examination, it signifies that the individual is certified to meet certain standards or competencies related to successful implementation of KM, as prescribed by the profession. The following are three such programs, but this does not represent an exhaustive list of KM certification programs that are available:

Knowledge Management Institute

The Knowledge Management Institute (KMI; http://www.kminstitute.org/) supports the paradigm of "learn anywhere and anytime." The KMI is dedicated to researching, defining, publishing, and sharing knowledge in a variety of formats, truly suited to learner needs. KMI programs provide what expert KM practitioners need to know to carry out successful enterprise KM and what all KM professionals need to know for greater career success in the knowledge age. KMI provides the following:

- Proven methodology implemented by public/private sector
- Curriculum licensed and actually taught by acclaimed institutions of higher learning
- Preferred training vendor for many US Department of Defense Agencies and Commands
- Preferred training vendor for all US Combatant Commands ("COCOMS")
- Trusted enterprise-wide training solutions for Fortune 500 companies
- Training solutions endorsed by leading government agencies and universities worldwide
- Both certification-level and modular training options, supporting the "learn anywhere and anytime" philosophy

In addition, KMI offers several KM programs to specifically address what the KM professionals will need in order to execute their job. These programs include certified knowledge manager (CKM); certified knowledge specialist (CKS); certified knowledge practitioner (CKP™); master classes—Special topics in taxonomy, information architecture (IA), innovation, knowledge capture, social KM, and community management; and a basic awareness series entitled KM101.

Contact the KMI for specific up-to-date information regarding their programs.

RightAnswers

Although RightAnswers is a KM software vendor (I try and stay away from endorsing any specific vendor and/or their products), they offer a unique KM certification program (http://www.rightanswers.com/training/rightanswers-knowledge-management-certification/) that focuses on knowledge-centered support (KCS) and information technology infrastructure library (ITIL). The program focuses on KCS principles and knowledge best practices, and how they are applied within the RightAnswers platform.

RightAnswers has indicated that the participant will learn the following:

- Industry best practices (ITIL and KCS)
- Knowledge architecture
- Knowledge segmentation
- User management and workflow
- Content development
- Taxonomy and attribute management
- Knowledge style guides
- Improving searching capability
- Knowledge analytics and measuring success

In addition, you will become certified in the use of the RightAnswers KM system tools. Contact RightAnswers for specific up-to-date information regarding their program.

Association for Talent Development

The Association of Talent Management (ATD; https://www.td.org/Education/Programs/Knowledge-Management-Certificate), which was formerly ASTD, states that they offer the following:

- Develop a vision and strategy for a knowledge-centric workplace, ensuring that it integrates with the organization's business strategy
- Evaluate and determine appropriate uses for current and emerging KM tools and technologies, including Web 2.0 approaches, to support work-centered learning and development
- Manage the information life cycle, from identifying, defining, and creating knowledge assets to assessing the value that KM brings to the organization
- Examine the design of workplace and social environments that encourage and facilitate knowledge creation, sharing, and innovation
- Analyze organizational readiness for KM and implement appropriate strategies to assure successful organizational implementation
- Articulate the benefits of KM as an important component of an organization's overall learning and performance strategy
- Develop strategies for creating requests for proposals and selecting a vendor for KM work
- Identify strategies that incorporate KM approaches in support of organizational learning programs and how the training and development function can incorporate KM into its repertoire

The content for this program is based, in part, on the ATD Competency Study and helps in preparation for obtaining the Certified Professional in Learning and Performance (CPLP) credential. Contact the ATD for specific up-to-date information regarding this program.

Key Learnings

The following are some key learnings from this chapter:

- Ensure that your human resources department plays an integral role in approving all KM roles along with their subsequent responsibilities and core competencies.
- Ensure that the KM curriculum development and delivery supports the paradigm of "learn anywhere and anytime."
- When implementing KM at your organization, incorporate KM competencies based on the details as described in the KM competency model.
- When determining a KM education program to enroll in, ensure that the program incorporates case studies of actual application of KM.

Tips and Techniques

The following are several tips and techniques that can be applied to understanding KM education and educational programs:

- When determining KM roles, responsibilities, and core competencies, leverage Table 13.1 as a guide.
- For KM education to be successful, knowledge services and knowledge strategy require an understanding of shared concepts and a mutual understanding about the elements and framework of KM.
- When developing a KM educational program or looking for one, make sure that the KM program allows for some flexibility in its curriculum choices.
- The curriculum must not only focus on concepts and theories but also on the practical aspects (based on real-world implementation of KM) as well as its implementation and use.

Chapter 14

"Big Knowledge!": Knowledge Management and Big Data

A goal of knowledge management (KM) is to capture and share knowledge wherever it resides in the organization. Leveraging the corporate collective know-how will improve decision making and innovation where it is needed. The proliferation of data, information, and knowledge has created a phenomenon called *Big Data*. KM when applied to Big Data will enable a type of analysis that will uncover the complete picture of the organization and be a catalyst for driving decisions. In order to leverage an organization's Big Data, must be broken down into smaller more manageable parts. This will facilitate a succinct analysis, which can then be regrouped with other smaller subsets to produce *big picture* results.

Volume, velocity, and variety are all aspects that define Big Data.

Volume: It is the proliferation of all types of data expanding to many terabytes of information.

Velocity: It is the ability to process data quickly.

Variety: It refers to the different types of data (structured and unstructured data such as data in databases, content in content management and KM systems/repositories, collaborative environments, blogs, wikis, sensor data, audio, video, click streams, and log files). Variety is the component of Big Data in which KM will play a major role in driving decisions. Enterprises need to be able to combine their analyses to include information from both structured databases and unstructured content.

Data, Information, and Knowledge

Because the focus here is about leveraging KM techniques to extract knowledge from Big Data, it is important to understand the difference between data, information, and knowledge (see Figure 14.1). *Data* refers to a discrete set of facts that are represented by numbers and words. *Information* is an organized set of data (puts context around data). This can result in an artifact such as a stock report and news article. *Knowledge*, on the other hand, emerges from the receiver of information applying his/her analysis (aided by their experience and training) to form judgments in order to make decisions. Erickson and Rothberg indicate that information and data only reveal their full value when insights are drawn from them (knowledge). Big Data becomes useful when it enhances decision making, which in turn is only enhanced when analytical techniques and an element of human interaction is applied (Erickson and Rothberg, 2014).

In a February 26, 2014, *KM World* article titled "Big Data Delivering Big Knowledge," Stefan Andreasen, chief technology officer at Kapow Software, Palo Alto, CA, indicates that "To gain a 360° view of their ecosystem, organizations should also monitor user-generated data, public data, competitor data and partner data to discover critical information about their business, customers and competitive landscape" (Andreasen, 2014, p. 1). The user-generated data, public data, competitor data, and partner data provide the variety of data needed to be analyzed by KM, and it's this type of data that will be examined more closely.

User-Generated Data

Customers are sharing information about their experience with products and services, what they like and don't like, how it compares to the competition,

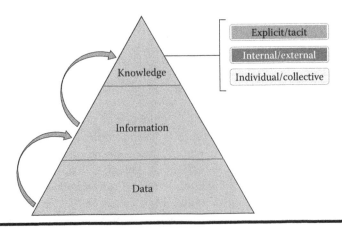

Figure 14.1 Knowledge management pyramid.

and many other insights that can be used for identifying new sales opportunities, planning campaigns, designing targeted promotions, or guiding product and service development. This information is available in social media, blogs, customer reviews, or discussions on user forums. Combining all these data contained in call center records and information from other back-office systems can help identify trends, have better predictions, and improve the way organizations engage with customers (Andreasen, 2014).

Public Data

Public information made available by federal, state, and local agencies can be used to support business operations in human resources, compliance, financial planning, and so on. Information from courthouse websites and other state portals can be used for background checks and professional license verifications. Other uses include monitoring compliance regulation requirements, bill and legislation tracking, or in healthcare obtaining data on Medicare laws and, which drugs are allowed per state (Andreasen, 2014).

Competitor Data

Information about competitors is now widely available by monitoring their websites, online prices, press releases, events they participate in, open positions, or new hires. This data allows better evaluation of the competition, monitor their strategic moves, identify unique market opportunities, and take action accordingly. As a retailer, for example, correlate this data with order transaction history and inventory levels to design and implement a more dynamic pricing strategy to win over your competition and grow the business (Andreasen, 2014).

Partner Data

Across your ecosystem, there are daily interactions with partners, suppliers, vendors, and distributors. As part of these interactions, organizations exchange data about products, prices, payments, commissions, shipments, and other datasets that are critical for business. Beyond the data exchange, intelligence can be gleaned by identifying inefficiencies, delays, gaps, and other insights that can help improve and streamline partner interactions (Andreasen, 2014).

To comb through the various sources of user-generated data, public data, competitor data and partner data leveraging KM analytics (data analysis, statistics, and trend analysis), and content synthesis technology (technology that categorizes, analyze, combines, extracts details, and reassess content aimed at developing new meanings and solutions) will be necessary.

Applying KM to Big Data

The emerging challenge for organizations is to derive meaningful insights from available data and reapply it intelligently. KM plays a crucial role in efficiently managing this data and delivering it to the end users to aid in the decision-making process. This involves the collection of data from direct, indirect, structured, and unstructured sources, and analyzing and synthesizing them to derive meaningful information and intelligence. Once achieved, the data must be converted into a useful knowledge base, storing it and finally delivering it to end users.

KM has the ability to integrate and leverage information from multiple perspectives. Big Data is uniquely positioned to take advantage of KM processes and procedures.

These processes and procedures enable KM to provide a rich structure, to enable decisions to be made on a multitude and variety of data. In the *KM World* March 2012 issue, it was pointed out that "organizations do not make decisions just based on one factor, such as revenue, employee salaries, or interest rates for commercial loans. The total picture is what should drive decisions." (p. 2) KM enables organizations to take the total picture Big Data provides, along with leveraging tools that provide processing speed to break up the data into subsets for analysis. This will empower organizations to make decisions on the vast amount and variety of data and information being provided.

As it pertains to KM and Big Data within organizations, the advancement of search technologies (see Chapter 4) on Big Data is making an impact. In *KM World*'s "100 Companies That Matter in Knowledge Management," they point out that search technologies' ability to implement, service, and manage Big Data environments is the key reason for their inclusion. The "findability" of information and knowledge within a large amount of unstructured data contribute to the ability to disseminate and reuse the knowledge of the enterprise.

Besides search technologies, there are several companies offering KM solutions to address Big Data. Some of these companies include CACI, which offers solutions and services to go from data to decisions; Autonomy (an HP Company) offers KM solutions that mine unstructured data, tag this data, and where appropriate make it available to the knowledge base; and IBM offers a Big Data platform that includes KM to address Big Data's vast amount of unstructured data. As organizations come to know more about Big Data and their management, and the use/reuse of the vast amounts of information and knowledge it provides, more software and consulting companies will provide the products and solutions organizations are looking for. Where is Big Data going? A 2013 Gartner Report stated that "Many global organizations have failed to implement a data management strategy but will have to as IT leaders need to support big data volumes, velocity, and variety," as well as "decisions from big data projects for decision support, and insights in the context of their role and job function, will expand from 28% of users in 2011 to 50% in 2014."

An emerging opportunity to apply KM to Big Data will be realized within research institutions (see Chapter 5). During the innovation activities where product/service development and R&D activities occur, several types of data are generated. Over a period, this proliferation of data, information, and knowledge is created in large volumes, which may be processed and then used/reused within a knowledge repository. This knowledge can be accessed to provide, for example, real-time intelligence to the research and product development teams, and provide knowledge for customer insights as well as competitive intelligence.

Having this access brings about efficiencies in developing new products and services as well as improving existing ones. In order to realize these benefits, organizations must start with a well-defined strategy to collect, store, synthesize, and disseminate knowledge in the form of product ideas, customer behavior patterns, voice of the customer (VotC), product trends from social networks, and listening platforms (among others).

Knowledge, when managed effectively, can help reduce project time, improve product quality, and increase customer satisfaction. In a knowledge-based organization, knowledge plays a crucial role in guiding the organization's actions and establishing a sustainable competitive advantage. The data and information that reside in the organization's systems, if integrated, can create a significant Big Data opportunity that the organization can leverage to create value. This is accomplished through establishing platforms for collaboration between a variety of groups (employees, suppliers, customers, and other stakeholders). This collaboration links useful knowledge obtained through Big Data analysis with rules and logic that will help deliver knowledge faster at the right time and in the right content. Leveraging KM with Big Data analysis will also lead to a "correct-the-first time" decision making, contain cost, and improve performance within and between your collaborative groups.

Social Network Analysis

Making sense of a large amount of disorganized information that is spread across the organization has always been the defining challenge of KM. The ability for organizations to capture, analyze, and understand information about themselves, their customers, and every facet of their business from the various Big Data sources is an ongoing challenge! An important KM tool in aiding organizations to extract knowledge from Big Data sources is to perform social network analysis (SNA).

Social networks are evolving and growing stronger as forms of organization of human activity. SNA is the mapping and measuring of relationships and flows between people, groups, organizations, computers, URLs, and other connected information/knowledge entities. The nodes in the network are the people and groups, whereas the links show relationships or flows between the nodes. SNA provides both a visual and a mathematical analysis of human relationships. This mapping present nodes of individuals, groups, organizations, and related systems that tie in one or more types of interdependencies; these include shared values, visions, and ideas; social contacts; kinship; conflict; financial exchanges; trade; joint membership in organizations; and group participation in events, among numerous other aspects of human relationships. To understand networks and their participants, we evaluate the location of actors in the network. Measuring the network location is finding the centrality of a node. These measures give us insight into the various roles and groupings in a network. This includes who are the connectors, mavens, leaders, bridges, isolates, as well as where the clusters are and who is in them.

In examining a social network, let's look at two nodes that are connected as if they regularly talk to each other, or interact in some way. For example, Tony regularly interacts with Tanya, but not with Sandy. Therefore, Tony and Tanya are connected, but there is no link drawn between Tony and Sandy. This network effectively indicates the distinction between the three most popular individual centrality measures: degree centrality, betweenness centrality, and closeness centrality.

Degree Centrality

Social network researchers measure network activity for a node by using the concept of degrees (the number of direct connections a node has). In the following example, Chris has the most direct connections in the network, making his node the most active in the network. He is a "connector" or "hub" in this network. Are more connections better? This is not always true. What really matters is where those connections lead to and how they connect the otherwise unconnected. Here, Donald has connections only to others in his immediate cluster—her clique. She connects with only those who are already connected to each other (Figure 14.2).

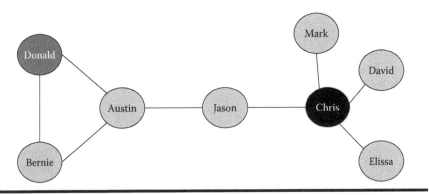

Figure 14.2 Degree centrality.

Betweenness Centrality

Although Chris has many direct ties, Jason has few direct connections, yet he has one of the best locations in the network. He is *between* two important constituencies. He plays a *broker* role in the network. The good news is that he plays a powerful role in the network; the bad news is that he is a single point of failure. Without him, Chris, Elissa, Davis, and Mark would be cut off from information and knowledge in Austin's cluster. A node with high betweenness has a great influence over what flows and does not flow in the network (Figure 14.3).

Closeness Centrality

Jason has fewer connections than Chris, yet the pattern of his direct and indirect ties allows him to access all the nodes in the network more quickly than anyone else. He has the shortest paths to all others, and closer to everyone else. He is in an excellent position to monitor the information flow in the network and therefore has the best visibility into what is happening in the network.

Let's take a look at other social network measures that contribute to gaining knowledge from the relationships in your networks. These include network centralization, network reach, network integration, boundary spanners, and peripheral players.

Network Centralization

Individual network centralities provide insight into the individual's location in the network. The relationship between the centralities of all nodes can reveal much about the overall network structure.

A very centralized network is dominated by one or a very few central nodes. If these nodes are removed or damaged, the network quickly fragments into unconnected subnetworks. A highly central node can become a single point of failure.

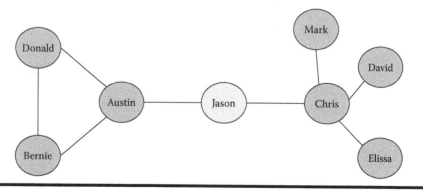

Figure 14.3 Betweenness centrality.

A network centralized around a well connected hub can fail abruptly if that hub is disabled or removed. Hubs are nodes with high degree and betweenness centrality.

A less centralized network has no single points of failure. It is resilient in the face of many random failures—many nodes or links can fail while allowing the remaining nodes to still reach each other over other network paths. Networks of low centralization seldom fail.

Network Reach

Not all network paths are created equal. In many instances, the shorter paths in the network are more important (see Figure 14.4). It is also to be noted that networks have horizons over which we cannot see, nor influence. In these cases, the key paths in the network are 1 and 2 steps and on occasions, three steps to all connections (direct and indirect). Therefore, it is important to know who is in your network neighborhood, who you are aware of, and who can you reach (network reach).

Network Integration

Network metrics are often measured using shortest paths. This measurement makes the (often incorrect) assumption that all information and/or influence flows along the network's shortest paths only. However, networks operate via direct and indirect, shortest, and near-shortest paths.

Boundary Spanners

Nodes that connect their group to others usually end up with high network metrics. Boundary spanners such as Austin and Jason are more central in the overall network than their immediate neighbors whose connections are only local, within their immediate cluster. A boundary spanner occurs via your bridging connections to

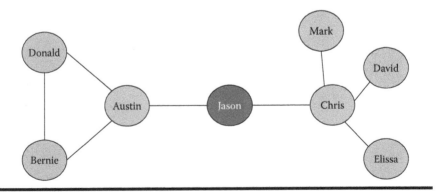

Figure 14.4 Closeness centrality.

other clusters or via your concurrent membership in overlapping groups. Boundary spanners are well positioned to be innovators, because they have access to ideas and information flowing in other clusters. They are in a position to combine different ideas and knowledge, found in various places, into new products and services.

Peripheral Players

Most people would view the nodes on the periphery of a network as not being very important. In fact, nodes such as Mark and David receive very low centrality scores for this network. Because individuals' networks overlap, peripheral nodes are connected to networks that are not currently mapped. Mark and David may be contractors or vendors that have their own network outside of the company, making them very important resources for fresh information not available inside the company.

SNA Graph/Knowledge Map

The SNA graph presents similar information as a knowledge map. A SNA graph is a tool used in SNA to represent information about patterns of ties among social actors, while a knowledge map is a graphical representation of people in an organization or within a network, indicating their expertise and understanding and the key knowledge holders, indicating what knowledge is essential or at risk to be lost if someone is removed from the network/organization.

Social scientists use graphs as a tool for describing and analyzing patterns of social relations. Instead of taking a deep dive into the specific terminology, presented here will represent some important ideas about social structure in a simpler more consumable manner. Once the basics have been mastered a deeper dive may be in order.

Graph theory provides a set of abstract concepts and methods for the analysis of graphs. This provides a visualization of social (as well as other) networks. As with knowledge maps, SNA graphs centers on relations between individuals, groups, and institutions. In studying a network in this manner, we are examining individuals as embedded in a network of relations rather than from an individual basis. Owing to the widespread availability of data, it is from this basis that SNA can be applied to a range of problems, including analyzing Big Data.

Social Media Networks

With the popularity of social media, many more people and groups are interacting. Through these interactions a proliferation of knowledge is created and shared. Social networks such as LinkedIn, Twitter, and Facebook facilitate a key component of KM: knowledge sharing. Through these networks a multitude of data can be analyzed, leading to enhanced decision making in many areas such as product marketing, and identifying key thought leaders and decision makers.

SNA is based on an assumption of the importance of relationships among interacting units. The social network perspective encompasses theories, models, and applications that are expressed in terms of relational concepts or processes. Along with growing interest and increased use of network analysis, there has been a consensus about the central principles underlying the network perspective. In addition to the use of relational concepts, we note the following as being important:

■ Actors and their actions are viewed as interdependent rather than independent, autonomous units.
■ Relational ties (linkages) between actors are channels for transfer or "flow" of resources (either material or nonmaterial).
■ Network models focusing on individuals view the network structural environment as providing opportunities for or constraints on individual action.
■ Network models conceptualize structure (social, economic, political, etc.) as lasting patterns of relations among actors.

The unit of analysis in network analysis is not the individual, but an entity consisting of a collection of individuals and the linkages among them. Network methods focus on dyads (two actors and their ties), triads (three actors and their ties), or larger systems (subgroups of individuals, or entire networks), which social media networks provide.

Big Data Sources and KM

The use of Big Data and its analysis is very closely driven by the available technologies in the organization, and the tight integration between hardware and software and other data generation mechanisms. A Big Data strategy requires the ability to sense, acquire, transmit, process, store, and analyze the data to generate knowledge that can be stored in a repository for later use.

Analyzing Big Data and understanding where KM can play a role start with analyzing the data, information, and knowledge within enterprise-wide systems. These systems include but are not limited to knowledge repositories/portals, content management (CM), enterprise resource planning (ERP), customer relationship management (CRM), material requirements planning (MRP), product life cycle management (PLM), and product data management (PDM) systems (see Figure 14.5).

The knowledge that can be gained from these systems include tacit (by identifying the key knowledge holders of the content, which in this reference includes information and knowledge) and explicit (through accessing the various types of market, technology, procedural, customer, and competitor knowledge that is captured and unstructured (see Table 14.1). Information and data are exchanged on a continuous basis with these systems as the product and services are being

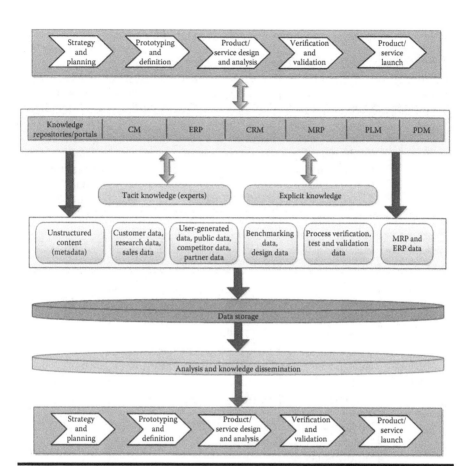

Figure 14.5 Enterprise view of Big Data sources and knowledge management. (Based on Rajpathak, T. and Narsingpurkar, A., Manufacturing Innovation and Transformation Group (ITG), TCS, Managing Knowledge from Big Data Analytics in Product Development. http://www.tcs.com/resources/white_papers/Pages/Knowledge-Big-Data-Analytics-Product-Development.aspx.)

realized. The unconventional, unstructured information comes from several sources such as simulation, sensors, blogs, employee experience, wikis, and customer experience and it should be harnessed.

Knowledge Classifications

Knowledge, in particular organizational knowledge, typically exists in large volumes dispersed across the enterprise. This lends itself to the fact that organizations need to find a way to discover, classify, capture, disseminate, and reuse this knowledge. Once the knowledge sources are discovered, an essential element to leverage KM in Big Data is to classify that knowledge.

Table 14.1 Mapping Knowledge Areas to Big Data Elements

Knowledge Type	Volume	Velocity	Variety	Value
Market knowledge	Customer data Competitor data User-generated data Public data Competitor data Partner data	Direct interactions Social media Surveys	Market analysis Demographic data Benchmarking data Trends	High value Customer data User-generated data Competitor data Partner data
Human (tacit) knowledge	Experience-based collaborative	Real-time decision making	Skill-based Experience-based Tacit knowledge	Heuristics
Technology knowledge	Standards Usage Materials Field data	Real-time data Acquisition	Cost Reliability Packaging Ergonomics	Patents
Procedural knowledge	Design knowledge Analysis Verification, testing, and validation Knowledge	Design knowledge Knowledge repository/ knowledge base	Procedures Job-aids Workflows	Best practices Process data Validation data

Source: Yuan, Q.F., Yoon, P.C., and Helendar, M.G., *J. Knowl. Manag.*, 10, 6, 50–63, 2006.

According to Yuan, Yoon, and Helendar, knowledge areas are classified into four types, collectively referred to as M-H-T-P: market knowledge, human (tacit) knowledge, technology knowledge, and procedural (explicit) knowledge. Based on these four knowledge areas, Table 14.1 depicts the mapping of knowledge areas with elements of Big Data (Yuan et al., 2006).

Although a small part of this information flows back into the enterprise systems, attempts should be made to capture this in a central repository, typically a single data warehouse. A deliberate attempt must be made to keep the data together, so that the data can be combined to create information, which can be analyzed to generate knowledge that loops back to the knowledge repository and into the organization.

Information Architecture and Big Data

As detailed in Chapter 4, IA is the art and science of labeling and organizing information, so that it is findable, manageable, and useful (Downey and Banerjee, 2010). IA also plays a significant role when applying KM to Big Data.

Big Data leverages techniques and technologies that enable enterprise to effectively and economically analyze all of its data. We need to remember that Big Data includes all data (i.e., unstructured, semi-structured, and structured). The characteristics of Big Data (volume, velocity, and variety) are a challenge to your existing architecture, and how you will effectively, efficiently, and economically process data to achieve operational efficiencies.

In order to derive the maximum benefit from Big Data, organizations must modify their IT infrastructure to handle the rapid rate of delivery and extraction of a huge volume of data, with varying data types. These can then be integrated with the organization's enterprise data and analyzed. Organizations, with legacy systems, must have a clear understanding of their historical data and how that data can be managed as a part of their overall Big Data picture.

IA provides the methods and tools for organizing, labeling, building relationships (through associations), and describing (through metadata) your unstructured content adding this source to your overall analysis. In addition, IA enables Big Data to rapidly explore and analyze any combination of structured and unstructured sources. Big Data requires IA to exploit relationships and synergies between information, aligning unstructured and structured data. This infrastructure enables organizations to make decisions utilizing the full spectrum of your Big Data sources.

To facilitate the inclusion of unstructured data (content), the metadata schema must be used (it is developed as part of the IA). Having a sound, IA will enable a consistent structure to Big Data in order for this data to provide value to the organization. The enterprise IA checklist will assist in enabling a consistent structure.

Elements of the enterprise IA checklist include content consumption, content generation, content organization, content access, content governance, and content quality of service. It is this framework (see Table 14.2) that will align your IA to Big Data, which will provide business value to be gained from all of your Big Data resources.

Some of the essential elements of the IA as it pertains to Big Data include the following:

Content consumption—which provides an understanding of the universe of relevant content through performing a content audit. This contributes directly to volume of available content.

Content generation—which fills gaps identified in the content audit by gathering the requirements for content creation/generation. This in turn will contribute directly to increasing the amount of content that is available in the organization's Big Data resources.

Table 14.2 Information Architecture Elements Align to Big Data

	Volume	Velocity	Variety
Content consumption	Provides an understanding of the universe of relevant content through performing a content audit. This contributes directly to volume of available content.	This directly contributes to the speed at which content is accessed by providing initial volume of the available content.	It identifies the initial variety of content that will be a part of the organization's Big Data resources.
Content generation	Fill gaps identified in the content audit by gathering the requirements for content creation/generation, which contributes directly to the increasing the amount of content that is available in the organization's Big Data resources.	This directly contributes to the speed at which content is accessed because of increase in volume.	It contributes to the creation of a variety of content (documents, spreadsheets, images, video, and voice) to fill identified gaps.
Content organization	Content organization will provide business rules to identify relationships between content, create metadata schema to assign content characteristic to all content. This contributes to the increasing volume of data that is available and in some ways leveraging existing data to assign metadata values.	This directly contributes to improvement in the speed at which content is accessed by applying metadata, which in turn will give context to the content.	The variety of Big Data will oftentimes drives the relationships and organization between the various types of content.

(Continued)

Table 14.2 (*Continued*) Information Architecture Elements Align to Big Data

	Volume	Velocity	Variety
Content access	Content access is about searching and establishing the standard types of search (i.e., keyword, guided, and faceted). This will contribute to the volume of data, oftentimes by establishing parameters such as additional metadata fields and values to enhance search.	This contributes to the ability to access content and the speed and efficiency in which content is accessed.	It contributes to the way the variety of content is accessed. The variety of Big Data will oftentimes drive the search parameters used to access the various type of content.
Content governance	The focus here is on establishing accountability for the accuracy, consistency, and timeliness of content; content relationships; metadata and taxonomy within areas of the enterprise; and the applications that are being used. Content governance will often "prune" the volume of content available in the organization's Big Data resources by only allowing access to pertinent/relevant content, while either deleting or archiving other content.	When the volume of content available in the organization's Big Data resources is trimmed through content governance, it will improve velocity by making available a smaller more pertinent universe of content.	When the volume of content available in the organization's Big Data resources is trimmed through content governance the variety of content available may be affected as well.

(Continued)

Table 14.2 (*Continued*) Information Architecture Elements Align to Big Data

	Volume	Velocity	Variety
Content quality of service	Content quality of service focuses on security, availability, scalability, usefulness of the content, and improves the overall quality of the volume of content in the organization's Big Data resources by • Defending content from unauthorized access, use, disclosure, disruption, modification, perusal, inspection, recording, or destruction. • Eliminating or minimizing disruptions from planned system downtime. • Ensuring that the content that is accessed is from and/or based on the authoritative or trusted source, reviewed on a regular basis (based on the specific governance policies), modified when needed and archived when it becomes obsolete • Enabling the content to behave the same, regardless of that application/tool that implements it; moreover, the content should be flexible enough to be used from both an enterprise level and a local level without changing its meaning, intent of use, and/or function. • Tailoring the content to the specific audience and ensuring that the content serves its distinct purpose, thereby being helpful to its audience and being practical.	Content quality of service will eliminate or minimize delays and latency from your content and business processes by speeding to analyze and make decisions directing affecting the content's velocity.	Content quality of service will improve the overall quality of the variety of content in the organization's Big Data resources through aspects of security, availability, scalability, and usefulness of content.

Content organization will provide business rules to identify relationships between content, create metadata schema to assign content characteristic to all content. This contributes to increasing the volume of data available and in some ways leveraging existing data to assign metadata values.

Content access is all about search and establishing the standard types of search (i.e., keyword, guided, and faceted) that will be needed. This will contribute to the volume of data, through establishing the parameters and oftentimes additional metadata fields and values to enhance search.

Content governance focuses on establishing accountability for the accuracy, consistency, and timeliness of content, content relationships, metadata, and taxonomy within areas of the enterprise and the applications that are being used. Content governance will often "prune" the volume of content available in the organization's Big Data resources by only allowing access to pertinent/relevant content, while either deleting or archiving other content.

Content quality of service, which focuses on security, availability, scalability, usefulness of the content, and improves the overall quality of the volume of content in the organization's Big Data resources by

 - Defending content from unauthorized access, use, disclosure, disruption, modification, perusal, inspection, recording, or destruction.
 - Eliminating or minimizing disruptions from planned system downtime.
 - Ensuring that the content that is accessed is from and/or based on the authoritative or trusted source, reviewed on a regular basis (based on the specific governance policies), modified when needed and archived when it becomes obsolete.
 - Enabling the content to behave in the same manner, regardless of the application or tool that implements it; moreover the content should be flexible enough to be used from both an enterprise level and a local level without changing its meaning, intent of use, and/or function.
 - Tailoring the content to the specific audience and ensuring that the content serves its distinct purpose, thereby being helpful to its audience and being practical.

Inclusion of additional types of data into the IA is needed. This includes semistructured data (i.e., data coming from sensors such as RFID, location information coming from the mobile devices, information from web logs, documents, and e-mails). These new data elements are often produced at much higher rates compared to the classical transactional data. There is a lot more data coming in at much higher rates and enterprises need to be able to manage these new types of data and incorporate them into their overall IA framework. These new types of data are one of the new characteristics of Big Data.

Key Learnings

The following represents some key learnings from KM and Big Data:

- Don't repeat solving the same problem. Perform root-cause analysis and focus your analytics to solve the "right problem!"
- The same principle that knowledge still exists within an organization's data still holds; however, the challenge is to manage the knowledge found by breaking it down into smaller consumable *chunks* and then bringing them together to form a complete picture.
- There must be a cultural change to enable the belief that all of the individuals in an organization are owners of both their own and the company's knowledge.
- Workers today must be coached to manage, organize, and take responsibility (or held accountable) for their content (information and knowledge) that they create at every step of their work process.
- Principles of KM are scalable as data grows.
- The security, availability, scalability, and usefulness of the content can only be achieved by executing a comprehensive content and data governance strategy.

Tips and Techniques

The following are some of the tips and techniques from deduced from reading this chapter:

- Leverage Big Data tools such as Apache's Hive, Mahout, and Hadoop to bring significant value to your Big Data analytics, which include but are not limited to
- Detecting abnormal behavior patterns
- Detecting trends through social media activities
- Detecting suspicious activities
- Identifying discrepancies in records across systems
- Aligning your organization's tacit knowledge (experts) to content (information and knowledge) through expertise locators, assignment of authoritative voice as a metadata field/value is an essential part of extracting knowledge from your Big Data sources
- Incorporating in your Big Data knowledge extraction efforts the understanding of the data, information and knowledge within your enterprise-wide systems, and the specific knowledge types that are important to your organization to capture
- Creating a comprehensive IA structure in order to enable unstructured data to be included into the mix of Big Data sources
- Aligning IA elements with Big Data components to enable consistencies when including unstructured data to the organization's Big Data environment

Chapter 15

"What Have You Done for the War Fighter Today?": Knowledge Management in the Military

The twenty-first century military will be predominantly characterized by a rapid pace and use of technology. This technological change will require a military that is able to gather and process knowledge and make rapid decisions once that knowledge is vetted. In addition, the policies, practices, operating procedures, and other doctrines will need to be modified to address these advancements and use in technology. The use of unmanned drones is an example of this. The use of unmanned aircraft in the form of drones is being utilized to gather intelligence for military operations in the form of surveillance, air strikes, as well as crowd monitoring and control (Henriques, 2014).

The use of warfare technology highlights the rising importance of utilizing KM to create a military advantage over adversaries. New technologies have resulted in increasingly dynamic, unpredictable, and complex operations that require people to filter and analyze data, information, and knowledge from multiple sources. Problem solving and decision making are more complex and more essential in military situations especially with the advancements in technology. This type of warfare requires superiority at all levels of command and control. It demands situational awareness tools that are superior to those of opponents for anticipating reactions, knowledge gathering, problem solving, and superior decision making. A comprehensive KM strategy that enables continuous evolution in operationalization effectiveness is essential to attain and maintain knowledge superiority, know how, and expertise in executing military operations.

On the human resources side, the military, like their corporate counterparts, recognize the important role of intellectual capital in the modern military enterprise. Rapid technological advancement means that training must become faster and more effective. Time for learning is reduced. Additionally, demographic changes to the work force, and the loss of military knowledge suffered through reduced military spending in the 1990s, have had a long-term impact on the military's corporate memory. Military personnel are rotated through positions for both operational experience and career development. They acquire vast resources of tacit knowledge through their experience; upon leaving the military, the expertise acquired during their service unless captured is lost. KM can be applied to address this issue and apply the necessary solutions.

Continuing KM Challenge of BRAC

When it comes to the movement and the loss of military (enlisted and civilian) personnel, base realignment and closure (BRAC) plays a significant role. BRAC presents the US military with a significant KM challenge. This is a human resources challenge that must be met in order for the US military to maintain its effectiveness. The BRAC specifically represents the challenge of capturing knowledge both tacit and explicit before it leaves a command from personnel shifts and loss due to a BRAC move. The US military has already experienced this knowledge loss and unless steps are taken at least a year in advance of a BRAC or similar move, this loss will continue to happen. The loss of knowledge has the potential to compromise mission activities and the soldier in theater. Leveraging the US military's ability to share knowledge through its established process and tools will help lessen the adverse impact of this knowledge loss. However, without process and tools to capture, catalog, and reuse knowledge, the US military will be challenged to keep the various commands fully operational and effective in a long term for the solider in theater. At the end of the day, KM in the military must be focused on providing actionable intelligence in order to save lives and to successfully complete missions.

This chapter will examine three of the major branches of the military (army, air force, and navy), and how KM is being adopted and the practical applications of this adoption. This chapter will examine the KM strategy each branch is deploying through tactical implementation of KM programs, systems, and initiatives. Special attention to the past performance and future execution of BRAC or similar movements and the knowledge needs that this presents will also be detailed.

Included in this chapter will be my own experiences as it applies to the BRAC, KM policies, procedures, strategies, methods, and systems being deployed within the military.

Department of Defense Knowledge Management Structure

The Joint Chiefs of Staff organizational structure provides the impetus for driving and aligning KM throughout the military. The Joint Chiefs of Staff Department of Defense (DoD) structure aligns the KM efforts from all branches of the military (see Figure 15.1). The Joint Chiefs of Staff structure has established the knowledge management cross-functional team (KM CFT). The KM CFT is a governing entity responsible for improving KM across the Joint Staff (JS), as well as mentoring and promulgating KM best practices across the services, combatant commands, and combat support agencies. The KM CFT ensures that lessons are learned and best practices are filtered up and across, while strategic guidance from the JS guides priority of effort.

The JS KM process has a bottom-up focus where lessons learned and best practices filtered up from the directorates, the services, combatant commands, and combat support agencies, while strategic guidance from the vice director of the JS guides priority of effort. To achieve this end, the KM CFT leverages the Knowledge Management Board (KMB) to develop the JS KM strategic roadmap and provide guidance and direction to the JS via the quarterly strategic guidance memorandum, in support of the Chairman's strategic direction. The KMB also provides the authority for staffing actions initiated by the services, combatant commands, and combat support agencies.

The designated lead for the KM CFT is the vice director of the JS. The Chief of the Information Management Division, Secretary Joint Staff (SJS IMD) will coordinate the day-to-day activities, act as the secretary and provide secretariat support for the KM CFT to include ensuring that minutes are taken and published from each meeting of the KM Board, KM synchronization cell, content management working group, joint KM working group, and other working groups when created. Each J-Dir and Director of Management (DOM) component will provide representation to the KM CFT.

KM Principles

The DoD understands that KM improves efficiency, effectiveness, and innovation across the JS and throughout the DoD. The DoD also understands that as a force, planning, training, operations, and engagement are improved/enhanced when the principles encapsulated in KM are applied (see Table 15.1).

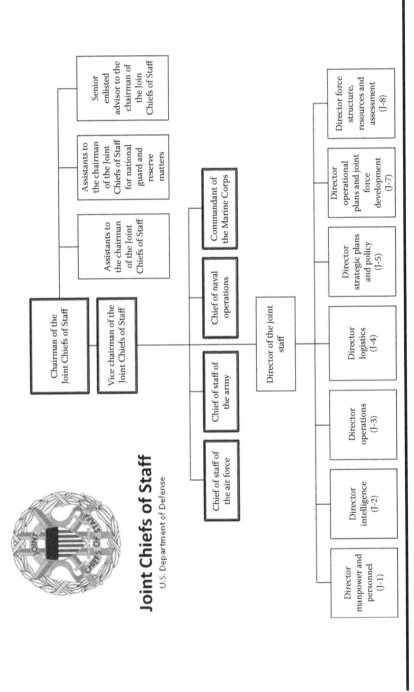

Figure 15.1 Joint Chiefs of Staff US DoD organization structure.

Table 15.1 KM Principles

KM Principles
1. Train and educate KM leaders, managers, and champions.
2. Reward knowledge sharing and make KM career rewarding.
3. Establish a doctrine of collaboration.
4. Use every interaction, whether face-to-face or virtual, as an opportunity to acquire and share knowledge.
5. Prevent knowledge loss.
6. Protect and secure information and knowledge assets.
7. Use legal and standard business rules and processes across the enterprise.
8. Embed knowledge assets (e.g., links, podcasts, videos, documents, simulations, and wikis) in standard business processes and provide access to those who need to know.
9. Use standardized collaborative tools sets.
10. Use open architectures to permit access and searching across boundaries.
11. Use a robust search capability to access contextual knowledge and store content for discovery.
12. Use portals that permit single sign-on and authentication across the global enterprise including partners.

KM Strategies in the US Army

Army Knowledge Management (AKM) is the Army's strategy to transform itself into a net-centric, knowledge-based force, and an integral part of the Army's transformation to achieve the future force. AKM will deliver improved information access and sharing while providing infrastructure capabilities across the Army so that war fighters and business stewards can act quickly and decisively. AKM connects people, knowledge, and technologies.

The goals of AKM are as follows:

■ Adopt governance and cultural changes to become a knowledge-based organization.

■ Integrate KM and best business practices into Army processes to promote the knowledge-based force.

■ Manage the infrastructure as an enterprise to enhance efficiencies and capabilities such as collaborative work, decision making, and innovation.

■ Institutionalize AKO/DKO as the enterprise portal to provide universal and secure access for the entire Army.

■ Harness human capital for the knowledge-based organization. The result of the AKM strategy is to align the Army enterprise knowledge and the information infrastructure with the DoD principles.

- Army organizations will develop communities of practice (CoPs) or communities of interest (COIs) as an integral part of the transformation to a net-centric, knowledge-based force.
- The use of online-secret (AKO-S) permits maximum sharing of Army information and knowledge resources across the Army enterprise and reduces the need for investment in duplicative IT resources. Army activities require collaborative tools to successfully execute missions.
- Use a single Army portal for authenticating Army users to gain access to enterprise systems and portals.
- Active Army, Army Reserve, National Guard, civilian, and appropriate contractor personnel will make full use of online resources and capabilities.
- All personnel must become familiar with the AKM strategy and goals. Commanders and activity heads must develop organizational initiatives to support the strategy and goals. The ability to store and find the right information, at the right time, and to deliver it to the right customer must be a major focus at all levels of command and especially with the information management (IM)/IT community of service providers.

The Army CIO/G-6 will issue policy to ensure an enterprise focus to KM efforts with adherence to Army KM principles. Army commands and organizations will develop KM practices and systems with an enterprise perspective with the latitude to tailor KM practices to specific missions.

Army KM Principles

Any discussion of Army KM should include a discussion of the Army KM principles that were signed by the Army Chief of Staff (General George W. Casey, Jr.) and the Secretary of the Army in 2008. The AKM principles are still in effect and have served as a basis for KM efforts in the Army and the Federal KM arena at large.

The Army KM principles create a consistent framework, so that war fighters and business stewards can innovate, evaluate alternate courses of actions within context of local conditions, and act quickly and decisively. The Army KM principles will help preserve tacit and explicit knowledge and accelerate learning as units and personnel rotate in and out of theaters or organizations. In addition, the Army KM principles anchor KM efforts as an Army-wide enterprise function.

The following are the Army KM principles. These principles align closely to the overall DoD KM principles.

People and Culture
   Principle 1: Train and educate KM leaders, managers, and champions. This will create a culture of collaboration, which will be leveraged to educate

the next-generation KM change agents who understand KM principles and technologies and can effect change to accelerate meeting mission objectives. This will lead to improved curriculum development and instructional delivery methods identified to train and educate the force in KM competency at all levels of the Army.

Principle 2: Reward knowledge sharing and make knowledge management career rewarding. The Army supports the statement "what gets rewarded in organizations gets done" and reward structures guide organizational and individual behavior. This will establish KM career fields, where appropriate, and insert performance elements to evaluate knowledge sharing contributions.

Principle 3: Establish a doctrine of collaboration. This will create a collaborative environment that fosters new ideas, understanding, and ways to execute the commander's intent. It is the intent for Army leaders to incorporate the core principles of collaboration into their business procedures and human resources practices. This includes (1) responsibility to provide— *need to share* should be replaced by *responsibility to provide*; (2) empowered to participate—soldiers and civilians are empowered to participate and share insights in virtual collaborative communities, without seeking prior permission; and (3) user driven—collaborative communities are self-defining, self-creating, and adaptable. Users own the collaborative community, not IT providers.

Principle 4: Use every interaction whether face-to-face or virtual as an opportunity to acquire and share knowledge. This is intended to foster continuous learning, and is an expected day-to-day activity. Learning faster than adversaries or competitors yields short- and long-term results. It is the expectation that Army leaders will frame day-to-day activities as learning opportunities to accelerate knowledge acquisition and transfer and promote learning in teams and in informal and formal social networks.

Principle 5: Prevent knowledge loss. The intent here is to understand that knowledge is perishable and it has a life cycle. The life cycle can't begin until it is documented and assessed for its value. The Army assesses what is valuable from a past activity, document it, and share with those who need to know.

Process

Principle 6: Protect and secure information and knowledge assets. The intent is to deny adversaries access to key information that gives the US and coalition forces the decisive advantage to securely communicate and collaborate across geographic and organizational boundaries. This includes balancing risks regarding *need to know* against *need to protect* and requires leaders of knowledge communities to comply with relevant information assurance regulations and policies.

Principle 7: Embed knowledge assets (links, podcasts, videos, documents, simulations, wikis, etc.) in standard business processes and provide access to those who need to know. The intent is to leverage digital media to add context, understanding, and situational awareness to operations and business activities. The Army insists that leaders creatively embed and use digital media (podcasts, videos, simulations, wikis, etc.) in training routines and operations to add to or leverage the existing knowledge assets of the Army. Convert intellectual capital (ideas, best known practices, etc.) to structural capital (anything that is digitized and accessible and searchable by others). Verify content for legality and desired outcome.

Principle 8: Use legal and standard business rules and processes across the enterprise. The intent is to establish business rules and processes that are repeatable, thus reducing learning curves and promoting consistent quality products and services. The Army expects its leaders to follow standard business rules and processes set by the Army and the DoD. Modify and evolve business rules to meet the commander's intent and quickly adapt business processes to meet or anticipate emerging threats or business opportunities (situational awareness). The Army and across the DoD leverage lean six sigma and continuous process improvement principles within the KM discipline.

Technology

Principle 9: Use standardized collaborative tool sets. The intent is to use common collaborative software tool sets for training, which reduces training and maintenance costs while creating a common platform for data, information, and knowledge exchange in theaters and with other partners and organizations. It reduces impediments to search for relevant knowledge across the enterprise. This promotes the use of the approved Army and DoD collaborative tool sets. Train and deploy with them. Provide access to structural capital to accelerate learning curves and adopt/modify best known practices.

Principle 10: Use open architectures to permit access and searching across boundaries. The intent is to create seamless and ubiquitous service on demand, when one client application requests one or more services for another application that provides complimentary services. The goals here are for KM applications to be designed and operated with an enterprise focus, permitting access, and searching across systems and organizations without technical or structural impediments.

Principle 11: Use a robust search capability to access contextual knowledge and store content for discovery. With the exception of classified information, the Army expects knowledge bases to be accessible and searchable by search engines that deliver contextual knowledge and information. As the Army delivers and operates its KM systems, leaders through the use of appropriate content management principles need to ensure that there are no organizational or technical barriers blocking access to digital media residing in knowledge bases.

Principle 12: Use portals that permit single sign-on and authentication across the global enterprise including partners. The Army will utilize authentication across its enterprise portal for access to lessen confusion for users and provide a standard process for accessing enterprise knowledge assets while reducing total cost of ownership of other portals, websites, or knowledge networks.

Army Knowledge Online

Army Knowledge Online (AKO; see Figure 15.2) represents the Army's information sharing environment offering a robust KM system and access to a network of enterprise services for Army personnel that will facilitate communication, collaboration, and the free exchange of ideas. This environment also provides access to more than 1200 applications that include e-mail, directory services, blogs, file storage, instant messenger, chat, and business process management capabilities as well as links and access to other related Army websites (e.g., Army Training Requirements and Resources System [ATRRS], Interactive Personnel Electronic Records Management System [iPERMS], and Medical Protection System [MEDPROS]).

Current Army KM Direction

Current Army KM direction as stated in the Department of the Army US Army Corps of Engineers 2015 KM Strategic Plan includes the US Army Corps of Engineers (USACE) development of an enterprise-wide integrated KM strategy to promote and drive quality and improve performance across the organization. As the world's

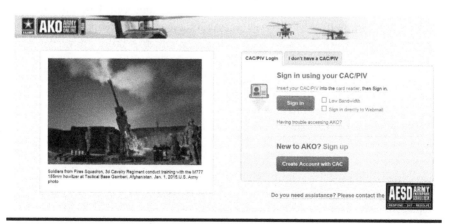

Figure 15.2 Army Knowledge Online portal main page. (Courtesy of US Army. https://www.us.army.mil/suite/login/welcome.html.)

largest public engineering, design, and construction management agency, more than 37,000 USACE personnel manage dams, canals, and flood protection projects throughout the United States, as well as a wide range of public works throughout the world. The strategy will drive a program that provides approaches, methods, and tools that enable KM best practices and promote the flow of actionable information with the goal of capturing critical knowledge and expertise of an aging workforce, transferring knowledge between teams, and improving collaboration and learning across the USACE enterprise. This strategy establishes the roadmap to how KM is implemented across the Department of the Army and creates an Army-wide picture of KM benchmarks and best practices.

KM Strategies in the US Air Force

Timely, accurate, and relevant information is imperative for planning and conducting air, space, and cyberspace operations within the Air Force. A lack of decision-ready, actionable knowledge degrades the Air Force's ability to conduct and support operations with the certainty required to support national military objectives. Turning raw data into information that enables the creation and transfer of knowledge requires an approach of careful collaboration, analysis, deliberation, and judgment. Air Force KM supports this approach by using a combination of technology, processes, and people to achieve mission superiority.

KM provides war fighters with the capability to rapidly access and exploit authoritative, accurate, and relevant information to plan CoAs and execute missions. This specifically includes virtual collaboration, tailored information presentation, integrated data and information, locating and accessing relevant information, sharing information and knowledge, managing information, and intelligence IA. This enables sharing of information and knowledge among CoI, CoP, and coalition partners in a common, collaborative information environment, supporting network services, improved search engine technologies, and integration of knowledge managers and training.

According to Jaggers (2014) of Air Force Public Affairs Agency, the Air Force revamped the KM career field, aiming to make its airmen into some of the service's top innovators working in newly established KM centers Air-Force-wide.

The KM career field split, announced in 2014, moved 80 percent of its airmen to the new Administration Air Force Specialty Code 3A1 × 1. Approximately 20 percent of airmen currently assigned to the KM AFSC 3D0 × 1 will remain, becoming a more specific, technically honed specialty.

According to Chief Master Sergeant Robert Jackson, KM career field manager, KM will undergo a significant technical training ramp-up to meet the challenge of making airmen into top innovators across the Air Force. They employ a process improvement mindset, analyze mission requirements, and recommend solutions. They are the consultants, trainers, and facilitators to connect people to the information they need. "The idea is to help airmen avoid searching through mountains of digital data to find what they're looking for," said Jackson (Jaggers 2014). "The real goal is capturing and reusing the wisdom, experience and lessons we learn over time."

In 2014, the Secretary of the Air Force's Chief Information Officer, Lt. Gen. Michael Basla, sponsored a pilot program to evaluate KM outreach in 15 organizations spanning the Air Force and Air National Guard, yielding promising results. "The pilot proved that real innovation can happen when we connect process improvement and technology," Basla said. "We are not just applying new technology to old processes, but rather looking to improve the process itself, harnessing our airmen's intellectual capital to enhance mission effectiveness."

One pilot KM center at Dover Air Force Base, Del., reinvented a process for producing thousands of letters of appointment. They used Microsoft SharePoint capabilities to produce an appointment letter management tool, cutting back on numerous hours and resources.

"If this kind of improvement can be made with appointment letters, imagine what is possible with our critical mission and business systems," Jackson said. "Airmen spend a lot of time on old paper-era processes, so KM can really help."

Air Force KM Goals and Objectives

The following represents the goals and objectives set forth by the implementation and execution of Air Force KM as mandated in the *Air Force Instruction 33–396 7 November 2014 Communications and Information Knowledge Management*:

- *Decision superiority*: Provides decision makers with a competitive advantage, enabled by an ongoing situational awareness
- *Information superiority*: The degree of dominance in the information domain that allows friendly forces the ability to collect, control, exploit, and defend information while denying this ability to opposing forces
- *Improved individual and shared awareness of the operational environment*: Allows Air Force, joint, and coalition information exchange and enables coordinated operations across all spectrums
- *Constantly evolving team-based learning*: Transforms the Air Force into a learning organization using continuous innovation to steadily feed new information, ideas, and concepts into an expanding base of tacit and explicit knowledge
- *Optimized knowledge processes*: The integration of knowledge principles in work environments assists airmen with optimizing their mapped processes through various KM methodologies and techniques

■ *Seamless access and unified communications*: Provide organizations' access to relevant information anywhere and anytime irrespective of hardware or software platforms utilized

■ *Knowledge assessment and prioritization*: Evaluate classification, sensitivity, mission criticality, and required levels of access for incoming data, information, and knowledge to ensure compliance with required management, handling, and security standards and practices

■ *Capabilities*: Through effective network services and a common collaborative information exchange, KM affords a specific set of capabilities. Success in KM is measured by the degree in which these capabilities are available and leveraged within an organization

■ *Virtual collaboration*: KM provides meaningful situational awareness to all leadership levels through the ability to globally monitor, display, store, distribute, access, and share information and knowledge

■ *Tailored information presentation*: KM connects airmen to authoritative, accurate, and relevant information by using an airman's role-based attributes provided and tracked automatically by EIS

■ *Integrated data and information*: The information environment supports the integration of relevant information from multiple sources and produces improved situational awareness for airmen, based on their role-based attributes and responsibilities

■ *Locate, assess, and refine information*: Airmen can locate required information, extract it, determine its veracity and relevancy, and manipulate it to further support mission goals. This also includes the ability to determine the authority of information and information services by identifying the source, currency, and conditions of use

■ *Identify, store, share, and exchange information and knowledge*: Airmen can identify, store, share, and exchange information and knowledge for collaboration and situational awareness. They are able to do this with other Air Force members, as well as joint and coalition partners, as required

■ *Manage information from creation to final disposition*: Airmen have the ability to store and manage all types of information and knowledge from creation to final disposition. This includes all actions necessary to store and maintain structured and unstructured information. Critical to this concept is the capability to identify and reuse authoritative information from multiple functional areas to eliminate redundant and potentially conflicting information. An integrated enterprise-wide metadata repository and services are essential to effective information discovery and accessibility

■ *Information architecture*: An established IA is essential to establish standardized criteria, processes, and procedures to store and share data, information, and knowledge, including cross-security domain solutions that connect Air Force capabilities with different environments and functional areas

Air Force Knowledge Now

Air Force Knowledge Now (AFKN) is a web-based collaborative environment developed by the Triune Group for the US Air Force (USAF; see Figure 15.3). From 1999 to 2012, AFKN grew to more than 19,000 CoPs and 400,000 members. In 2004, Air Force CIO John M. Gilligan designated AFKN the Air Force Center of Excellence for KM, making it the USAF's only certified and accredited enterprise-wide KM program. By focusing on social, behavioral, and cultural aspects of knowledge sharing, AFKN evolved beyond traditional KM systems, which focused on capturing information through technology.

The Triune Group has been the prime contractor for the AFKN program since 2004. Although the AFKN site has been shutdown and transitioned to Air Force Net (AFNet) effective August 1, 2013, the USAF extended the AFKN contract through 2015.

Figure 15.3 Air Force Knowledge, new portal main page. (http://www.slideshare.net/joannhague/walkingincloudshaguefinal; https://afkm.wpafb.af.mil.)

The program had the following two focus areas:

1. *Collaboration suite*: Provides management and maintenance of the AFKN application; a web-based platform providing knowledge sharing and collaboration through virtual workspaces (called CoP) offering Web 2.0 functionality. The AFKN approach has always been technology agnostic, and the program has embraced new technologies as they have become available
2. *KM services*: Provides consulting services throughout the Air Force to help organizations design and implement knowledge-centric solutions, typically on the AFKN application. These solutions include KMMM, knowledge retention and transfer (KRandT) process, and KM workshops (taxonomy development, implementation, governance, etc.)

KM services capabilities that support AFKN included the following:

■ Comprehensive workshops
■ Online virtual collaboration and sharing
■ Robust document management
■ Expertise locators
■ Integrated e-learning
■ Search/discovery
■ Shared network folders
■ Threaded discussion forums
■ Validated practices library

KM Strategies in the US Navy

The KM strategy for the Department of the Navy (DON) identifies goals and objectives for continued KM implementation throughout the DON. At the DON departmental level, KM is defined as the integration of people and processes, enabled by technology, to facilitate the exchange of operationally relevant information and expertise to increase organizational performance.

Although Navy and Marine Corps personnel have shared information and collaborated since the services began, KM as a recognized discipline with explicit processes has been pursued only for the past 15 years in the DON. Numerous DON commands have benefitted from the implementation of KM processes, procedures, and programs. An updated KM strategy is necessary to keep up the momentum.

Most KM efforts can be grouped into two overlapping categories: command support and commander support. Command support links people to who they need to know and what they need to know to do their jobs better. It seeks to stop *reinventing the wheel* and to take advantage of the DON's tremendous experience and intellectual capital. Commander support includes efforts to ensure that there is a

■ Common understanding of the Commander's intent from the headquarters to the tactical edge or furthest echelon.
■ Shared situational awareness with all concerned.
■ Process to provide the information and knowledge requisite for timely, high-quality decisions.

The tenets of KM are a significant complement to the next generation enterprise network, the joint information environment, and every other environment that connects people and information.

The DON vision for KM is to create, capture, share, and reuse knowledge to enable effective and agile decision making, increase the efficiency of task accomplishment, and improve mission effectiveness. To achieve this vision, the DON KM community will continue to share and leverage the significant KM experience and resources existing within the department. Currently, DON KM is a centralized vision executed through decentralized implementation.

The goals and objectives for DON KM are to

1. Continue to expand departmental awareness that KM applied to operational and business processes will enable significant improvements in mission accomplishment.
2. Instill KM principles and methodologies into the DON culture. This includes the following:
   – Expanding and supporting the DON KM CoP and other KM stakeholders
   – Sharing experiences, key learnings, and results to foster collaboration, enable shortened learning cycles, and assist other efforts.
   – Providing KM training and education across the department. Include KM material in appropriate Navy and Marine Corps training courses
   – Assisting those new to KM to expeditiously locate the support and resources needed to gain an understanding of KM
3. Maximizing the utility of existing DON KM experience and resources. This includes the following:
   – Assisting commands in building upon the KM experiences and resources of others
   – Collect; catalogue; and advertise existing plans, documents, topical guides, and other resources to assist command KM programs and projects
   – Maximizing utility of existing technology resources (those already paid for) to support KM implementation
4. Drive toward a more centrally supported universally available and executed DON KM program

According to Mr. Jim Knox, DON CIO KM team lead, the DON continues to "support the use of KM principles and methodologies as an enabler to improve war fighting and business processes. Though KM is driven by the specific mission requirements and needs of individual commands, it is important to continue to share KM know-how and lessons learned across the department. In the current fiscally challenging environment, commands should recognize the benefits of KM as an enabler to facilitate mission accomplishment" (Jaggers 2014).

Some of the guiding principles of KM established by the Navy include the following:

- KM must align with the commander's vision and mission.
- Enable knowledge capture, sharing, and collaboration.
- Improve Navy performance using the people, and tools available to them.
- KM is critical to integrating disparate functions and units, including functional silos, geographically dispersed domain members, and critical strategic initiatives.
- Follow the knowledge management maturity model (KMMM). This model served as a road map to guide us through the KM process. The KMMM was based on the same concept as the capability maturity model for software.
- Effectively communicate and collaborate. Implementation of collaborative tools that would allow sharing of documents and enable collaboration
- Utilize standardized administrative processes.
- Foster an environment of continuous improvement, innovation, and learning. KM uses CoP as cross-functional teams that can sustain change and focus on the quality of knowledge flows, assets, and key learnings.

Navy Knowledge Online

Navy Knowledge Online (NKO) is the Navy's knowledge portal used by active duty, reserve, and retired enlisted and officers of the US Navy (see Figure 15.4). NKO provides information and resources such as career management, personal development, and leadership. Allowing Navy retired personnel access to NKO increases the pool of knowledge available that can be shared between current active duty and reserve personnel. Sharing knowledge is primarily done through the NKO forum. The NKO Community of Practice (CoP) program provides the ideal way for Navy personnel to share their knowledge. The CoP facilitates sharing of best practices, advice, and expertise in organizational, functional, and operational knowledge in a specific interest group. The focus is on continuous learning, mutual exchange, and collaboration.

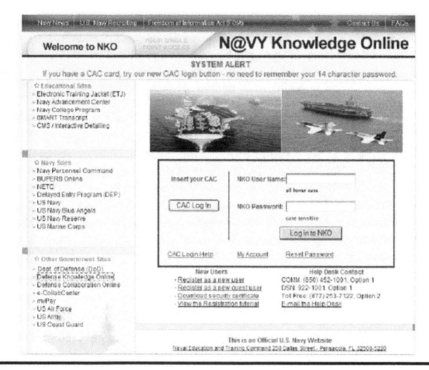

Figure 15.4 Navy Knowledge Online portal main page. (http://www.slideshare. net/joannhague/walkingincloudshaguefinal; https:/wwwa.nko.navy.mil/portal/ home.)

KM and BRAC

The Congress established the 2005 BRAC Commission to ensure the integrity of the base closure and realignment process. At the onset of a BRAC movement, there will be many personnel who will not transition with the command as it moves to their new location. Losing these personnel will cause a gap in both tacit and explicit knowledge. Leveraging KM in support of BRAC movements will provide a mechanism to capture and retain this knowledge for the command as it transitions. This paper will focus on the KM principles, practices, and techniques to transition knowledge from individuals and make it available as a corporate knowledge asset that can be retrieved, examined, and leveraged by the entire command.

A BRAC move has to synchronize people, the information systems they use and the knowledge they have. The organization (command) experiencing the BRAC must carefully manage the change and the transition with precise planning and attention to detail. There must be a realization of what roles/positions are and are not transitioning along with an understanding of the effect of what losing knowledge would do for the command and how this will be addressed.

One of the objectives of the BRAC is to transition and execute change management without an interruption or dilution of mission services and/or activities. An essential component of this is the personnel and the knowledge they possess to effectively carry out the missions of the command. Capturing, cataloging, and retaining critical knowledge of the command before it leaves during a BRAC move are at the core of applying KM to BRAC movements. The problem occurs because the loss of knowledge will have an adverse effect on the missions and the activities of the command that can be detrimental to the personnel in theater. The solution will be to apply KM as a mechanism to capture and retain this knowledge for the command and make it available as a corporate knowledge asset that can be retrieved, examined, and leveraged by the entire command. This knowledge should continue to be updated after the BRAC is completed.

Summary of Contributing Factors

Table 15.2 outlines the key contributing factors related to the opportunity/problem the BRAC presents.

Addressing the BRAC Problem

To begin to address this problem of potential loss of knowledge, a KM strategy must be created. Creating a KM strategy presents a holistic approach to capturing, cataloging, and making available the various knowledge assets of the command. Creating a single integrated knowledge repository is a major deliverable for cataloging and making available the various knowledge assets. This knowledge repository should support the KM principles as depicted in Table 15.1.

The critical task for the command is to determine what knowledge they should retain and share. KM content management should link to what people know, and how they use the knowledge to support the mission, objectives, and activities of the command. It draws on human competency, intuition, ideas, and motivations. It is not a technology-based concept even though utilizing the correct technology KM tools is important. The short-term KM goal for the command is to determine what knowledge to collect from its personnel who are going to leave prior to the final BRAC move while supporting the long-term KM goal to refine and implement the strategic KM plan. The final state of KM at the command will provide enterprise knowledge and services that are necessary to improve operations and decision making across the command. Table 15.3

Table 15.2   Contributing Factors to Capturing Knowledge

#	*Contributing Factors*	*Effect on Organization*
1	Some personnel will not transition to the new location	Cohesiveness of mission activities could be compromised because of lack of skilled personnel
2	Explicit knowledge (SOP's, lessons learned, templates, examples) not properly captured and cataloged	Loss of documented knowledge that could compromise the effectiveness and efficiency of personnel performing the job at the new location
3	Tacit knowledge (specific *know how* from experienced personnel) not properly captured and cataloged	Loss of knowledge (specific "know how") that could compromise the effectiveness and efficiency of personnel performing the job at the new location
4	Lack of understanding of who are the key knowledge holders and what knowledge they possess	Potential of losing key personnel with substantial knowledge of mission critical activities. This personnel has a high impact on the effectiveness and success of missions/activities once the BRAC is completed
5	Lack of understanding of the "knowledge gaps" that will exist once the BRAC transition is made	Understanding and identifying the gaps in knowledge will enable the command/organization to plan and execute a strategy to fill these gaps. This strategy could consist of training, additional skilled personnel (temp employees), new hires, creating SOP's, etc.

presents a BRAC chart showing possible KM needs, goals, and objectives for Stakeholders for potential services.

The KM program for the command will optimize the organization, exchange, currency, and accessibility of knowledge so that personnel spend less time looking for what they need in order to make critical decisions and complete the mission. The KM efforts and initiatives will add value by

- Facilitating better, more informed decisions.
- Contributing to the intellectual capital of the organization.
- Encouraging the free flow of ideas that leads to insights and innovation.
- Eliminating redundant processes and streamlining operations.
- Improving efficiency and overall productivity.

Table 15.3 BRAC Chart Showing Possible KM Needs, Goals, and Objectives for Stakeholders

KM Strategic Initiative	1. Develop Sites in Support of Tacit Knowledge Collaboration	2. Train and Educate Leaders, Managers, and Users on KM	3. Establish a Doctrine of Collaboration as a Way of Doing Business	4. Reward Knowledge Sharing and Make KM Career Rewarding	5. Use Open Architecture to Permit Access and Searching Across Boundaries	6. Manage KM Resources	7. Coordinate KM Across the Command	8. Elicit Requirements for KM Tools
Stakeholder Knowledge Management Needs								
e-learning	✓	✓	✓				✓	✓
Web-conferencing	✓	✓	✓					✓
Collaborative software	✓	✓	✓					✓
Email lists	✓	✓	✓					✓
Wikis	✓	✓	✓	✓				✓
Blogs	✓	✓	✓	✓				✓
Communities of practice	✓	✓	✓	✓	✓		✓	✓
Content management systems	✓				✓	✓	✓	✓
Knowledge bases and networks	✓				✓	✓		✓

(Continued)

Table 15.3 (Continued) BRAC Chart Showing Possible KM Needs, Goals, and Objectives for Stakeholders

KM Strategic Initiative	1. Develop Sites in Support of Tacit Knowledge Collaboration	2. Train and Educate Leaders, Managers, and Users on KM	3. Establish a Doctrine of Collaboration as a Way of Doing Business	4. Reward Knowledge Sharing and Make KM Career Rewarding	5. Use Open Architecture to Permit Access and Searching Across Boundaries	6. Manage KM Resources	7. Coordinate KM Across the Command	8. Elicit Requirements for KM Tools
Stakeholder Goals and Objectives								
Create and enable a learning and sharing environment	✓	✓	✓	✓	✓	✓	✓	✓
Connect people with other knowledgeable people	✓	✓	✓	✓	✓	✓	✓	✓
Connect people with information	✓	✓	✓		✓		✓	✓
Enable the conversion of information to knowledge	✓	✓	✓		✓		✓	✓
Encapsulate knowledge to facilitate its transfer	✓	✓	✓	✓	✓		✓	✓
Disseminate knowledge	✓	✓	✓	✓	✓		✓	✓

Any KM program will need to concentrate on developing the following practices among individuals and groups, and must be reflected in management processes and behaviors, becoming an integral part of the organizational culture:

■ Recognition and valuing of individual knowledge
■ Recognition and valuing of knowledge held by others
■ An enthusiasm to search for new knowledge
■ The skills to search for that new knowledge
■ An enthusiasm for sharing knowledge with others, and a capacity to link personal and shared knowledge to organizational goals and performance

A well-structured and consistent approach to facilitating knowledge capture, cataloging, and retention within the command is needed to support the diversity of content and the locations where it resides; there is tremendous content in both physical repositories and within the minds of individuals. Understanding and managing that content so that it can be shared and applied is vital to increasing overall effectiveness of personnel.

An understanding of the knowledge and content being managed is an essential first step to enable effective knowledge capture, cataloging, and retention. Raw data can be transformed to increasing levels of trust and authority through the application of cognitive practices of the command. This results in a spectrum of knowledge that must be managed through structured practices and business rules so that there is cohesion of understanding and application.

The knowledge and content that must be understood and managed range from the unexpressed or tacit that is in the heads of individuals across the spectrum of the command to the formal, approved content such as regulations and manuals. At each level, the authority and trust of the material are balanced by the risk of applying that content. There is little risk in following a regulation, whereas applying an observation that is provided verbally from a peer may be considered potentially risky.

As the KM BRAC process is worked, it will benefit from a well-defined knowledge/content hierarchy and knowledge capture, and transformation rules. These provide a framework that is at the core of the KM BRAC process and tool.

Missed KM Opportunity of BRAC

Impending BRAC moves have the potential to bring considerable personnel turnover, which will lead to knowledge loss and gaps in operations. During my time in executing BRAC movements within the military, there was a missed opportunity when it came to adequately capturing and cataloging knowledge loss to enable reuse. To close this gap, there are several steps that need to be considered. These steps include the following:

1. Determining existing and potential sources, flows, and constraints including environmental factors that could influence knowledge flow
2. Identifying and locating where the explicit and tacit knowledge exists
3. Creating a knowledge map depicting the flow of knowledge within the organization
4. Identifying what knowledge is missing within the organization that is needed in order to achieve stated goals and objectives and who needs the missing knowledge within the organization to effectively perform their duties
5. Identifying possible improvements and recommendations regarding KM activities within the organization

Key Learnings

The following are some key learnings from this chapter:

- One of the takeaways from this chapter is about how the military structures KM to be aligned to the overall DoD principles and structure, with a focus on the individual KM principles of each branch. KM by design is given a strategic alignment with a specific tactical focus depending on the needs of the particular branch of the military.
- All organizations can learn from the DoD structure of KM and apply it by aligning KM to the overall corporate strategy, enabling KM through senior leadership support (C-suite executive support), and aligning specific KM strategies and tactical implementations across departments to the overall policies and objectives stated in the organization's enterprise KM strategy.

Tips and Techniques

The following are some tips and techniques that stood out from this chapter:

- The chart indicating KM needs, goals, and objectives for stakeholders is a good tool to utilize for BRAC initiatives, and it can be applied to any KM initiative that focuses on determining the knowledge to capture and the knowledge services that are required to improve operations and decision making.
- Developing an understanding of contributing factors to capturing knowledge as indicated in Table 15.2 is an essential tool in understanding the effect of knowledge loss and what has to occur in order to capture knowledge.
- When the organization knows that a location move is eminent, the need to capture, catalog, and store knowledge from individuals that may leave

the organization becomes imperative. Understanding this from experience, a knowledge transfer/capture effort must start anywhere from six months to a year in advance of the move. This timeframe is established to adequately validate the knowledge being captured and to ensure individuals will be engaged and incentivized long enough to transfer their know how.

Chapter 16

Drinking the Knowledge Management Kool-Aid: Knowledge Management Adoption

"Drinking the KM Kool-Aid" is a metaphor to indicate the adoption of KM (program, policies, procedures and the methods, and systems that enable it) throughout your organization. KM is a multidisciplinary approach to enabling the right knowledge, to get to the right people, in the right context, and at the right time. This knowledge can be tacit (in the minds of individuals) and/or explicit (written down/documented in various forms, for example, knowledge articles, frequently asked questions (FAQs), job aids, standard operating procedures (SOPs), and key learnings). To enable knowledge to flow quickly through your organization and to support the processes and procedures that have been defined, the implementation of methods (i.e., knowledge sharing, collaboration, knowledge capture, and knowledge reuse), and the governance (maintenance and management) of your knowledge assets, a systems (KMSs), must be deployed. So, in this case, adoption will have to occur at many levels within the ecosystem of your organization's KM structure.

Once the need for a KM program has been determined, immediately after its official launch, efforts must be on the way to initiate its adoption. In order to initiate the adoption of your KM program, an effort to market the program and its various components has to be an intentional endeavor.

Marketing and communication are critical ongoing activities that are aimed at creating awareness and spreading the system benefits to the end user.

A high-impact and effective marketing campaign should be included in the project plan both during and after a system launch. Marketing will help create a buzz about the KMS and also help showcase the success that has been achieved. Marketing strategy should ensure that all user segments and stakeholders of the project are impacted.

Communication Channels

The following channels should be leveraged for communicating the KM program and need to be detailed in the communications plan:

- *Newsletter*: Created by the marketing team and published monthly. Using an interview format, a feature article is written by a reporter from the team. The article is then written and published in the newsletter.
- *News brief*: Published once a week. The content is coordinated and submitted to the communications team.
- *Leadership thought message*: Part of newsletter. A message is highlighted once a month from one of the leadership teams. A schedule for the year is created at the start of each year by the communications team and the chief information officer. Topics of messaging are left to the monthly leader but recommended by the communications team.
- *Project manager forum and mentoring sessions*: Mentoring sessions are held daily for any PMs requiring assistance. The project management office (PMO) also holds project management forums periodically for sharing major news and addressing process efficiency issues pertaining to the KM program.
- *Town hall meetings*: Everyone are invited to attend town hall meetings, which can be scheduled as needed. Schedules and marketing of these meetings are coordinated through the communications and marketing teams.
- *Corporate broadcast messaging*: Advertisement agency type static messages flashed via the corporate intranet. This is utilized to drive corporate associates to news brief and newsletter articles and also to create awareness to events (e.g., town hall meetings). The communications team creates the actual visuals and controls pushing those out to the organization. This is an essential vehicle that should be utilized to socialize the KM program and energize the adoption process.

Adoption Activities

In an effort to socialize and adopt your KM program inclusive of its policies, practices, methods, and systems, there are certain activities that will impact in a positive way on the success of your adoption efforts. The following is a representation of some of these activities:

■ *Lunch-n-learn*: At its simplest, a learning at lunch program is a training (or learning) event scheduled during the lunch hour. The attendees bring their lunches and eat them during the presentation session. The training is usually less formal and less structured than normal. This promotes a comfortable atmosphere where the attendees feel free to not only learn from the presenter but also share knowledge among themselves.

■ *Knowledge café (see Chapter 5)*: A knowledge café is a means of bringing a group of people together to have an open, creative conversation on a topic of mutual interest to surface their collective knowledge, to share ideas and insights, and to gain a deeper understanding of the subject and the issues involved. As a KM tool, a knowledge café is used to share tacit knowledge. The knowledge café can be used within teams, communities of practice (CoP), across several teams both colocated and distributed, to help facilitate learning from others and gain a deeper collective understanding of a subject through interactive conversation.

■ *Business social*: Business social represents utilizing social media capabilities within the organization. Social media has become an important consequence to organizational communication processes because social media concepts and tools afford behaviors that were difficult or impossible to achieve in combination before these new technologies entered the workplace (Treem & Leonardi, 2012). These technologies speak to the way people interact outside of the corporation and enable a familiar and effective way to promote awareness of the KM program and positively influence its adoption.

Key Adoption Challenges

With any effort there will be some challenges to a successful adoption. These adoption challenges will be analyzed and detailed in this chapter. Typically, the adoption challenges faced during the lifetime of the KM program are as follows:

■ Unclear KM strategy
■ Lack of personal return on investment (ROI)
■ Lack of organizational culture
■ Lack of organizational commitment
■ Failure to communicate effectively
■ Poor maturity of tool deployed

In this chapter, an examination of the communication and marketing efforts to support adoption will be presented in detail. Also, implementation strategies, cultural barriers, and other adoption challenges will be examined. In addition, a demonstration of how the task–technology fit (TTF) model can be applied to increase adoption of the KM program and its various components will be detailed.

Communications and the Adoption Approach

The communications plan should include messages from leadership to employees that create an awareness of the KM initiative, prepare the organization for adoption, and educate key stakeholders to get them up to speed on activities that are required. The goal of the communications plan should be to move from disparate or nonexistent knowledge sources and content to organizational knowledge value through adoption of the KM strategy. A critical component of success in KM adoption is setting the expectation and communicating a vision of what your organization is trying to achieve in the short term, mid term, and long term. Successful adoption means people change the way they work, it is not just implementing a system. The more personalized the message the greater the understanding of change is for each employee. The approach utilized for the communications plan should include (but not limited to) the following:

- Leveraging existing communications channels (create new ones if needed) — see communication channels listed in this chapter
- Communicate in some way at least once per week
- Develop core messages that your organization can leverage through the remainder of the initial year of KMS implementation and postimplementation
- Communicate to multiple levels in the organization—leadership and associate

The Communications Plan

At the heart of communication (and KM) lie the development of information and the sharing of that information with others to add insights about it—turning information into knowledge. KM takes the matters further to (a) ensure information is well-organized and accessible (i.e., information management), (b) optimize the frequency and richness of dialogues (through various channels) that take place to solve current/upcoming issues and come up with new solutions (i.e., social learning and innovation), and (c) keep a learning attitude at various levels to ensure continuous improvement of these information and knowledge processes.

The KM communications plan should include the following items in its structure:

- The challenges and opportunities of setting up a KM program
- The scope of the KM program
- KM communication objectives
- Communication channels (see Table 16. 1)
- Activities proposed per objective
- Activities identified in the communications calendar

Town Halls and Communication Messaging

Town Hall Content

In addition to organizational news brief messaging, a town hall meeting is the other broad communication channel that can be utilized. Best practices for these types of sessions include the following: dynamic lead off, several speakers to change things up, make things interactive, and be clear about the major messages to communicate. Two town hall sessions are recommended on the communication calendar. The first session will educate on the topic and how it affects each associate and work process. The second session is recommended to market any changes in the direction or initiatives within the program.

Goals of a KM Town Hall Session Are as Follows:

- *Sell the vision* of the *enterprise KM program* messages:
  - Why KM?
  - Not a system, a different way to work together
  - Link knowledge to help address major pain points within the organization
    - Lack of SME identification
    - Lack of available corporate knowledge
    - The ability to find knowledge when it is needed
- *Create awareness* of the KM Program
- *Explain*
  - How each associate is expected to participate
  - What is different from how they work today
  - What KM is and why they need to care about it
- *Educate regarding KM program rollout and adoption plan*

Communication Messaging

The recommendation for communicating about KM and setting the expectations is a two-prong approach: (a) The executive management and KM program leadership share similar messaging as it pertains to implementing the KM program. They will be expected to push the messaging down through their organizations. (b) KM champions or key management for an area will communicate the same message with their subordinates as they work to adopt aspects of the KM program.

Sample Messaging

XYZ Company is rolling out an enterprise KM program (EKMP). We listen to your concerns and needs for such a program and are asking your support to enable the

EKMP to realize its vision and achieve its mission: "Deliver the right knowledge, to the right people, in the right context, and at the right time."

Critical to successful KM is the depth and breadth of the knowledge available. We expect (appreciate?) your support in transferring all pertinent knowledge assets into the enterprise KM system, making it the single location for corporate intellectual capital.

We've received the questions concerning when the new knowledge sharing methods (KSM) will be available. To eliminate silos of information/knowledge, a news brief and calendar indicating availability of knowledge sharing technology is now available to everyone via the corporate intranet.

Thanks for your support in changing the way we work together. A timeline for understanding KM impacts in your area will be provided by your KM champion. Table 16.1 indicates sample communication audience, channels, and message points

Table 16.1 Sample Communication Audience/Channels

Audience	Channel	Messages	Target Dates
Executive leadership	Executive-level meetings	Goals of KM program Rollout and adoption progress and the role of the executive	Established in communications calendar
KM program leadership	Program leadership meetings	Expectations during KM program operationalization	Established in communications calendar
Company associates	News article, news briefs, town hall meetings	Vision for KM program Rollout and adoption status	Established in communications calendar
KM administrators	Specific communications from KM program leadership News article, news briefs	Vision for KM program Features of the KM system (if available) Rollout and adoption status	Established in communications calendar
KM champions/ KM team	Specific communications from KM program leadership News article, news briefs		Established in communications calendar

Adoption and the KM Implementation Strategy

To ensure adoption and usage of KMS, the implementation strategy should be people centric rather than technology centric. The key activities that are critical during KM project management are discussed next:

Project discovery is a structured and analytical approach to assess the business value that the KM tool would deliver and also to develop an implementation strategy for the KM tool.

Discovery involves the following:

- Develop scenarios to identify how employees will use the system and how value will be delivered
- Develop implementation strategy based on the organization's use case scenario, assessment of barriers in connecting and collaborating, recommendations for measuring the value delivered, and tactics for driving usage and adoption
- Leadership and cultural assessment questionnaires to identify leadership interest and organizational culture support in making KM a success

Business objectives and success metrics: It is a prelaunch activity that determines the metric tracking, reporting, and success guidelines of the project. This includes identifying your corporate objectives and business objectives that help achieve your corporate goals, as well as determining project-tracking metrics based on business objectives and identifying suitable ranges. Metrics should be measureable, actionable, and quantifiable. Examples of metrics are as follows: knowledge transactions, reuse of knowledge content, and expertise search and location.

Champion program: The role of a champion is crucial for long-term adoption strategies as they will evangelize the system within their respective user groups and directly impact usage. It is important to recruit champions across the organization (by location, function, and community) who can positively influence the adoption within their user segments. Create a structured champion program to motivate, manage, and provide incentives to champions.

Community development and prepopulation strategies: They should be developed based on the feedback gathered during the project discovery. Communities can be based on technology or business disciplines, departments, functions, products, business process, or special interests. During community development, ensure that the communities are not more than three-level deep; they are prepopulated and have an active champion identified. Prepopulation focuses on ensuring a great first experience to the user of the system. The strategies are to be aimed at building user profiles, expert profiles, and bringing the existing content by integrating content repositories such as file shares or emails with the KMS.

Integration: It involves integrating the KM tool with other existing tools and resources within the organization. Integration coupled with prepopulation ensures that users are able to use the system to its fullest potential right from the start and are also able to access the other resources made available to them earlier. A highly integrated environment ensures that the tool is better used and also easier to use.

Training: Training users to utilize the system helps the users in using the system more effectively and it has also been seen that a trained user is more likely to return to the system. Training sessions will also help in showcasing the benefits and use of the system and drive user acceptance.

Lunch-n-learn: This will provide a less formal approach to training and will not consume additional time; attendees would spend getting their daily work accomplished. Typical lunch-n-learn programs when used to facilitate adoption efforts would include the following:

- *Skills training*: This can range from teaching customer service representatives how to answer the phone correctly to providing leadership training to first-line managers.
- *Product training*: If your company has many products or services, a program of learn at lunch sessions can help all employees better understand the product differences.
- *Professional development*: Give people an opportunity to learn what people in other departments do. Do you have someone in IT who could teach a course in programming basics or someone in accounting who could explain how financial forecasting works? Maybe someone in HR could teach a session on how to interview better.
- *Personal development*: A learn at lunch program does not have to be strictly business. You could offer an occasional session on any talent any of your employees is willing to teach, from wood carving to painting or drawing.
- *Life skills*: You could bring in a guest speaker to explain to your employees the different types of insurance and the benefits of each. Or have a class in household budgeting, first aid, or fire safety, anything that helps your employees learn.

Incentive management: This involves driving usage by encouraging participation through the use of rewards, performance reviews, and other motivators. Incentive management in itself becomes crucial, as an incorrect program would impact the usage of the system. While implementing an incentive program, identify all possible incentives, get key stakeholder buy in, and publicize the incentive plan.

Tactics for culture change: To promote KM culture within an organization, the project team must use the KMS to its fullest and evangelize the system. The culture change can be brought about by maintaining a rewards and recognition program for KM adopters, by gathering feedback from early adopters in terms of high personal ROI and sharing broadly, and in some cases by undoing the organization's past history of unsuccessful attempts at KM. The project team must also work to get full commitment and support from key executives at the organization.

Metrics measurement, reporting, and ROI: As an ongoing exercise, metrics need to be monitored and reported in a formal manner by the project team. The objective of this exercise is to ensure that the system is being used as per expectation and, if there is any deviation, the project team is able to preempt it by taking a corrective course correction. Many KM implementations are unsure of how to link KM efforts to ROI. This should be addressed by identifying a set of metrics that best correlate to business impact that can be traced to actions taken by users on the KMS such as time taken to solve problems, project execution times, new product ideas or feedback gathered, time taken to solve customer issues, and reduction in manufacturing-related defects.

Usage optimization: It is a continuous exercise to measure and enhance the value of a KM implementation and to monitor the health of the system. Usage optimization process should

- Gather, analyze, and report actual usage and adoption metrics against expected metrics.
- Carry out root cause analysis of the usage and adoption issues.
- Develop a set of tactics to impact these root causes.
- Set goals and timeline for next optimization exercise.

Adopting KM Systems

To succeed in executing your KM strategy, it is imperative that the adoption of the system within the user base is achieved. The focus of the implementation and socialization of the KMS should be on increasing and maintaining the usage of the system in terms of the number of users participating, increasing the number of transactions on the system, and improving the quality of the transactions.

Failure in meeting adoption translates into slow growth and an underutilized and ineffective KMS. We will focus on two primary areas (a) key adoption challenges faced by organizations and (b) a framework to guide project teams to overcome these challenges.

The recommended approach to adoption followed critical elements of technology transfer, which included taking into consideration the input from the user community concerning their KMS needs, providing assurances of confidence and trust that the knowledge and content contained in the KMS was relevant and up-to-date, messaging changing attitudes from a silo organization to an open accessible organization when it came to sharing, and the ability to obtain knowledge and its associated content.

Implementing Information Architecture

Information architecture (IA) focuses on organizing, structuring, and labeling content in an effective and sustainable way. The goal is to help users find, share, and collaborate regarding content (information and knowledge) in most cases in order to complete certain tasks. The purpose of your IA is to help users understand where they are in the system, how to find what they need, know what they've found, and what to expect from the system. As a result, your IA informs the content strategy through identifying word choice as well as informing user interface/user experience (UI/UX) through influencing wire framing and the KMS development. The IA brings in the understanding of the interdependent nature of users the content and context of information.

IA as it is applied to create a KMS provides a user-centric approach to the KMS implementation. IA (see Chapter 4) and its involvement of users contribute to the user's ability to understanding how the KMS works by providing intuitive and user-friendly functionality, which contributes to the adoption and effective use of the system. By establishing clarity upward into the UI and downward into the system architecture, contributing to simplifying design, development, and implementation, the IA creates a common ground bridging the gap between the users, designers, and developers. A well-defined IA will provide consistent experiences for the users that will also contribute to the successful adoption of the KMS.

TTF Model

The examination of the TTF theory by Huang and Lin (2008) is predicted to be a significant precursor to KMS usage (Huang & Lin, 2008). The Huang and Lin study has shown that the TTF theory is suitable for understanding the specific KMS needs of the group by determining and prioritizing their technology needs (Huang & Lin, 2008; Simmons, 2013). The significance of Huang and Lin's study determines that the TTF theory can be applied to examine the motivation of users to leverage a KMS to perform their organizational tasks and that applying the TTF theory to the KM program can have a positive effect on the success of the KM program.

In addressing the application of the TTF theory and how it could be applied to a KM program, the first step is an examination of the components of a KM program. According to an article by Robert Simmons on implementing a KM program, he points out eight specific steps as follows:

Step 1—Establish KM program objectives: Simmons points out that articulating the end state is important to establishing the appropriate program objectives and identifying the business problems and the business drivers that will provide momentum and justification for the endeavor.

Step 2—Prepare for change: Simmons indicates that a major component of establishing a KM program is to execute change management. The change management strategy will address the cultural changes that need to take place on how employees perceive and share knowledge as well as addressing the changes within the organization's norms and shared values that need to take place. A change management strategy will establish an approach for managing cultural change and produce a knowledge sharing, knowledge-driven culture end state of the KM program.

Step 3—Define high-level process: To facilitate the identification, capture, cataloging, use, and maintenance of the corporation's knowledge assets, an effective KM process needs to be established (Simmons, 2013).

Step 4—Determine and prioritize technology needs: Simmons indicates that depending on the program objectives that have been established, as well as the process controls and criteria that have been defined, a prioritization of the KM technology needs can occur (Simmons, 2013). It is important to understand how the KM technology will address the knowledge processing and cultural knowledge needs of the organization as well as how the KM solution will be adopted by its users.

Step 5—Assess current state: Assessing the current state of KM within your organization should focus on the five core KM components: people, processes, technology, structure, and culture (Simmons, 2013). This assessment, according to Simmons, should uncover the gaps between current and desired states, and the recommendations for addressing/closing these gaps. This assessment will become the foundation for the KM roadmap (Simmons, 2013).

Step 6—Build a KM implementation roadmap: Simmons stresses that "before going too far, you should reconfirm senior leadership's support and commitment, as well as the funding to implement and maintain the knowledge management program" (Simmons, 2013). This is crucial to the development and execution of the program.

The KM program strategy should be presented as a "roadmap of related projects, each addressing specific gaps identified by the assessment" (Simmons, 2013). The roadmap will indicate timelines, milestones, and dependencies. The roadmap should indicate the initiation of specific projects to execute the KM program strategy.

Step 7—Implementation: Implementing a KM program and maturing the overall effectiveness of your organization can require significant personnel resources and funding. Implementation of the KM program will involve the execution of the roadmap, ensuring that short-term goals and wins are realized to gain momentum and maintain the support of key stakeholders (Simmons, 2013).

Step 8—Measure and improve the KM program: In order to understand if your KM program and its associated initiatives (projects) are effective, establishing the appropriate metrics/measurements are necessary. These metrics must be utilized in a way to measure the actual effectiveness and comparing that to anticipated results (Simmons, 2013).

Applying the TTF Model

When applying the TTF theory to the KM program, a determination of where the TTF theory fits within the KM program structure must be identified. The TTF theory (see Figure 16.1) holds that IT is more likely to have a positive impact on individual and group performance if it is aligned with the tasks the users perform (Huang & Lin, 2008). When incorporating the KMS into the KM program, the system is aligned with the KM processes that have been identified that the KM program will support (Simmons, 2013). The KM processes of the KM program reflect how workers within the organization use knowledge to perform their tasks. The TTF theory is suited to measure this usage and can be leveraged to understand not only how the KMSs are being used but will guide the KM program administrators on the best way to increase adoption and contribute to increasing the performance of the workers who use the KMS.

The Huang and Lin (2008) examination of KMS application of the TTF theory included the application of the TTF theory to analyze its usefulness. This examination indicated that the TTF theory is predicted to be a significant precursor to KMS usage (Huang & Lin, 2008).

Furthermore, the Huang and Lin study has shown that the TTF theory is suitable for understanding the specific KMS needs of the program contributing to step 4 (determine and prioritize technology needs) of the KM program (Huang & Lin, 2008; Simmons, 2013). The TTF theory will also contribute to the KM program roadmap as it pertains to the alignment of technology to the specific milestones and objectives identified in the roadmap; in addition, the TTF theory will contribute to understanding what are the key aspects to adoption of the KMS by the organization's users and provides mechanisms to measure the rate of adoption contributing to step 8 of the KM program, to measure and improve the KM program (Simmons, 2013).

The Huang and Lin (2008) research into the TTF theory as it applies to the adoption of KMS indicates that KMS can play a major role in the facilitation of KM policies, processes, and procedures throughout an organization (Huang & Lin, 2008). The significance of this research determines that the TTF theory can be applied to examine the motivation of users to leverage a KMS to perform their organizational tasks and that applying the TTF theory to the KM program can have a positive effect on the success of the KM program.

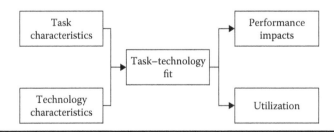

Figure 16.1   Task–Technology fit (TTF) model.

The examination of the TTF theory by Huang and Lin (2008) is predicted to be a significant precursor to KMS usage (Huang & Lin, 2008). The Huang and Lin's study has shown that the TTF theory is suitable for understanding the specific KMS needs of the group by determining and prioritizing their technology needs (Huang & Lin, 2008; Simmons, 2013).

The significance of Huang and Lin's study determines that the TTF theory can be applied to examine the motivation of users to leverage a KMS to perform their organizational tasks and that applying the TTF theory to the KM program can have a positive effect on the success of the KM program.

Organizational Culture

Understanding the culture of your organization will mitigate cultural resistance to KM adoption. Knowing if your organization's culture is knowledge hoarders or knowledge sharers, resistant to change or welcomes change, adoption leaders, or adoption laggards will play a significant role on the messaging, activities, and objectives that are placed on adoption initiatives.

Hsu, Lawson, and Liang state that diverse enterprise cultures and leadership styles may lead enterprises to a different management pattern. Three primary factors affect the adoption of KM: senior management support, a knowledge-friendly culture, and a clear strategy for managing knowledge (Hsu, Lawson, & Liang, 2007).

Important to the adoption of KM is the organizational culture regarding the importance and use of knowledge. This may be the most difficult component to fully mitigate (Davenport & Prusak, 1999). The enterprise culture represents a company's values, which become the norms of its employees' activities, opinions, and conduct. A method to mitigate an organization's cultural barrier to KM is to take an individual knowledge and attitude approach toward KM adoption. Changing user perceptions and attitudes is the key to a user's participation.

In numerous studies, top management support and high-ranking management positive participation have been found to be crucial to the successful adoption of KM by an organization's employees (Hsu, Lawson, & Liang, 2007).

Key Learnings

The following are some key learnings from this chapter:

- Best practice organizations use a variety of channels including e-mail, the intranet, and leadership involvement to promote KM to employees.
- Do not take a *one size fits all* approach to KM and KM adoption. A recommendation is to structure each communication to convey the value of KM participation to a specific audience. When your employees understand the

organizational (global) picture of how they as individuals fit and will benefit, they are much more likely to make the effort to adopt the KM program and its various initiatives.

■ By applying the task characteristics of the roles within the group to the functionality of your organization's KMS, you are able to ascertain the gaps in knowledge and content provided by the system.

■ The TTF model indicates that the greater the fit of IS design with task characteristics of its users along with the ability of the KMS to address the knowledge needs of the users, the better the performance of the users.

Tips and Techniques

The following are several tips and techniques that can be applied to adopt your organization's KM program (policies, procedures, methods, and systems):

■ In adopting a KMS, it is important that the user's knowledge needs are met and trust that the knowledge and content contained in the system is relevant and up-to-date.

■ The TTF theory can also contribute to the group enhancing the KM program roadmap as it pertains to the alignment of technology to the specific roles within your organization.

■ In measuring value and rate of adoption of the KMS, it is similar to other software implementations. However, it has a significant difference. Instead of quantitative measures to value a KMS such as the number of contributions or number of uses, "measures of KMS success are rather related to intention to use (end users) and intention to contribute (contributory users) and can be assessed with the help of the perceived benefit model." (see Figure 16.2; Baloh, 2007).

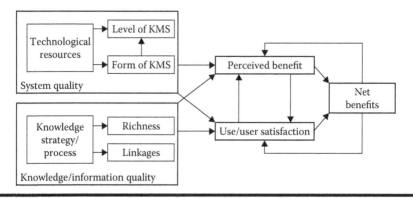

Figure 16.2 Perceived benefit model.

■ The TTF is leveraged to analyze the context through an analysis of the characteristics of knowledge needs (instead of tasks) where task and technology contingencies are internally consistent and aligned. Baloh also indicates that "the more technology is aligned to knowledge needs, the greater their intentions to contribute and use KMS will be" (Baloh, 2007).

Chapter 17

Failure Is Not an Option: Why Do Knowledge Management Programs and Projects Fail?

Why do knowledge management (KM) programs and projects fail?

Let's begin by determining the difference between a KM program and a KM project. In a blog post dated December 31, 2012, I have stated what in my experience designates a KM program and a KM project. In many of my KM engagements, organizations look to initiate KM through a specific initiative or project. Once that project is concluded, many of these organizations believe that their KM involvement is done and they move on to the next initiative. In order to have a sustainable KM presence in an organization, we must move from the tactical approach of a KM project to that of a strategic approach of a KM program. In order to accomplish this, a KM strategy has to be developed.

To increase the opportunity for success, the KM strategy must be positioned at the program level, and this strategy will drive specific initiatives that align with the mission and objectives of the KM program. The KM strategy includes formal procedures to collect knowledge throughout the organization, a well-established infrastructure, networks for transferring knowledge between employees, and tools to facilitate the process. The KM strategy will lay the foundation to align specific tools/technology to enhance individual and organizational performance.

This is accomplished by incorporating the following three components into the fabric of an organization's environment:

- People—those who create, organize, apply, and transfer knowledge; and the leaders who act on that knowledge
- Processes—methods of creating, organizing, applying, and transferring knowledge
- Technology—information systems used to put knowledge products and services into organized frameworks

According to an April 2013 article by Robert Simmons, a principal within Forsythe's information technology (IT) operations management practice on implementing a KM program, he points out eight specific steps as follows:

Step 1: Establish KM program objectives—Simmons points out that articulating the end state is important to establishing the appropriate program objectives, and identifying the business problems and the business drivers that will provide momentum and justification for the endeavor (Simmons, 2013).

Step 2: Prepare for change—Simmons indicates that a major component of establishing a KM program is to execute change management. The change management strategy will address the cultural changes that need to take place on how employees perceive and share knowledge, and the changes within the organization's norms and shared values that need to take place. A change management strategy will establish an approach for managing cultural change and produce a knowledge-sharing, knowledge-driven culture end state of the KM program (Simmons, 2013).

Step 3: Define high-level process—To facilitate the identification, capture, cataloging, use, and maintenance of the corporation's knowledge assets, effective KM process need to be established (Simmons, 2013).

Step 4: Determine and prioritize technology needs—Simmons indicates that depending on the program objectives that have been established as well as the process controls and criteria that have been defined, a prioritization of the KM technology needs can occur (Simmons, 2013). It is important to understand how the KM technology will address the knowledge processing and cultural knowledge needs of the organization as well as how the KM solution will be adopted by its users.

Step 5: Assess the current state—Assessment of the current state of KM within your organization should focus on the five core KM components: people, processes, technology, structure, and culture (Simmons, 2013). This assessment, according to Simmons, should uncover the gaps between current and desired states, and the recommendations for addressing/closing these gaps.

This assessment will become the foundation for the KM roadmap (Simmons, 2013).

Step 6: Build a KM implementation roadmap—Simmons stresses that "before going too far, you should re-confirm senior leadership's support and commitment, as well as the funding to implement and maintain the knowledge management program" (Simmons, 2013, p. 1). This is crucial to the development and execution of the program.

The KM program strategy should be presented as a "roadmap of related projects, each addressing specific gaps identified by the assessment" (Simmons, 2013, p. 1). The roadmap will indicate timelines, milestones, and dependencies. The roadmap should indicate the initiation of specific projects to execute the KM program strategy.

Step 7: Implementation—Implementing a KM program and maturing the overall effectiveness of your organization can require significant personnel resources and funding. Implementation of the KM program will involve the execution of the roadmap, insuring that short-term goals and wins are realized to gain momentum and maintain the support of key stakeholders (Simmons, 2013).

Step 8: Measure and improve the KM program—In order to understand if your organization's KM program and its associated initiatives (projects) are effective, establishing the appropriate metrics/measurements are necessary. These metrics must be used in a way to measure the actual effectiveness and comparing that to anticipated results (Simmons, 2013).

The failure rates for KM initiatives are at 50% (Frost, 2014). Knowing this we must determine, what is the cause and effect? Is it because of lack of senior leadership/support? Is a cultural issue? Or much more? The reasons why KM initiatives fail are varied, and it stems from the following key indicators:

In examining why KM programs/projects fail, besides the lack of a KM strategy other key indicators include the following:

- Lack of executive leadership/sponsorship
- Inadequate budgeting and cost expectations
- Lack of participation from all levels of a corporation
- Inadequate processes and technology
- Lack of knowledge and resources
- Lack of education and understanding of KM
- KM does not become ingrained into the corporations work culture
- Lack of a knowledge sharing environment
- Lack of metrics to measure the impact of KM on the corporation or insufficient/incorrect metrics being captured
- Lack of monitoring and controls in place to ensure the knowledge is relevant and is current and accurate. The organization must view

KM more than just a function of the call center or a cost of doing business. KM is a method of enhancing the collective know-how of the organization, improving productivity, and enhancing overall organizational value. KM will improve efficiencies that will increase a corporations' profitability, enhances the quality of work, performance, and overall value of the corporation. KM allows tacit knowledge to be leveraged, transferred to increase the quality of work performed across the organization. This tacit knowledge allows KM to eliminate the "reinvent the wheel" syndrome. This transfer of knowledge is a core value of KM.

Lack of Executive Leadership/Sponsorship

Successful KM initiatives depend greatly on management backing and have been documented and proven over many years of implementing KM initiatives (Davenport, De Long, and Beer, 1998; Chong and Choi, 2005; Wu et al., 2010). In contrast, failure of KM initiatives have been a consequence of inadequate management support (Singh and Kant, 2008; Weber, 2007; Pettersson, 2009).

Developing and operationalizing a KM strategy and subsequent program involves the creation, acceptance, and adoption of processes, values, and systems that are either company-wide or in the very least span across functions, departments, and communities. The implementation and long-term success of such far-reaching changes require top and central management backing, not only from the perspective of resource and political support but also to ensure day-to-day acceptance and use of the KM.

Sustained management support, in particular, senior leadership support is necessary for continued KM success because of the following factors:

■ KM requires strong guidance, decision making, and change implementation.
■ KM efforts require a clear vision and the example set by management, as well as implementing policies that serve as a way to legitimize KM and highlight its importance in the organization.
■ In order to prevent lack of enforcement of responsibilities and lack central management responsibility.
■ Failure can occur due to a lack of leadership support in the organization.
■ When KM is used as a political instrument to gain influence and leverage within an organization.
■ To incentify the use of KM as a standard for rewarding that enforce appropriate behavior need to be set by management. The extent to which this is useful should be discussed among leadership.

- Management must provide the resources necessary for KM implementation. KM requires a great deal of financial, human, and material resources; this includes the assignment of competent professionals and a sufficient budget.
- Management must stem the lack of understanding of the benefits, complexity, and requirements of KM by instituting an awareness campaign that includes but is not limited to lunch-n-learn briefings, KM training both instructor lead and online, and the ability to attend and participate in KM conferences.
- Management needs the ability to present return on investment (ROI). The need for solid performance indicators is extremely important for management to continue investing in KM.
- KM must not be just another task to do, but it should be a part of what is done by everyone in the organization. It must become part of the corporate DNA to have longevity and lasting success.

Without the enforcement of managerial responsibilities, an organization may end up with no control of the shared or reused knowledge. Management can mitigate this through the creation of the knowledge manager, KM liaison, and KM champion (see Table 17.1) roles within the organization. These roles will be an extension of management, and will facilitate the distribution of managerial responsibilities of KM and increases the level of KM acumen and at all levels of the organization.

Table 17.1   KM Extension Roles

KM Extension Role	Description
Knowledge manager	This management role is the extension of the chief knowledge officer (or equivalent role), whose primary duty is to implement knowledge initiatives and manage KM efforts, including change management.
KM liaison	The KM liaison serves as extended KM team members across the organization that has the responsibility of carrying out specific KM initiatives within their area.
KM champion	The KM champion promotes KM in an organization often by championing/supporting and evangelizing specific KM initiatives that align with organization strategy and direction.

Inadequate Budgeting and Cost Expectations

Successful KM requires adequate financing as well as sound financial management. Appropriate or inappropriate budgeting depends on leadership and management support. Budgeting in turn affects the ability to develop a KM program/project and the technology that supports and enables KM.

Many KM projects do end successfully, while many others are outright disasters. However, it's common to complete a project but be over your deadline or over your budget, or to have a dissatisfied client or a miserable team. To keep your KM projects from ending up in this gray area (or in the failure range), you must avoid making the single biggest project management mistake that leads to cost and budget overruns and that is inadequate project definition and planning.

Before the KM project work begins, it is essential that the work is properly understood and agreed to by the project sponsor and key stakeholders. Working with your sponsor and stakeholders to ensure that there is a common understanding of KM and what the project will deliver, when it will be complete, what it will cost, who will do the work, how the work will be done, and what the benefits will be. The larger the project, the more important it is to complete upfront planning and budgeting to prevent problems caused by differing understanding on the various KM deliverables and the basic terms of the project.

Usually, a KM project needs to have a budget and deadline before it is started. In many cases, if the definition and planning are not done ahead of time, the KM project team starts off with inadequate resources and time. Many KM projects that could be successful are viewed as failures (about 50%), because they overrun their budgets and deadlines. Inadequate budgeting and cost expectations contribute to the following failure factors:

- Inappropriate method or lack of budgeting
- Excessive cost of KM implementation
- Lack of a separate budget
- Maintenance cost of a KM strategy

Need for Organizational Participation

Organizational participation and the lack thereof is another key reason contributing to the failure of KM projects and programs. Many factors can be attributed to this, including lack of contribution because stakeholders were not asked/encouraged to contribute, because stakeholders were unable to contribute, or because stakeholders were unwilling to contribute.

This can include adding to the corporate knowledge base, improving KM initiatives, and actively participating in knowledge-sharing activities. Lack of contribution because stakeholders were not asked/encouraged to contribute (Weber, 2007) indicates that KM initiatives risk failure when they are designed without input from all the organization's stakeholders, pointing to the importance of community processes and organizational culture.

More often than not, limiting KM activities based on organizational boundaries contributes to KM failure both from a program and project perspective, because it ignores valuable external sources such as customers. A lack of involvement can also occur when an organization's members are unable to contribute with their knowledge. Inadequate technology may impose limitations on how users can share their knowledge and is another barrier to organizational participation (Weber, 2007).

Inadequate technology, which can put barriers up for users to contribute, also adds to the lack of willingness among users to contribute to the KM efforts. Knowledge sharing depends on organizational culture and its ability to foster reciprocity, openness, and trust. The lack of reciprocity, openness, and trust contributes to fearing the results and ramifications of contributing to KM (which begins at knowledge sharing). Having a holistic execution of a communication plan allows for open communication and is key to creating trust. However, the lack of willingness to share knowledge and communicate is also a contributor to KM failure. This is a problem when knowledge is regarded as a source of power or when a corporate culture places value on individual genius rather than collective work, and in some organizations, in some cases, individuals may perceive accessing another member's knowledge as a sign of inadequacy.

Inadequate Processes and Technology

Technology has always been a rather tricky issue within KM, and knowledge management system (KMS) is a key component to KM success and its failure. There are three general problems that an organization may encounter when implementing a KMS:

1. Poor performance
2. Poor fit with organizational processes and culture
3. Overreliance on technology

Problems related to KMS performance include poor technical infrastructure, poor representation of knowledge, and poor usability, which contribute to inadequate process and technology in KM. Failure can occur due to KM systems that can either not handle the demand placed on them, which represent knowledge in a way that does not meet the needs of its users, or that are not user-friendly.

Achieving organizational goals depends upon organizational processes, and therefore, failure will occur if KMS is not integrated with organizational processes (Weber, 2007). In addition, the organizational culture plays a role in determining whether the system is accepted by members of the organization or not. Chapter 16 details a proven method: task–technology fit (TTF) for adopting KM systems and the adoption of the KMS plays a key role in the success of the KM program/project.

However, an overreliance on technology in KM can lead to a neglect of tacit knowledge. We must understand that tacit knowledge is still best transmitted from person to person and the more tacit the knowledge, the less high-tech the solution has to be. Failure is likely to occur when the IT system is seen as a solution in itself. Moreover, failure can also occur if the limitations of the IT systems, particularly in regard to tacit knowledge, are not well understood and should be adopted only when it is suitable to the task (Weber, 2007).

Lack of Knowledge and Resources

Staff defection and retirement can lead to failure in KM implementation. Failure to plan ahead and transfer key knowledge can lead to problems for the organization. This points to the need to implement a knowledge transfer program to transfer key knowledge before employees retire. Liebowitz addresses knowledge retention, who indicates that the process of retaining knowledge should be integrated into the organization from the moment the employee is hired. (This is also addressed in the human capital management section of Chapter 6.) According to Liebowitz, few organizations have formal strategies in place for knowledge retention (Liebowitz, 2009). Once retired, key employees can still act as a valuable resource for the firm and can be brought back. As indicated in Chapter 6, this is still a temporary fix if the knowledge is not captured and transferred to the current workforce. At the end of the day, if the organization does not plan ahead and identify and protect its key knowledge resources, its KM initiatives risk failure.

Need for Education and Understanding of KM

It is extremely important that the staff facilitating KM activities have an understanding of KM. This understanding must align with the organization's KM goals and objectives and must be consistent as KM is adopted throughout the organization.

Knowledge managers and knowledge workers comprise the entire spectrum of KM-related positions, and may include titles/roles such as chief knowledge officer (CKO), knowledge champion, knowledge analyst, and knowledge systems engineer, among others.

As a KM practitioner who has (and continues to) work across various and different sectors and industries of the knowledge economy, I recognize that every organization is different and therefore the success of KM, in each industry, and company is going to depend on how well the elements of KM align with the corporate objectives, unique management methodologies, and leadership structures of the various organizations implementing KM programs and projects.

The skills required of KM personnel will depend on the role(s) being performed within the KM program. The following are some typical KM roles:

The skill requirements for a knowledge manager/worker could vary drastically depending on his specific areas of responsibility. For instance, a CKO would require very strong strategy and business skills, as well as management, learning, and communication (KM Skills Map, 2000). The CKO would not need to be as strong in IT skills as, for example, a systems engineer in charge of developing a KMS.

KM is likely to fail if there is a lack of availability of relevant skills: The right business and technical skills must be present to sustain the project. Skills can also be developed through training, providing that this is implemented with clear, measurable goals (Wu et al., 2010).

The selection of KM role must have the corresponding skills and be appropriate to the KM initiative.

Role	Role Description	Responsibilities
Chief knowledge officer (CKO) (or equivalent position, i.e., vice president)	Leader of enterprise KM and key figure for all knowledge from the program level as it relates to enterprise	CKO executes the KM strategy at the organizational level; leads efforts to move the organization to knowledge centricity; requires a dedication to KM principles, the ability to discuss the benefits of knowledge sharing and the vision to ensure that KM initiatives are adopted by the organization; ensures that the best, relevant information for the area of practice is accessible to all personnel and implements the knowledge sharing strategy in alignment with corporate guidelines; champions cross-organizational communities of practice; forms relationship with HR, IT, librarian, organizational learning; establishes incentive programs for knowledge sharing and reuse; fosters cultural change; defines roles, skill set, and opportunities for knowledge workers and facilitates training and education of knowledge workers
KM author	The primary person(s) involved in creating knowledge within the knowledge repository	See KM author capabilities below

(Continued)

Role	Role Description	Responsibilities
KM administrator	The KM administrator promotes, facilitates, and supports the KMS within the organization—with optimized outputs and process management	The KM administrator coordinates and executes governance of knowledge within the knowledge repository
KM lead	See KM manager	See KM manager
KM liaison	The KM liaison is the KM resource assigned to various teams across the organization that executes KM-specific duties for their teams on behalf of the CKMO	Responsibilities: • Execute KM initiatives on behalf of the specific KM director • Serve as KM champion for the CKMO and specific KM director program • Serve as the primary SME for the specific KM director area
KM champion	The KM champion promotes KM in an organization often by championing/ supporting and evangelizing specific KM initiatives that align with organization strategy and direction	
KM specialist	The KM specialist is engaged to support the KM policy and planning research and metrics for KM	KM specialist responsibilities include • Lead/contribute to the development of a KM strategy and associated implementation plan • Lead/contribute to the development and execution of the KM governance plan • Develop a comprehensive mapping of KM information sources and knowledge, including processes

(Continued)

Role	Role Description	Responsibilities
		• Contribute to the development and ongoing maintenance of the KMS • Create an approach for guiding ongoing analyses needed to address observed KM gaps and for identifying opportunities for innovation, process, procedure, and policymaking/adjustments • Oversee capacity building and support for internal knowledge acquisition, management and sharing; ensure relevant communities of practice are developed and strengthened. Support development of staff, consultants, and key partners on all aspects of KM
KM system administrator	The KM system administrator is the person(s) with administration rights and privileges within the specific knowledge repository	Responsibilities include the following: • Maintains the knowledge repository • Can serve as a KM author • Subject matter expert (SME) for all knowledge repository upgrades, capability issues, and approved configuration updates
Knowledge architect	The knowledge architect is a cross-organizational and interdisciplinary role. This role has knowledge of taxonomies, ontology analysis/ design/creation, understanding and creating knowledge flows to capture tacit and explicit knowledge	This person is charged with the design of dynamic systems of knowledge creation and transfer, the design of semantic structures that range from taxonomies to models of knowledge flows (explicit and tacit) within an organization. It also deals with the development of those semantic structures and designing for their use and application. A critical part of creating these designs is

(Continued)

Role	Role Description	Responsibilities
		research into an organization's knowledge, the knowledge contained in the people of the organization, and the information/knowledge component of the activities of the organization
KM writer	A member of the KM staff that applies plain language and information design to the construction of knowledge-specific content (knowledge articles, FAQs, and job aids) being housed within the KM repository/system	Responsibilities include the following: • Plain language • Information design • Collaboration with key SMEs • Establish/maintain, adherence and governance of style guide
Knowledge manager	Knowledge manager works with the CKO to implement KM initiatives	The knowledge manager has the following responsibilities: • Manages KM efforts (often serves as a KM project manager or product owner) • Looks across KM processes to capture tacit and explicit knowledge • Balances technology, information, processes and individuals, and organizational learning within a culture of shared values • Creates ways to maintain a sustainable competitive advantage
KM analyst	The KM analyst analyzes and proposes improvements to the overall effectiveness and efficiency of the KM program at all levels	KM analyst's responsibilities include the following: • Implements a range of methods and tools to capture and document knowledge

(Continued)

Role	Role Description	Responsibilities
	by applying advanced KM methods and practices for all users of KM at enterprise	• Contributes to the analysis and configuration of knowledge maintenance approaches and practices • Contributes to the analysis and configuration of knowledge-sharing approaches and practices • Works closely with the other staff members of the specific KM director and/or CKMO to ensure that new elements of KM using innovative technology and media are retained and developed, and advises on the mechanisms for their implementation

KM and the Corporate Culture

Culture is expressed by patterns of thinking and serves as the basis of creating employee's attitudes and their behaviors in particular to situations demonstrating their values and norms. This means that organizational culture describing the enterprise is understood and shared by employees. The system of cultural values will have an influence on the implementation of KM programs/projects, and this impact can be either strengthening or hindering.

The presence of an appropriate organizational culture is almost universally accepted as one of the key aspects of successful KM implementation. Culture plays a critical role in the willingness of organizational members to share knowledge. The willingness to share knowledge affects trust, the willingness to accept knowledge from others, without it being perceived as a personal shortcoming, the willingness and ability to learn, openness to change and the desire, and the ability to experiment and innovate.

Culture can vary on an organizational or community level. Because KM initiatives span functions and departments, an understanding of all the facets of an organization's culture is critical. The process of changing culture is particularly difficult; an organization's culture could persuade or discourage individuals to make use of KM techniques and technologies to create, codify, and share knowledge.

However, the management of culture to ensure and support sharing, learning, and innovation is essential for successful implementation of KM programs and projects. Organizational cultures vary in terms of their attitudes toward KM and the cultural obstacles that are experienced. We can conclude to some degree that KM is approached differently depending on the organization and its culture, and that those KM techniques and technologies that are successfully implemented in one organization might fail in another, owing to the influence that corporate culture has on the extent to which these techniques and technologies are used.

Creating an Environment for Knowledge Exchange

The structure of the organization plays an important role in determining how knowledge is distributed, how decisions are made, the degree to which people feel comfortable sharing, and the barriers that exist between different groups and individuals. Organizational structure therefore strongly influences the ability and willingness of people and communities to share and create knowledge, and it also determines the management of the KM program.

Centralization: The degree to which decision making is centralized. In highly centralized organizations, decisions are made by a few managers at the top of the organization. This puts a heavy demand on the cognitive capacity of these managers. Research and experience have identified that decentralized structures as being more suited for KM.

Formalization: It is the extent to which behaviors in an organization are governed by rules and policies (Wu et al., 2010). Conversely, it can be the degree to which informal networks are discouraged, tolerated, or encouraged within the organization. In general, rigid, formal structures are regarded as being detrimental to KM.

Complexity is seen as being composed of many, not necessarily, interrelated parts. Organizations are divided by function, region, business unit, or division, and this tends to hinder KM, because each of these is usually worried about its own bottom line and tends to operate as silos. Simpler organizational structures, which lead to fewer silos, tend to make it easier for KM to be implemented. The complexity of the organizational structure also affects its management and the necessary managerial roles to effectively implement KM.

Although there is no specific formula for determining the best environment for exchanging knowledge, we know that corporate structure influences KM on many levels, and an improper structure can lead to a variety of problems with knowledge sharing, organizational learning, effective decision making, and effective management of KM initiatives.

Poorly Measuring the Impact of KM

The ability to determine whether a project or initiative is succeeding or failing and whether it is a worthwhile endeavor for the organization is crucial for its long-term success. Performance indicators are therefore required so as to assess progress, devise improvements, and compare one's own situation to that of a different organization (Wu et al., 2010). KM must be linked to economics, meaning that its value must be made apparent.

Although performance indicators are not always listed among the top failure reasons, I have chosen to outline them first because they influence several other causal factors, including management support and the ability to plan and evaluate. The effect of KM is notoriously difficult to evaluate, particularly in monetary terms. The intangible nature of knowledge and the fact that value creation is often indirect and long term makes such an assessment very difficult. Yet, performance indicators are crucial for management to continue investing in KM (Wu et al., 2010).

Successful KM implementation depends upon the integration of many different aspects of an organization. Waltz (2003: 102) indicates that "KM provides a strategy and organizational discipline for the integration of people, processes, and IT into an effective enterprise."

Proper planning and continuous evaluation are needed to ensure that all aspects of KM are being implemented effectively and work well together. The implementation of KM requires a long-term and practical outlook.

The ability to evaluate progress depends on having good performance indicators. Without these, it becomes extremely difficult for management to track the effectiveness of the program. Therefore, very broadly, inadequate evaluation can result either from a lack of ability, due to the absence of solid performance indicators (Wu et al., 2010), or alternatively, due to the lack of a systemized approach during the implementation of the KM initiative. Although there is no specific formula that will guarantee success, planning, and evaluating your KM program/project are critical for setting goals and delegating responsibility, integrating different KM enablers into a KM strategy, aligning the KM strategy to the overall organizational strategy, improving KM effectiveness at the program and project level, anticipating and detecting problems, determining successes and failures, forecasting costs and determining budgets, and implementing corrective measures.

Lack of Monitoring and Controls

KM enables the retrieval, creation, sharing, collaboration, and management of knowledge. The management of knowledge resources can mean the difference between success and failure in a competitive environment. This encourages organizations to look for better ways to manage their knowledge assets. The lack of monitoring and controls for knowledge leads to improperly managing, maintaining, and keeping your organizational knowledge relevant; this in turn will quickly cause the KM program and/or project to be branded as a failure. One way to address this is to implement and execute a comprehensive KM governance plan.

KM governance ensures policy adherence and contributes to the sustainability of the KM program/project. KM governance provides controls to guarantee that the knowledge stored in the various systems, portals, and/or repositories provide the best value for the organization. Governance will detail how the knowledge will be managed. It describes the policies, procedures, roles, and responsibilities that are needed to successfully maintain and keep your knowledge relevant. Effective governance planning and the application of the governance plan are critical for the ongoing success of any KM program and/or project.

The governance plan will establish the processes and policies to

- Avoid knowledge proliferation by periodically reviewing knowledge assets for accuracy and relevance.
- Ensure that knowledge assets quality is maintained for the life of the solution by implementing quality management policies.
- Establish clear decision-making authority and escalation procedures, so that policy violations are managed and conflicts are resolved on a timely basis.
- Ensure that the solution strategy is aligned with business objectives, so that it continuously delivers business value.
- Ensure that knowledge assets are retained in compliance with knowledge retention guidelines of your organization.

Benefits of good KM governance

- Provide a business-wide common infrastructure for knowledge assets.
- Ensure that the KM delivers relevant knowledge to its users in an effective way.
- Employ best practices that will improve usability (through information architecture).
- Provide transparent mechanisms for risk management, evaluation, and measurement.
- Provide mechanisms to maintain performance management in order to match or exceed the predefined standards and objectives.
- Slow the proliferation and increases the relevance of available knowledge through consistent review, modification, and archiving of knowledge.
- Lower total cost of knowledge development and management through increased efficiencies throughout the KM life cycle.

Key Learnings

The following are some key learnings deduced from this Chapter:

Plan for success by executing a KM strategy that incorporates/champion these components into your organization:

- People—those who create, organize, apply, and transfer knowledge; and the leaders who act on that knowledge

- Processes—methods of creating, organizing, applying, and transferring knowledge
- Technology—information systems used to put knowledge products and services into organized frameworks

We must keep in mind that successful KM initiatives once completed and funded correctly can increase the organization's profitability, enhance the quality of work, encourage and stimulate innovation, and increase the value of the organization through an increase valuation and accountability of knowledge assets.

To decrease the probability of failure (and thus increasing the success rate!), the following must be resolved:

- Expecting KM technologies to replace KM processes or create processes where none exists
- Lack of participation from all levels of a corporation
- Forcing inadequate processes into new technology
- Lack of maintenance and resources after initial standup
- Lack of education and understanding of what KM means to the individual
- KM does not become ingrained into the corporations work culture
- Lack of involvement in creating and evolving KM content
- Lack of metrics to measure the impact of KM on the corporation or insufficient/incorrect metrics being captured
- Lack of monitoring and controls in place to ensure the knowledge is relevant and is current and accurate

Tips and Techniques

The following are some of the tips and techniques that can be applied to understand the reason for failure of KM programs/projects in hopes of avoiding them!

When developing your KM strategy for success, incorporate Robert Simmons' eight steps on implementing a KM program:

- Step 1: Establish KM program objectives
- Step 2: Prepare for change
- Step 3: Define high-level process
- Step 4: Determine and prioritize technology needs
- Step 5: Assess current state
- Step 6: Build a KM implementation roadmap
- Step 7: Implementation
- Step 8: Measure and improve the KM program

When establishing your KM program incorporate the following:

- Your KM program should be designed to support communities of practice. Being a community of practice implies that its members share the same interests. Sharing same interests allows for consistency in the quality of knowledge artifacts, as they are geared to positively impact the same target processes.
- Your KM program should integrate people, processes, and technology. The people component should consist of knowledge facilitators and users (i.e., knowledge workers) who work together to understand the community processes and master the technology.
- Your KM program should be designed in collaboration with different stakeholders. It takes a variety of stakeholders from all levels of management, KM champions from departments across the organization, human resources department to support new and evolving KM-specific positions, and all other employees (knowledge workers) to make the KM program successful and sustainable.
- Your KM program's strategy should align with the overall corporate strategy. This will support the buy-in that is necessary from senior leadership to get the KM program established and operational.
- Your KM program's outcomes should be measurable and accountable to the organization. Establishing a set of straightforward key performance indicators and metrics is just the beginning. In addition, having scheduled communication to leadership and the organization as a whole on the successes, challenges, and impacts to the organization KM is having is essential to creating a sustainable and successful KM program.

Chapter 18

Summary

Knowledge Management in Practice provides knowledge management (KM) professionals and those obtaining training and formal education in KM a practical examination on how KM is being applied. The use of its principles, practices, and procedures has expanded enormously in recent years. This expansion has also brought about the proliferation of KM systems in many forms (customer relationship management [CRM], content management, document management, knowledge repositories/ libraries, social media applications, decision support systems, etc.). The inclusion of KM from a strategic point of view to streamline revenue, increase revenue, improve performance, attract/retain customers, and manage human capital has enabled organizations to maintain and/or improve their competitive edge. To compete in a local, national, and/or global market, organizations including educational, government, and military are looking for that differentiator and KM has proved to be just that.

This book provided techniques and insights that the KM practitioner and organizations can utilize in order to be successful when implementing KM. This included detailed information on applying KM practices, procedures, and techniques to solve real-world problems. This chapter presents a synopsis of what has been presented in this book. It will also present some forward-looking statements about the future of KM and what we can look forward to in the near term.

What the reader has taken away from this book:

In reading this book undoubtedly you may have come away noticing several concepts and approaches, and patterns in delivering how KM has emerged. From examining the case for KM in Chapter 2, which focuses on why your organization may need a KM program, to techniques such as knowledge capture, knowledge sharing, expertise locators, information architecture, search, and governance that provide the methods and enablers for KM, to the industries such as research, human resources/talent management, healthcare, insurance, finance, military, and law, I attempted to present a holistic view of KM based on my experience. I approach implementing KM from a perspective that the scholar and practitioner alike can gain valuable insight from.

In addition, I presented an examination of KM in a few areas that I believe KM will be making a significant impact. These areas included social media, KM education programs, emergency and disaster preparedness, customer service (particularly within the insurance and financial industries), M&A transactions, and big data.

Social Media

Chapter 3 presented social tools and mediums such as blogs, wikis, Twitter, Facebook, and LinkedIn that represent the mechanisms to enable people to engage and share openly. These social tools put knowledge-sharing power in the hands of the users themselves, and this power has business and government taking notice. In this chapter, social media as it pertains to the key principles of KM were examined. These key principles included knowledge sharing, knowledge capture, and knowledge reuse. This chapter included a template for developing your organization's social media strategy as well as some proven tips and techniques to successfully execute this strategy.

Education Programs

Acknowledging that KM is a professional area of practice and to begin a formal discussion of the educational foundation needed to support this area of professional practice was the focus of Chapter 13. This chapter presented KM education delivery and options within universities and colleges as well as in KM certification organizations. This chapter covered topics that included strategic roles and responsibilities of knowledge professionals in organizations today and the educational needs of these professionals, standard KM competencies, KM curriculum development and delivery, and teaching methodologies.

Emergency and Disaster Preparedness

KM applied to emergency and disaster preparedness, response, and recovery presented in Chapter 7 focused on implementing a KM strategy centered on emergency preparedness and response by first responders. A detailed analysis of a comprehensive emergency alert system was presented. This chapter examined specific areas of a comprehensive emergency alert system that is a catalyst in delivering knowledge to the right people in the right context and at the right time in an emergency preparedness, response, and/or recovery situation.

Customer Service

KM in customer service continues to be the focus of many organizations. This is evident especially within the insurance and financial sectors as presented in Chapters 10 and 11. When KM is applied to customer service, we saw that it led to a faster speed to answer customer questions, which has been directly linked to higher satisfaction rates, better long-term loyalty, higher degrees of trust, and higher levels of revenue. In addition, some of the soft benefits included better engagement and a higher likelihood to recommend your organization to other potential customers.

M&A Transactions

The impact of KM on M&A transactions specifically when it comes to understanding who the key knowledge holders are and to properly give a valuation to a firm's knowledge is an essential value addition for applying KM to M&A transactions. We found in Chapter 8 that the effect of mergers will and often leads to a loss of valuable knowledge from both sides of the merger/acquisition equation. The question that was addressed is how do we identify who the key knowledge holders are and what knowledge do they hold? Also, has it been determined what knowledge is viable to the *new* organization going forward? In this chapter a discussion of implementing a comprehensive KM strategy with a human capital management component that would address the many intellectual capital issues that are caused by a merger/acquisition was examined.

Big Data

Big data continue to make an impact and present a challenge in the industry, which specifically points to how KM will be positioned to gleam knowledge from the various repositories of structured and unstructured data contained within the organization. As we read in Chapter 14, infusing big data with KM will provide organizations with a competitive edge to not only bring about significant innovations, but deliver knowledge across the enterprise to the right people at the right time and in the right context.

However, an examination of KM in practice would not be complete without adding an examination of KM adoption (Chapter 16) as well as why KM programs and projects fail (Chapter 17). In order to apply the principles, practices, and methods presented in this book, I also highlighted tips and techniques and key learnings. All these will provide a *jump start* to executing KM at your organization.

The Future of KM

One of the major areas in which KM will make an impact is within the customer service industry. Customer service is the area in which most customers will have their only connection and interaction with your organization. It is this area where customers will form their opinions about the organization and determine if they remain a customer or move on to another competitor. Because of this scenario (and others), organizations invest a major portion of their revenue and attention to improving their customer service.

In an August 2014 *Harvard Business Review* article titled, "The Value of Customer Experience, Quantified," Peter Kriss states that "Intuitively, most people recognize the value of a great customer experience. Brands that deliver them are ones that we want to interact with as customers that we become loyal to, and that we recommend to our friends and family." Also, he notes that the "value of delivering such an experience is often a lot less clear, because it can be hard to quantify." Delivering consistent and concise knowledge to provide answers to customer inquiries in an efficient way leads to providing value to the customer and improving the overall customer experience.

In support of this trend of KM in customer service, the author of Forrester's "Top Trends for Customer Service in 2015," Kate Leggett, highlights in trend 4 KM's impact when she states "Knowledge will evolve from dialog to cognitive engagement. Organizations will look at ways to reduce the manual overhead of traditional knowledge management for customer service. They will start to explore cognitive engagement solutions, interactive computing systems that use artificial intelligence to collect information, automatically build models of understanding and inference, and communicate in natural ways. These solutions have the potential to automate knowledge creation, empower agents with deeply personalized answers and intelligence, scale a company's knowledge capability, and uncover new revenue streams by learning about customer needs."

IBM Watson is playing a significant role in the evolution of applications that automate knowledge creation by providing deeply personalized answers and intelligence. This technology will affect customer service as well as a multitude of industries with its capability to extract knowledge from big data sources. The IBM Watson ecosystem will provide deep content analytics and intensive scientific discovery that will lead to improved cognition contributing to an organization's knowledge capabilities. This supports Kate Leggett's research and points out that KM will continue to play a significant role in delivering knowledge and decision-making capabilities to the customer service industry for the foreseeable future.

Technology Services Industry Association Research

In the Technology Services Industry Association's (TSIA) 2014 second annual survey on KM, TSIA documents the people, process, and technology components of technology service KM programs. It examines core metrics and practices related to knowledge capture, sharing, and maintenance, as well as video, crowd sourcing, and expertise management.

The TSIA research indicates that KM is no longer just of interest to technical support and call centers (I definitely agree with this!). The TSIA survey response was from groups other than customer support, which included 24% from professional services organizations. The TSIA research states that "KM is seen as a key way to improve efficiency, and a third of respondents said they could improve productivity by 30% or more if they were sharing knowledge effectively."

The TSIA results centered on the effect of search (see Chapter 4), knowledge capture (see Chapter 6), and social media (see Chapter 3), and how these factors contribute to the overall KM strategy. In regard to search, the TSIA results indicate that a KM strategy "that enables unified search is becoming increasingly important, not only across service divisions, but across the entire enterprises." "The digitalization of the workplace, i.e., the shift toward all enterprise technologies and processes being accessible online, is driving this trend." To further support the need for search, the TSIA research states that "case-deflecting and case-resolving content typically resides across the enterprise, and making it easily findable and usable by customers and employees alike has elevated the role of search."

In regard to knowledge capture, the TSIA research indicates that there are growing concerns about senior workers leaving organizations and taking their knowledge and expertise with them. The research results show that CIOs are pushing company-wide knowledge programs in order to capture knowledge/learning from employees in a searchable and shareable format.

In regard to social media, the TSIA research indicates that younger employees and customers having grown up in the social media era are more open to sharing information than previous generations. With adoption of enterprise collaboration tools on the rise, new streams, formats, and sources of enterprise knowledge are being created. This consists largely of unstructured content (social chats, team forums, etc.), and this must be incorporated into a broader KM strategy, and be made easily accessible/findable by customers and employees (see the section on information architecture in Chapter 4 to see how content can be made better accessible).

State of KM Survey

In the *State of Knowledge Management* survey of customer experience, which was conducted in order to better understand how they're using KM, Esteban Kolsky and IntelliResponse indicate the following:

■ A total of 56% of organizations have a KM program in place, whereas 44% do not. A primary use of KM is in the customer service area. Actual percentage breakdowns when asked to select all that apply are customer service 83%, sales 33%, marketing 44%, accounting/finance 12%, human resources 11%, and training 33%.

■ Organizations as a whole have a lot to learn about KM. The survey indicates that the majority of organizations today do not have high competencies in KM.
■ Organizations are not realizing the benefits of KM that was originally projected.

This might reveal a level of misunderstanding in companies as to precisely how KM should be expected to deliver value. And yet organizations that do have a handle on how to use KM to drive value are able to clearly identify the value they have derived.

KM solution engagement is lower than expected. A high percentage (44%) of companies cites *lack of usage* as the main challenge with their KM initiative. Knowing that people tend to avoid using what they don't understand, plenty of ground can potentially be gained by companies that do a better job of promoting their KM strategy—including what it is, how their KM tools are to be used, and the benefits the company and employees should expect to achieve.

KM investment is growing. The survey indicates that half of the companies surveyed report some growth in their KM investment. The survey supports the need for a KM strategy that includes metrics and key performance indicators (KPIs) that will deliver measurable expectations. In addition, a KM strategy must indicate an understanding of what technologies will best serve the goals for delivering knowledge to customers, and a means to report on the success of KM initiatives.

Global View of KM

In reviewing the 2015 *Global Knowledge Management Observatory Report*, David Griffiths, Abi Jenkins, and Zoe Kingston-Griffiths state "The Knowledge Management function in many organizations is in a state of general decline." This, as they indicate, is due to the following factors:

■ Satisfaction in KM's contribution to strategic and operational objectives within organizations is often poor.
■ KM lacks maturity and integration within the vast majority of organizations.
■ KM continues to be predominantly seen as a technology-led function.
■ Satisfaction with technology-led KM solutions is not improving.
■ Many KM professionals do not appear to have the necessary awareness and/ or permissions required to respond to unmet demand for KM activities in organizations.
■ KM, as a field or area of practice, is argued to be suffering from a lack of specialist practitioners.
■ The value and/or significance of KM activities is still not being appropriately recognized or reported within most organizations.

Solutions that address many of the findings of the 2015 *Global Knowledge Management Observatory Report* have been presented in this book; they include producing a comprehensive KM strategy, KM education options, adopting KM programs, project and systems, and why KM programs/projects fail. The findings in this report present a tremendous opportunity for growth in the KM field.

Future Edition of *Knowledge Management in Practice*

A future edition of *Knowledge Management in Practice* will include more in regard to KM's impact on customer service, how KM and big data are evolving, internal KM, KM in politics, the integration of KM and CRM systems, and personal KM and wearable technology.

KM Impact on Customer Service

KM's impact on customer service will continue to focus on speed to provide answers to questions, improve customer satisfaction, and eliminate churn when it comes to finding and communicating knowledge to the customer.

- *Speed to answer*: Customers want answers fast. Customers are not likely to wait long for answers, even less in a social media setting. The overabundance of channels has made it impossible for organizations to deliver proper answers via all channels fast. However, the rise of self-service using KM has led to great results in speed and accuracy of answers. As customers find the answers on their own (assisted in part by knowledge bases, but also via social media communities), the need for fast answers is met by better use of technology powered by KM.
- *Customer satisfaction*: This is a byproduct of faster speed to answer. By providing the right answer quickly, customer satisfaction is increased. In order to meet customer expectations for the right knowledge, at the right time, in the right context, KM is used as a critical tool. Not having access to the right knowledge is the most critical time wasted in preparing any answer for a customer. If the knowledge is not available quickly, it is nearly impossible to deliver against expectations. Using KM appropriately to fulfill the need for the right knowledge leads to meeting customer expectations.
- *Churn*: Among the leading reasons for employees churning in any job is lack of proper tools, and this is even more prevalent in customer service. Having to *hunt* for knowledge among different systems, tools, and channels causes churn. In addition, as customers take to more channels and processes become automated, only complex processes will be left to be resolved by customer service, and, in those cases, the right tools can make a difference between

a resolution and a frustrated caller that needs to be escalated to yet further service levels. Finding the right knowledge is a key to delivering the right answer to the customer. When customer service representatives have the right access to the right knowledge, they will more happily answer the interactions fast and effectively eliminate the chances for churn.

More on KM and Big Data

In recent years, the ability to manage data, information, and knowledge to gain competitive advantage and the importance of business analytics for this process has been well established. Organizations continue to investigate ways to efficiently and effectively collect and manage the data, information, and knowledge that they are exposed to. As the proliferation of structured and unstructured data continues to grow, we will continue to have a need to uncover the knowledge contained within these big data resources. KM and analytics will be key aspects in extracting knowledge from big data. Strategy, process-centric approaches, and interorganizational aspects of decision support to research on new technology and academic endeavors in this space will continue to provide insights into how we process big data.

Internal KM

Internal KM focuses inward within the organization. This inward focus is aimed at maximizing the intellectual capital found in the organization. This intellectual capital resides both within the organization's human capital and within the various systems (i.e., knowledge repositories, portals, wikis, blogs, CRMs, and collaborative environments). Internal KM specifically supports the organization's flow of substantive expertise and is aimed at improving operational efficiency. An organization's KM framework must support its internal knowledge needs. This support will yield improved quality and efficiency of staff, outside consultants, and project teams.

Internal KM will enable your organization to gain the advantage of leveraging all existing knowledge resources available through your organization's entire network of available explicit and tacit (people) knowledge. Enabling and improving the mechanisms that deliver internal KM will continue to be prevalent as KM matures within an organization. This is a key reason for examining this area of KM in a future edition of *Knowledge Management in Practice*.

KM in Politics

KM as a political activity, made by and instituted by political leaders, will be the subject of this chapter. The research is interesting because given that we live in a knowledge society, in the information era, it is more or less obvious that the political leaders should also do KM. Illustrating the ideas of KM implementation and use with the example of President Obama and other politicians has incorporated KM in executing their political strategy. KM always was and nowadays is pervasive in the activity of political leaders.

Incorporating the use of blogs, YouTube, and other social networking sites (Facebook, Twitter, and LinkedIn), President Obama's team was able to push out the latest news, information, and knowledge about every aspect of his campaign. This increased the involvement of every supporter enabling them to feel a part of the campaign from start to finish. Supporters received text messages and emails at every turn encouraging them to hold parties with friends to *get out the vote* and donate their time and yes their money.

Leveraging the internet in a precise strategic manner that supports the mission of political campaigns is exactly how all organizations leveraging KM (getting the right knowledge to the right people at the right time) are positioning themselves in this evolving paradigm. I believe that many politicians and political organizations will utilize KM, and undoubtedly this will become a new trend in American politics.

KM and CRM

The business environment is transforming from product centric to customer centric. CRM as a customer-oriented business approach is considered as one of the powerful capabilities in organizations that help transform themselves to a customer-centric environment. The utilization of CRM is directly related with increase in customer knowledge, which in turn has a positive effect on customer satisfaction. By using KM, companies can improve their relationship with their valuable customers, thus creating loyal customers and obtaining a competitive advantage.

Organizations can create new ideas and provide improved and new services by the help of KM and the knowledge originating from CRM. The customer knowledge as an integral element of relationship between KM and CRM could help organizations to tailor their products and services and even the entire relationship with customers to increase customer satisfaction and finally economic profitability.

Personal KM and Wearable Technology

With all of the advances in technology becoming accessories for us to wear, have you thought about all of the information that is at your fingertips! Fitbits, Apple watch, Google glasses, and more... all deliver and collect information that allow us to make personal decisions during the course of the day. What to eat, drink, wear, how much we're exercising (or not) are all decisions in some part influenced by our wearable tech!

Wearable technology is gathering information not only about us but also the environment around us. Where is this all taking us? Will our physicians have the capability to tap into all of this personal information? How about potential advertisers? How can we capture the decisions we make from this information to improve our own lives? Is personal KM the key to taking control of our personal information created by these devices? These and more questions will be addressed in this future chapter.

Closing Statement

The goal of this edition of *Knowledge Management in Practice* was to provide the reader with specific key learnings, along with tips and techniques that will enable the KM practitioner to be more productive in their application of KM, and provide those who are being educated in KM with an understanding of the pertinent issues KM is solving across a variety of industries. In future editions, I will continue to present the evolution of KM, its importance, and how it can be of leverage for a competitive advantage. In summary, it is my hope that *Knowledge Management in Practice* will be a definitive KM reference for anyone entering into the field and/or currently practicing KM.

Appendix A

KM Business Case Template

The following is a template that can be used when constructing a KM business case:

Executive Summary

Summarize each of the sections in this document concisely by outlining the following:

- Problem or opportunity
- Solution alternatives
- Recommended solution
- Implementation approach

Business Problem

Environmental Analysis

Outline the core aspects of the business environment that were instrumental for this KM initiative to take place. These may include the following:

- Business vision, strategy, or objectives
- Business processes or technologies that are not operating efficiently
- New competitor products or processes that have been identified
- New technology trends (or opportunities resulting from new technologies introduced)
- Commercial or operational trends that are driving changes in the business
- Changes to statutory, legislative, or other environmental requirements

Provide any facts or evidence to support the conclusions drawn above.

Problem Analysis

Outline the fundamental business problem or opportunity that the resulting KM initiative will directly address.

Business Problem

Provide a summary of the core business problem, including:

- A generic description of the core issue to hand.
- The reasons why the problem exists.
- The elements that create it (e.g., human, process, and technology).
- The impact it has on the business (e.g., financial, cultural, and operational).
- The timeframes within which it must be resolved.

Business Opportunity Outline the business opportunity that has been identified, including:

- A summary of the generic opportunity.
- Any supporting evidence to prove that the opportunity is real.
- A timeframe within which the opportunity will likely exist.
- The positive impact that realization of the opportunity will have on the business.

Available Options

This section provides a full listing of all solution options, their benefits, costs, feasibility, risks, and issues. Options suggested may include doing nothing or doing something that will achieve a better result than the current state.

Option X (Provide the Name of the Option)

Description Provide a summarized description of the option identified. This will include the general approach to be taken, and a summary of the core elements of the solution (e.g., people, process, organization, and technology).

Benefits, Goals, and Measurement Criteria Describe the tangible and intangible benefits to the company upon implementation of the solution. One of the obvious benefits described will be that the business problem/opportunity outlined above will be addressed. Complete the following table (Note: the benefits are examples only, refer to your established KM metrics and KPIs, including your performance figures for specific benefit information):

Category	Benefit	Value
Financial	• New revenue generated • Reduction in costs • Increased profit margin	$ x $ x $ x
Operational	• Improved operational efficiency • Reduction in product time to market • Enhanced quality of product/service	x % x hours x %
Market	• Increased market awareness • Greater market share • Additional competitive advantage	x % x % Describe
Customer	• Improved customer satisfaction • Increased customer retention • Greater customer loyalty	x % x % Describe
Staff	• Increased staff satisfaction • Improved organizational culture • Longer staff retention	x % Describe x %

Costs and Funding Plan   Describe the tangible and intangible costs to the company upon implementation of the solution. The costs of the *actual* KM initiative should be included as well as any negative impact to the business resulting from the "delivery" of the KM initiative. Complete the following table:

Category	Cost	Value	Budgeted
People	• Salaries of KM initiative staff • Contractors/outsourced parties • Training courses	$ x $ x $ x	Yes No Yes
Physical	• Building premises for KM initiative team • Equipment and materials • Tools (computers, phones, etc.)	$ x $ x $ x	No No No
Marketing	• Advertising/branding • Promotional materials • PR and communications	$ x $ x $ x	Yes No No
Organizational	• Operational down-time • Short-term loss in productivity • Cultural change	$ x $ x Describe	No No No

Feasibility   Describe the feasibility of the solution. To adequately complete this section, a feasibility study may need to be initiated to quantify the likelihood of achieving the desired KM initiative result. To assess the overall feasibility of this option, break the solution down into components and rate the feasibility of each component in the following table:

Component	Rating (1–10)	Method Used to Determine Feasibility
New KM technology	5	A KM technology prototype was created to assess the solution
New people	8	A survey was completed to identify skill set availability
New processes	3	Processes within similar organizations were reviewed
New assets	9	Physical assets were inspected

To ensure that the feasibility ratings are accurate, use all appropriate methods possible to identify the likely feasibility of the solution. For example, when adopting a new KM technology, develop a small prototype and test it to see if the resultant benefits match those expected from the exercise.

Risks   Summarize the most apparent risks associated with the adoption of this solution. Risks are defined as any event which *may* adversely affect the ability of the solution to produce the required deliverables. Risks may be strategic, environmental, financial, operational, technical, industrial, competitive, or customer related. Complete the following table:

Description	Likelihood	Impact	Mitigating Actions
Inability to recruit skilled resource	Low	Very high	Outsource KM initiative to a company with proven industry experience and appropriately skilled staff
Technology solution is unable to deliver required results	Medium	High	Complete a pilot KM initiative to prove the technology solution will deliver the required results
Additional capital expenditure may be required in addition to that approved	Medium	Medium	Maintain strict cost management processes during the KM initiative

To complete this section thoroughly, it may be necessary to undertake a formal risk assessment (by documenting a *risk management plan*). To reduce the likelihood and impact of each risk's eventuating, clear "mitigating actions" should be defined.

Issues   Summarize the highest priority issues associated with the adoption of this option. Issues are defined as any event which *currently* adversely affects the ability of the solution to produce the required deliverables. Complete the following table:

Description	Priority	Resolution Actions
Required capital expenditure funds have not been budgeted	High	Request funding approval as part of this proposal
Required computer software is only at "beta" phase and has not yet been released live	Medium	Design solution based on current software version and adapt changes to solution once the final version of the software has been released
Regulatory approval must be sought to implement the final solution	Low	Initiate the regulatory approval process early, so that it does not delay the final roll-out process.

Upon approval of the business case, each issue should be formally recorded and tracked using an issue management process, forms, and register.

Assumptions   List the major assumptions associated with the adoption of this option. Examples include the following:

- There will be no legislative, business strategy, or policy changes during this KM initiative.
- Prices of raw materials will not increase during the course of this KM initiative.
- Additional human resource will be available from the business to support this KM initiative.

Recommended Option

This section compares the key characteristics of each solution option and recommends a preferred solution option for implementation.

Reasons for Recommended Option

Based primarily on the highest total score achieved above, list here the "Recommended Option" for business case approval. Summarize the primary reasons why this option was chosen over the other options previously identified.

Implementation Approach

This section provides an overview of the general approach undertaken to deliver the preferred solution option and derive the resultant business benefits.

KM project initiation: Outline the method by which the KM initiative will be defined, the KM initiative team formulated, and the KM initiative office established.

KM project planning: Define the overall planning process to ensure that the KM initiative phases, activities, and tasks are undertaken in a coordinated fashion.

Project execution: Identify the generic phases and activities required to complete the "build" phase of the KM initiative.

KM project closure: List the generic steps necessary to release the deliverables to the business (once complete), close the KM initiative office, reallocate staff, and perform a post-implementation review of the KM initiative.

KM project management: Describe in brief how the following aspects of the KM initiative will be managed:
- Time management
- Cost management
- Quality management
- Change management
- Governance management
- Risk management
- Issue management
- Procurement management
- Communications management
- Acceptance management

Appendix B

Fire Fighter First Responder after Action Review Template
Executive Summary
Summarize the goal and objectives of the AAR and describe how it was conducted.
Strength
Describe what the team did well.
Opportunities
Describe what the team could have done better.
Recommendations
Describe the most important recommendations and follow up actions.
Event Overview
In this section, provide an overview of the event being reviewed and capture the highlights of the event timeline.
Analysis of Outcomes
In this section, describe the results of the analysis of how well the team achieved the expected outcomes. The focus of this analysis is on outcomes rather than on output or processes. (The distinction here is between organizational/team outcomes as opposed to human output or effectiveness of processes.)
Analysis of Critical Tasks
In this section, describe critical tasks that were done well and those that could be improved upon. Alternatively, this section could focus on themes and explore the same topics thematically.

Task (ID number): (Task Title)
Issue 1: (Issue concerning this task)
Reference: (Where to find a description of how the task should be performed. i.e., SOP)
Summary of Issue: (Summary of the issue)
Consequence: (Describe the impact of this issue, i.e., why and how did this issue create a problem)
Analysis: (Explain the root cause for this issue)
Recommendations and Improvements
Recommendation 1: (Describe the recommendation and actions or steps that are proposed)
Action 1:
Action 2:
Action 3:
Alternatively, choose appropriate themes and describe results of the analysis of the themes:
THEME I:
THEME II:
THEME III:
THEME IV:
Lessons Learned
Describe lessons learned that could be applied by this and other groups, teams, etc. in the future
Remaining Issues
(Describe any issues or problems that were not resolved, their importance, their impact if not resolved, and any recommendations to resolve the issues)
Recommendations to the Management
This section could outline recommendations that the AAR team would like to make to management. Many if not all of these recommendations should already be documented in previous sections; therefore, a summary table of action items could go here.

IMPROVEMENT PLAN MATRIX				
Task/Issue	Recommendation	Improvement Action	Assigned To	Status/Due Date
Conclusion				
In this section, reflect on the event being reviewed and provide general recommendations on how the next similar event should be conducted/ managed.				

Source: Adapted from the General Services Administration—PBS Knowledge Management AAR Guide.

Fire Department First Responders Knowledge Management (KM) Strategy—Template
Introduction
The following represents a template for instituting a KM strategy for first responders. This KM strategy takes into account the following characteristics:
Executive Summary
This section summarizes where the organization is now, where it wants to be, and how the organization intends to get there as it pertains to KM and creating a knowledge organization.
KM Mission Statement
This section encapsulates the KM mission of the organization and sets the definition of knowledge and KM for the organization to follow.
KM Vision
This section encapsulates the vision of organization's KM program.
KM Roles and Responsibilities
This section details the KM roles and responsibilities in order to support the vision and execute the initiatives.

Knowledge Recognition Needs Assessment and Allocation
The key issues and knowledge needs of the organization will be summarized here (knowledge audit findings) and will include any knowledge resources, processes, and tools that will be needed to effectively execute the KM strategy.
KM Feedback and Evaluation
The following outlines the actions, activities, next steps as well as the timing involved in performing the after action reviews as it pertains to the organization's KM initiatives.
Knowledge Acquisition
The key issues and knowledge needs of the organization will be summarized here and will include any knowledge resources, processes, and tools that will be needed to effectively execute the KM strategy.
Knowledge Transfer
Knowledge transfer is a culture-based process by which adaptive organizational knowledge that lies in people's heads and which lies in documents, programs, reports, and so on is exchanged with others. This section will indicate how knowledge transfer will play a role in the overall KM strategy.
Incident Command Structure
This section details the strategy and execution of the policy, procedure, and protocols of incident command.
Expertise Coordination Practice (ECP)
This section details the strategy and execution of the policy, procedure, and protocols of the ECP.
Command and Control Structure
This section details the strategy and execution of the policy, procedure, and protocols of command and control.
Initial KM Initiatives
This section details and prioritizes the initiatives necessary to carry out the execution of the KM strategy.
Dependencies
This section will detail critical dependencies such as the availability of key personnel, approval of budgets, and available technologies to initiate the KM strategy. This section will also analyze the effect of not executing the KM strategy at all.

Ongoing KM Support
To continue to foster an atmosphere of sharing, transferring, harvesting, and creating knowledge within the organization, an adherence to this strategy will be imperative. Ongoing support will include the following:
Identifying the key knowledge holders within the organization (perform knowledge audit)
Creating an environment that motivates people to share
Creating opportunities and utilizing tools to harvest knowledge
Creating opportunities to foster knowledge creation
Designing a sharing mechanism to facilitate the knowledge transfer
Measuring the effects of executing the knowledge strategy
Establish a KM Initiative Board
The KM Initiative Board is comprised of the senior management and core team members and is the vehicle for implementing and keeping under review the KM initiatives that will be championed by the organization.

References

Chapter 1

Tjaden, T. (2010). *Legal Research and Writing*, 3rd Edition. Irwin Law, Toronto, Canada.

Chapter 2

Clare, M. (May/June 2002). Solving the knowledge value equation: How to estimate the value of the intangible benefits of KM. *Knowledge Management Review*, 5(2), 14–15.

Cohn, M. (2013). What is scrum methodology. http://www.mountaingoatsoftware.com /topics/scrum. Accessed on December 8, 2013.

Project management book of knowledge (PMBOK). http://www.pmi.org/pmbok-guide-and-standards/pmbok-guide.aspx. Accessed on April 25, 2016.

Rhem, A. (2011). Knowledge acquisition unified framework (KAUF). The knowledge management depot. http://theknowledgedepot.blogspot.com/2011_06_01_archive.html. Accessed on September 15, 2012.

Wiley, A. (2012). Iterative software development approach. https://wiki.nci.nih. gov/display/CommonProjects/Iterative+Software+Development+Approach. Accessed on September 8, 2013.

Chapter 3

Allen, A. (2012). The impact of social media on knowledge management. Accessed on July 2, 2013. http://knowledgebird.com/the-impact-of-social-media-on-knowledge-management/.

Corbett, J. (2010). *Participatory Mapping and Communication: A Guide to Developing a Participatory Communication Strategy to Support Participatory Mapping*. International Fund for Agricultural Development (IFAD), Washington, DC.

Palmert, C. (2012). Knowledge management in the social media era. tcworld 7/2012. http://www.tcworld.info/e-magazine/content-strategies/article/social-media-in-the-coffee-corner/. Accessed on March 3, 2014.

Pirkkalainen, H. and Pawlowski, J. (2013). Global social knowledge management: From barriers to the selection of social tools. *The Electronic Journal of Knowledge Management*, 11(1), 03–17. Available at www.ejkm.com.

Chapter 4

U.S. Department of Health and Human Resources. www.usability.gov.

Downey, L. and Banerjee, S. (2011). Building an information architecture checklist. *Journal of Information Architecture*, 2(2) Available at http://journalofia.org/volume2/issue2/03-downey/. Accessed on April 16, 2016.

Usability.Gov (n.d.). What and Why of Usability. http://www.usability.gov/what-and-why/information-architecture.html.

Chapter 5

Clare, M. (2002). Solving the knowledge value equation (part one): How to estimate the value of the intangible benefits of KM. *Knowledge Management Review*, 5(2): 14–17, Melcrum Publishing Ltd.

http://www.fastcompany.com/1651431/work-smart-brainstorming-techniques-boost-creativity. Accessed on January 2, 2014. Fast Company.

Johansson, F. (2014). *The Medici Effect*. What Elephants and Epidemics Can Teach Us About Innovation, Harvard Business School Publishing, Boston, MA.

Lasseter, J. (2012). Pixar Headquarters and the Legacy of Steve Jobs, http://officesnapshots.com/2012/07/16/pixar-headquarters-and-the-legacy-of-steve-jobs/. Accessed on January 30, 2014.

Office snapshots blog—Pixar headquarters and the legacy of Steve Jobs. http://officesnapshots.com/2012/07/16/pixar-headquarters-and-the-legacy-of-steve-jobs/. Accessed on January 30, 2014.

Passuello, L. (2008). The Medici Effect Mind Map, http://www.biggerplate.com/mindmaps/d182919/the-medici-effect.

Robitaille, D. Surviving root cause analysis. http://www.thecqi.org/Knowledge-Hub/Resources/The -Quality-Survival-Guide/Surviving-root-cause-/. Accessed on January 4, 2014.

Trapani, G. (2010). *Work Smart: Brainstorming Techniques to Boost Creativity.* Wenger, E. (n.d.). Communities of practice: A brief introduction. http://www.fastcompany.com/1651431/work-smart-brainstorming-techniques-boost-creativity. Accessed on June 20, 2014.

Chapter 6

Bersin, J. (2010). A new talent management framework. http://www.bersin.com/blog/post/2010/05/A-New-Talent-Management-Framework.aspx. Accessed May 24, 2016.

Bersin, J., Harris, S., Lamoureux, M., and Mallon, D. (2010). The talent management framework: Executive summary. Bersin & Associates Research Report V.1.0.

Heathfield, S. (2016). What is talent management—Really! http://humanresources.about.com/od/successionplanning/g/talent-management.htm. Accessed March 30, 2016.

Kilburg, R. R. (2000). *Executive Coaching: Developing Managerial Wisdom in a World of Chaos*, American Psychological Association, Washington, DC, pp. 65, 67.

Chapter 7

Anderson et al. (2008). http://www.fema.gov/media-library-data/20130726-1824-25045-1942/national_incident_management_system_2008.pdf.

Baker, F. (2008). Fireground Strategies & Tactics: Understanding the capabilities and limitations of the fire department, Professional Safety, February 2008.

Balogun, O., Balogun E., Ntuen, C., Turner, A. (2006). Supporting command and control training functions in the emergency management domain using cognitive systems engineering. *Egonomics*, 49 (12–13), 1415–1436. Taylor & Francis, New York.

Bartczak, S.E., England, E.C., and Turner, J.M. (2008). *Challenges in Developing a Knowledge Management Strategy: A Case study of the Air Force Materiel Command.* IGI Publishing, Hershey, PA.

Bohmann, T., Greiner, M.E., and Krcmar, H. (2007). A strategy for knowledge management. *Journal of Knowledge Management*, 11(6): 3–15. ABI/INFORM Global.

Burstein, F., Mitchell, S., Owen, J. (2004). Knowledge reuse and transfer in a project management environment. *Journal of Information Technology Cases and Applications (JITCA)*, 6(4), Ivy League Publishing, Marietta, GA.

Coleman, R.J. (2007). Guessing the role of EMS & fire is no game. *Fire Chief*, 9, 28–36.

Crilly, T., Lusignan, S.D., Rowlands, G., Shaw, A., and Wells, S. (2005). A knowledge audit of the managers of primary care organizations: Top priority is how to use routinely collected clinical data for quality improvement. *Medical Informatics and the Internet in Medicine*, 30(1), 69–80. Taylor & Francis Group, New York.

Department of Homeland Security. (2008). National Incident Management System. http://www.fema.gov/national-incident-management-system.

Ekionea, J. and Swain, D. (2008). Developing and aligning a knowledge management strategy: Towards a taxonomy and a framework. *International Journal of Knowledge Management*, 4(1), 29–45. IGI Publishing, Hershey, PA.

Elearn Training Company. (2007). *Making Sense of Data and Information*. Elsevier Philadelphia, PA.

Faraj, S., Xiao, Y. (2006). Coordination in fast-response organizations. *Management Science*, (2006), 15, 1155–1169.

General Services Administration – PBS Knowledge Management AAR Guide. (2010). http://www.pbsworks.com/documentation/support/PBSProUserGuide10.4.pdf.

Haggie, K and Kingston, J. (2003). Choosing Your Knowledge Management Strategy, *Journal of Knowledge Management Practice*, 4 (June, 2003), http://www.tlainc.com/jkmpv4.htm.

Kruger, J. and Snyman, R. (2004). The interdependence between strategic management and strategic knowledge management. *Journal of Knowledge Management*, 8(1): 5–19. ABI/INFORM Global.

Leeson, P.T., Sobel, R. S. (2007). The use of knowledge in natural-disaster relief management, *The Independent Review*, Spring 2007, 14, 519–532.

McLaughlin, S. (October/November 2007). Managing knowledge for success. *Engineering Management*, 17(5), 42.

Nicolas, R. (2004). Knowledge management impacts on decision making process. *Journal of Knowledge Management*, 8(1), 20. ABI/INFORM Global.

NIMS. (2008). http://www.fema.gov/media-library-data/20130726-1824-25045-1942/national_incident_management_system_2008.pdf. Accessed on 28 June, 2014.

Nonaka, I. and Takeuchi, H. (1995). *The Knowledge-Creating Company.* Oxford University Press, New York.

Rhem, A.J. (2006). *UML for Developing Knowledge Management Systems.* Taylor and Francis Group. Boca Raton, FL.

Riege, A. (2005). Three-dozen Knowledge-sharing barriers managers must consider. *Journal of Knowledge Management.* 9(3), 18. ABI/INFORM Global.

Smith, A.D. (2004). Knowledge management strategies: A multi-case study. *Journal of Knowledge Management,* 8(3): 6–16. ABI/INFORM Global.

Turoff, M., Carver, L. (2007). Human-computer interaction: The human and computer as a team in emergency management information systems. *Communications of the ACM,* 6, 33–38.

United States Agency International Development (USAID). (2006). *After-Action Review Technical Guide.* Washington, DC.

Walker, S. (2006). 12 steps to a successful KM program. *KM Review,* 9(4), 8–9.

Chapter 8

Apple market cap. https://ycharts.com/companies/AAPL/market_cap. Last accessed April 23, 2016.

Braverman, M. (2007). The human side of due diligence: Protecting the M&A investment. http://www.bravermangroup.com/services/OrgConsult/text/The%20Human%20 Side%20of%20M%26A.pdf. Accessed on June 2, 2014.

Clare, M. (May/June 2002). Solving the knowledge value equation. *Knowledge Management Review,* 5(2), 14–17. Melcrum Publishing Ltd.

Coveo. (2013). *Measuring Return on Knowledge in a Big Data World.* Coveo, San Mateo, CA. http://www.coveo.com/~/media/Files/WhitePapers/Coveo_Measuring_Return _on_Knowledge_in_a_Big_Data_World.ashx. Accessed on June 2, 2014.

Brown, C. (2002). Contextual intelligence (CI): The key to successful consulting. http:// headinthegame.net/resources/library/contextual-intelligence-ci-the-key-to-successful- consulting/. Accessed on June 2, 2014.

Investopedia. (2010). The basics of mergers and acquisitions. http://www.investopedia. com/university/mergers/. Accessed on June 2, 2014.

Khanna, T. (2014). Contextual Intelligence. https://hbr.org/2014/09/contextual-intelli- gence. Accessed on December 1, 2014.

Rhem, A. (2010). Leveraging knowledge management (KM) for mergers and acquisitions. http://EzineArticles.com/4791792. Accessed on June 2, 2014.

Robert, S. (2012). Why half of all M&A deals fail and what you can do about it. http:// www.forbes.com/sites/forbesleadershipforum/2012/03/19/why-half-of-all-ma-deals -fail-and-what-you-can-do-about-it/. Accessed on June 2, 2014.

Chapter 9

Beal, A.C., Doty, M.M., Hernandez, S.E., Shea, K.K., and Davis, K. 2007. Closing the divide: How medical homes promote equity in health care: Results from The Commonwealth Fund 2006 Health Quality Survey. The Commonwealth Fund, New York.

Bordoloi, P. and Islam, N. (2012). Knowledge management practices and healthcare delivery: A contingency framework. *Electronic Journal of Knowledge Management*, 10(2), 110–120.

Chauhan, B., George, R., and Coffin, J. (November–December 2012). Social media and you: What every physician needs to know. *Journal of Medical Practice Management*, 28(3), 206–209.

Institute for Healthcare Improvement. (September 2, 2015). Schedule the discharge to improve the flow. Retrieved from http://www.ihi.org/resources/Pages/Changes/ScheduletheDischarge.aspx.

Lambert, K.M., Barry, P., and Stokes, G. (2012). Review risk management and legal issues with the use of social media in the healthcare setting. *Journal of Healthcare Risk Management*, 31(4), 41–47.

Lusignan, S. and Tringali, M. (2005). Foundations of a healthcare knowledge management application system. *American Medical Informatics Association Annual Symposium Proceedings*. http://www.ncbi.nlm.nih.gov/pmc/articles/PMC1560470/. Accessed date October 9, 2015.

Richardson, W.S., Wilson, M., and Guyatt, G. (2002). *The Process of Diagnosis*. American Medical Association, University of California, San Francisco, CA.

Chapter 10

J.D. Power McGraw-Hill Financial. http://www.jdpower.com/industry/financial-services. Accessed on February 2, 2013.

Chapter 11

Davenport, T.H. and Prusak, L. (2002). *Working Knowledge How Organizations Manage What They Know*. Harvard Business School Press, Boston, MA.

Dimension Data's 2015 Global Contact Centre Benchmarking Report, © Dimension Data 2009–2015. https://www.dimensiondata.com/Global/Downloadable%20Documents/2015%20Global%20Contact%20Centre%20Benchmarking%20Summary%20Report.pdf. Accessed on November 1, 2015.

Chapter 12

Gianakos, L.K. (2013). The intersection of knowledge and legal project management. https://info.legalsolutions.thomsonreuters.com/signup/newsletters/practice-innovations/2013-mar/article4.aspx.

Palomaki, S. and Wagner, F. (2011). Legal project management from the inside: 10 things law firm leaders need to know about implementing legal project management. *Law Practice Today.* www.lawpracticetoday.org. American Bar Association.

Precedent/Case Law. http://new.justcite.com/kb/editorial-policies/precedence-3/.

Rhem, A. (2012). Knowledge management in law firms. http://theknowledgedepot.blogspot.com/2012/03/knowledge-management-in-legal.html#!/2012/03/knowledge-management-in-legal.html. Accessed on September 1, 2013.

Solomon, M. http://www.forbes.com/sites/micahsolomon/2014/02/04/transform-your-law-firms-client-service-starting-today-a-five-step-legal-industry-client-service-initiative/.

Staudt, R.W. (2003). *Perspectives on Knowledge Management in Law Firms.* Miamisburg, OH, LexisNexis®.

Chapter 13

Green, A. (2011). Webinar, PLANT the Right Seeds to GROW: A Harvest of Knowledge http://kmef.iwiki.kent.edu/KMEFwebinar03152001.

R. Heer, A Model of Learning Objectives based on A Taxonomy for Learning, Teaching, and Assessing: A Revision of Bloom's Taxonomy of Educational Objectives. Center for Excellence in Learning and Teaching, Iowa State University, Ames, Iowa.

KMEF. (2011). http://kmef.iwiki.kent.edu/.

Yunginger, D. (2013). Knowledge management challenges top the CEO agenda. http://www.lminfo.us/blog/knowledge-management-challenges-top-the-ceo-agenda/. Accessed on February 4, 2014.

Chapter 14

Andreasen, S. (2014). Big data delivering big knowledge. *KM World.* http://www.kmworld.com/Articles/Editorial/Viewpoints/Big-Data-Delivering-Big-Knowledge-95057.aspx. Accessed April 18, 2015.

Downey, L., & Banerjee, S. (2011). Building an Information Architecture Checklist. Journal of Information Architecture. Vol. 2, No. 2. [Available at http://journalofia.org/volume2/issue2/03-downey/].

Erickson, S. and Rothberg, H. Big Data and knowledge management: Establishing a conceptual foundation. *The Electronic Journal of Knowledge Management*, Volume 12, Issue 2, pp. 108–116. Available at www.ejkm.com.

Gartner Press Release (Sept 17, 2014). Gartner Survey Reveals That 73 Percent of Organizations Have Invested or Plan to Invest in Big Data in the Next Two Years. http://www.gartner.com/newsroom/id/2848718.

LoPresti, M. (2014). The long tail of knowledge: Big data's impact on knowledge management. http://www.econtentmag.com/Articles/News/News-feature/The-long-tail-of-knowledge-big-datas-impact-on-knowledge-management-96285.htm. Accessed February 4, 2015.

Rajpathak, T. and Narsingpurkar, A. Manufacturing Innovation and Transformation Group (ITG), TCS. Managing Knowledge from Big Data Analytics in Product Development. http://www.tcs.com/resources/white_papers/Pages/Knowledge-big-data-analytics-product-development.aspx. Accessed March 2015.

Yuan, Q.F., Yoon, P.C., and Helander, M. G. (2006). Knowledge identification and management in product design. *Journal of Knowledge Management*, Volume 10, Issue 6, pp. 50–63.

Chapter 15

Army Knowledge Management Principles. A4 Doc 1 AKM Principles, June 25, 2008.

Chairman of the Joint Chiefs of Staff Instruction, Charter of the Knowledge Management Cross-Functional Team. (2013). DOM/SJS, CJCSI 5124.01, Distribution: A, C, https://archive.org/stream/Charter-of-the-Knowledge-Management-Cross-Functional-Team-12-Apr-2013/Charter%20of%20the%20Knowledge%20Management%20Cross-Functional%20Team,%2012%20Apr%202013_djvu.txt. Accessed December 2, 2014.

Communication and Information: Knowledge Management. Air Force Instruction 33–96, November 7, 2014.

Department of the Army US Army Corps of Engineers. (2015). *Knowledge Management Strategic Plan.* Department of the Army U.S. Army Corps of Engineers, Washington, DC.

Henriques, J. (2014). Use of unmanned drones for military and civilian use. http://www.globalresearch.ca/unmanned-aerial-vehicles-uav-drones-for-military-and-civilian-use/5374666.

http://www.doncio.navy.mil/ContentView.aspx?id=4980.

Senior Airman Jamie Jaggers, Air Force Public Affairs Agency Operating Location-P. (2014). Knowledge management centers roll out Air Force-wide. http://www.af.mil/News/ArticleDisplay/tabid/223/Article/484529/knowledge-management-centers-roll-out-air-force-wide.aspx. Accessed on December 2, 2014.

Chapter 16

Baloh, P. (2007). The role of fit in knowledge management systems: Tentative propositions of the KMS design. *Journal of Organizational and End User Computing*, 19(4), 21, 22–41.

Boyer, E.L. (1990). *Scholarship Reconsidered: Priorities of the Professoriate. The Carnegie Foundation for the Advancement of Teaching*, New York.

Buckland, B.K., and Zigurs, I. (1998). A theory of task/technology fit and group support systems effectiveness. *MIS Quarterly* 22(3) 313–334.

Cane, S., and McCarthy, R. (2009). Analyzing the factors that affect information systems use: A task-technology fit meta-analysis. *The Journal of Computer Information Systems*, 50(1) 108–123.

Davenport, T.H., and Prusak, L. (1999). *Working Knowledge—How Organizations Manage What They Know*. Harvard Business School Press, Boston, MA.

Goodhue, D.L., and Thompson, R.L. (1995). Task-technology fit and individual performance. *MIS Quarterly*, 19(2) 213–236.

Hsu, R.-C., Lawson, D., and Liang, T.-P. (2007). Factors affecting knowledge management adoption of Taiwan small and medium-sized enterprises. *International Journal of Management and Enterprise Development*, 4(1), p. 1.

Huang, C.-C., and Lin, T.-C. (2008). Understanding knowledge management system usage antecedents: An integration of social cognitive theory and task technology fit. *Information Management*, 45(6) 410–417.

Kim, D. (2009). Adoption of personal information system: Innovation diffusion theory and task-technology fit. *Proceedings of the Academy of Information and Management Sciences*, 13(2) 50–55.

Reh, F.J. Learn a Lunch. A Program to help Employees Grow http://management.about.com/od/trainingsites/a/LunchandLearn.htm. Accessed on February 3, 2015.

Rogers, E.M. (2003). *Diffusion of Innovations*, 5th Edition. The Free Press, New York.

Simmons. R. (2013). *8 Steps to Implementing a Knowledge Management Program at Your Organization*. Forsythe, Skokie, IL.

Treem, J.W., and Leonardi, P.M. (2012). Social media use in organizations: Exploring the affordances of visibility, editability, persistence, and association. *Communication Yearbook*, 36, 143–189.

Chapter 17

Chong, S.C. and Choi, Y.S. (June 2005). Critical factors in the successful implementation of knowledge management. *Journal of Knowledge Management Practice*, available at: http://www.tlainc.com/articl90.htm.

Davenport, T.H., De Long, D., and Beer, M.C. (1998). Successful knowledge management projects. *Sloan Management Review*, 39(2), 43–57.

Davenport, T.H. and Prusak, L. (2000). *Working Knowledge: How Organizations Manage What They Know*. Harvard Business School Press, Boston, MA.

Davenport, T.H. and Volpel, S. (2001). The rise of knowledge towards attention management. *Journal of Knowledge Management*, 5(3), 212–221.

Frost, A. (2014). A synthesis of knowledge management failure factors, available at: http://www.knowledge-management-tools.net/.

Liebowitz, J. (2009). *Knowledge Retention: Strategies and Solutions*. CRC Press, Boca Raton, FL.

Simmons, R. (2013). *8 Steps to Implementing a Knowledge Management Program at Your Organization*. Forsythe, Skokie, IL.

Singh, M.D. and Kant, R. (2008). Knowledge management barriers: An interpretive structural modeling approach. *International Journal of Management Science and Engineering Management*, 3(2), 141–150.

Weber, R.O. (2007). Addressing failure factors in knowledge management. *Electronic Journal of Knowledge Management*, 5(3), 333–346, available at: www.ejkm.com/issue/download.html?idArticle=117.

Wu, J., Du, H., Li, X., and Li, P. (2010). Creating and delivering a successful knowledge management strategy: in M. Russ (Ed.), *Knowledge Management Strategies for Business Development*. Business Science Reference, Hershey, PA, pp. 261–276.

Chapter 18

Griffiths, D., Jenkins, A., Kingston-Griffiths, Z. (2014). The 2015 Global Knowledge Management Observatory Report. K3-Cubed Ltd. Edinburgh, UK.

Kolsky, E. (2015). The State of Knowledge Management: A Special Report. IntelliResponse Systems Inc. Toronto, ON, Canada.

Kriss, P. (2014). The value of customer experience quantified. https://hbr.org/2014/08/the-value-of-customer-experience-quantified/. Accessed on February 6, 2015.

Leggett, K. (2014). Forrester's top trends for customer service in 2015. http://blogs.forrester.com/kate_leggett/14-12-17-forresters_top_trends_for_customer_service_in_2015. Accessed on February 6, 2015

Ragsdale, J. (2014). The current state of knowledge management culture. http://blog.tsia.com/blog/infographic-the-current-state-of-knowledge-management-culture. Accessed on March 1, 2015.

Index

Note: Page numbers followed by f and t refer to figures and tables, respectively.